Mahlon

D0097574

En Route to Global Occupation

Gary Kah

Huntington House Publishers

Huntington House Publishers
P.O. Box 53788
Lafayette, Louisiana 70505

Library of Congress Card Catalog Number
91-71072
ISBN   0-910311-97-8

Unless otherwise indicated all Scripture quotations are taken from
the New International Version,© 1978 by New York International
Bible Society and published by Zondervan Corp.

Dedication

To the memory of my mother-in-law, Marcella Liechty, who went to be with the Lord during the writing of this book. It was her godly example and steadfast encouragement that helped me to keep writing when times were difficult. Her prayers and heartfelt desire for people to know Jesus Christ as Lord live on with this book.

Contents

Introduction

During the early 1980s, I was on the fast track of a successful government career, which took me around the world dealing with American embassies, foreign government officials, international business leaders, and, at times, members of the press and media. It was in many respects the perfect job, the kind that most people only dream of having. The last thing I ever thought I'd do was to research and write a book on the seemingly obscure subject of globalism and the occult. But I now realize that God had different plans.

Through my travels and job-related contacts, I became aware of plans being laid worldwide for the establishment of a one-world government, most frequently referred to by insiders as the New World Order. Most of my insights were gained over a three year period as a result of several experiences. Had I learned about this information from someone on the streets, I probably would have dismissed it as nonsense. However, because of the circumstances surrounding my experiences and the caliber of people through whom I learned of these things, I had no choice but to take the information seriously.

Each trip, it seemed, provided a new insight or discovery, taking me further and further into a New World Order plot. Whenever a deception or contradiction was brought to my attention, I would begin to look into the matter for myself in search of the truth—I am by nature a curious person who likes to get to the bottom of things.

My investigation ultimately extended around the world, from Taiwan to Israel to the Soviet Union. In the meantime, I also became aware of preparations being made for the New World Order here in the United States. I soon realized that this movement was not only economic in nature, but also contained a political dimension, and indeed, a spiritual motivation. I found the inter-connections between the three to be extensive.

Unless one is already aware of the far-reaching influence of occult societies in global politics and corporate boardrooms, one might find much of this information difficult to believe. However, more than ten thousand hours of research have led me to conclude that we are rapidly being pushed toward a one-world government by powerful Luciferic forces rooted in age-old secret societies.

These forces, incredibly evil in intent, fully expect to accomplish their mission during the 1990s. I myself have had a rare glimpse into the forming of the world government by being involved in an organization participating in this effort. One of these organizations is the the World Constitution and Parliament Association (WCPA) whose plans and documents have been reproduced in the exhibits in Part Two of this book. This material should serve as ample evidence that the drive to create a one-world government is for real. Only a few thousand people currently know about the WCPA. However, this will soon change.

The WCPA's efforts have become increasingly blatant in recent months as it is preparing to launch its public campaign. Unless this book reaches significant numbers of people quickly, the organization could soon be operating out in the open. Its campaign will be extremely deceptive and will receive the full support of unsuspecting people throughout the world.

Although Bush, Gorbachev, De Cuellar, and various members of Congress have openly been talking about the "New World Order," none of these leaders has dared to explain the true meaning of the term. This is because the public would try to stop them if they understood what it really meant. Secrecy has been crucial to the progress of the plan. By communicating in their own esoteric language, insiders hope to be able to further their plan with little resistance, to the point where it will soon be impossible to stop.

I have chosen to release this message at this time because of my belief that the New World Order is drawing near. I have taken this stand at a considerable risk to myself and my family. It is my prayer that those reading this book would spread the message as quickly as possible while there is still time to effectively expose this satanic deception.

As the present age draws to a close, it is important for us to be apprised of the relentless strategies employed by the prince of this world to bring humanity under his rule. Only if we are adequately informed and prepared can we effectively carry out God's plan during the time that remains. This book will help equip you with the knowledge and spiritual discernment needed both for the present and for the days ahead.

Part 1
The Emerging World System

Why do the nations rage and the peoples plot in vain? The kings of
the earth take their stand and the rulers gather together against
the Lord and against his Anointed One.
Psalm 2:1-2

Chapter 1
Global Economics

It all began one day when my department received an invitation from an international corporation to tour their plant. We were informed that they were preparing to announce a major expansion and wanted us to become familiar with their operation. My guess is that the company was laying the groundwork to approach the government for some financial assistance for their expansion.

Two of us went as representatives of our department to meet with these corporate officials, along with members of a U.S. senator's office and the mayor's office.

After receiving an impressive tour of the facility, one of the members in our group asked why the firm was planning such a major expansion. The corporate official in charge of the tour replied, "We are one of three companies being considered by the U.S. Treasury Department to build the printing presses that will be printing the new U.S. currency."

We all looked at each other as if to say, "What new U.S. currency?" But no one said anything. Here we were, all of us government officials learning about the planned new currency through the grapevine from a private non-governmental source. The corporate official, when probed about the matter, claimed he didn't know much beyond what he had already told us. However, as I returned to my office, I couldn't help but wonder what this was really all about.

Over the next few weeks I spent my free time investigating the new currency and the purpose behind it. I discovered that other people were asking questions as well. One of those individuals was Congressman Ron Paul of Texas who served on the congressional committee dealing with the Treasury Department on this matter.

To make a long story short, I learned that the plans to issue a new currency were international in scope; at least a dozen major countries were also planning to come out with new money. They included Switzerland, the United Kingdom, Japan, Canada, France, Germany, Australia, Brazil, and others.

I did some more digging and discovered that several countries had already issued new currencies in various denominations. Most of these currencies had two things in common—they had bare spots about the size of a fifty-cent piece, usually on the left-hand side of the bill; and they contained metallic strips, enabling special devices to detect the currencies as they passed through airports or across international boundaries. (Some of these currencies are pictured on the following pages.)

If the currencies are held over a light, a three-dimensional image (or hologram) becomes apparent in the area of the blank spot. The images, barely visible to the naked eye, are always of prominent world figures and cannot be reproduced on copiers. The effort was clearly being internationally coordinated. Rumor had it that the currencies might later receive a common image linking them together in an international monetary system.

Several years have passed since I first learned about the proposed new currency; for some unknown reason the issuance of new money has been delayed. Based on my information, if we were to enter into a world government within the near future, the next step from a monetary standpoint would still include the establishment of an international currency system. However, because of the rapid advances in electronic banking technology and the proven willingness of consumers to quickly adapt to these changes, the chances of bypassing the next step entirely and going directly to an electronic (cashless) system are increasing. If the powers-that-be perceive the public to be prepared for such a move, I believe they wouldn't hesitate to make this jump all at once, in spite of the large investment that has already been made toward the new currency.

If this were to be the case, the main focus of international finance would shift toward promoting the debit cards, which are already

Bank of England 5 pound note (reduced)

Banque de France 20 franc note (reduced)

Australian 10 dollar note (reduced)

German 10 deutsche mark note (reduced)

gaining acceptance rapidly because of their convenience. To make a purchase, your card is passed through a scanning device. After making a positive identification your bank account is automatically debited. The willingness of consumers to accept a single card for worldwide use is already being tested by the credit card and telecommunications industries—by now, most people have seen AT&T's intriguing television commercial, "One World . . . One Card."

Once the debit card has become widely accepted, everything would be in place for the next and final step, which would be to force each individual to be tagged with a personal identification code without which he would be unable to buy or sell. The technology for such a worldwide electronic system is already in place, and experiments with such a mark have been conducted in several countries.

Other developments are underway as well. In the not too distant future, products on our grocery shelves may become labelled with an invisible bar code. The Universal Product Code (UPC), which many have complained is an eye sore on product packaging, will still be there. However, only the scanner will be able to read it. Once this transition to an invisible code begins to take place, it will only be a matter of time before humans are tattooed with a similar mark.

It is not unrealistic to expect this process to come to fruition during the 1990s or the first part of the next century. If globalists have their way, such a system could be operational as soon as 1994.

While looking into these global financial developments, I discovered that our money was controlled by just a few people devoted to the cause of world government.

Recently passed interstate banking laws have made this centralization possible by allowing big banks to swallow up smaller banks at an alarming rate. Over a twelve state region stretching from New England to the Carolinas, for example, three New York super-banks now control over 85 percent of the banking assets.

Small local banks were first bought out by larger in-state. Bigger regional banks then purchased these large state banks. Once this process had been completed, the regional banks were merged with the New York super-banks in unprecedented acquisitions until a few banks controlled nearly everything. This all happened during the late 1970s and early 80s. This same process is now being repeated throughout the rest of the country.

Little did I know at this point that I was still only scratching the surface on these matters. I would soon discover that the same forces behind the big bank mergers already controlled the American banking industry indirectly via the Federal Reserve System. This has been the case ever since the Fed's establishment in 1913. Contrary to public belief, the Federal Reserve is not a government institution. It is a privately held corporation owned by stockholders. Until a few years ago, however, the names of those who owned the Federal Reserve was one of the best kept secrets of international finance due to a proviso on passage of the Federal Reserve Act agreeing that the identities of the Fed's Class A stockholders not be revealed.[1]

Mr. R.E. McMaster, the publisher of a financial newsletter called "The Reaper," was able to determine who the Fed's principal owners were through his Swiss and Saudi Arabian contacts. According to McMaster, the top eight stockholders are Rothschild Banks of London and Berlin; Lazard Brothers Banks of Paris; Israel Moses Seif Banks of Italy; Warburg Bank of Hamburg and Amsterdam; Lehman Brothers Bank of New York; Kuhn, Loeb Bank of New York; Chase Manhattan Bank of New York; and Goldman, Sachs Bank of New York. These interests own the Federal Reserve System through approximately three hundred stockholders, all of whom are known to each other and are sometimes related to one another.[2]

A great deal of big bank maneuvering and deception surrounded the passage of the Federal Reserve Act. The original proposal calling for a central bank operated by private interests was presented by Senator Nelson Aldrich (the maternal grandfather of today's Rockefeller brothers) under the Aldrich Bill. Congress, however, seeing through the hidden motives of those sponsoring the bill and aware of the unconstitutionality of such a system, voted the bill down with strong backing from the small bank lobby. * A short time later, however, the same bill with only a few minor modifications was reintroduced under a different name and passed as the Federal Reserve Act (officially, the Owen-Glass Act).

Those who had led the congressional opposition to the Aldrich Bill felt that the battle had been won and were guilty of letting their guard down. Many of these individuals had already left for the Christmas holidays when the bill was reintroduced and rammed through Congress on 23 December 1913.

Because of the way in which the Federal Reserve System was designed by its founders, whoever controls the Federal Reserve Bank of New York essentially controls the system. For all practical purposes the Federal Reserve Bank of New York "is" the Federal Reserve. Cur-

*Article 1, Section 8 of the U.S. Constitution prohibits private interests from issuing money or regulating the value thereof. This power belongs only to Congress. Thus, according to our Constitution, the Federal Reserve System is an illegal enterprise.

rently, more than ninety of the one hundred largest banks in the United States are located within this district.

Class A stockholders control the system by owning the stock of the largest member banks in the New York Federal Reserve Bank. The controlling interest is held by fewer than a dozen international banking establishments, only four of which are based in the United States. The rest of the interests are European, with the most influential of these being the Rothschild family of London. Each of the American interests are in some way connected to this family. Included among these are the Rockefellers who are by far the most powerful of the Fed's American stockholders. (The Rockefeller's holdings in the Federal Reserve are primarily through Chase Manhattan Bank.)

The Rothschild family, I would later discover, has been allied with the Masonic Order (Freemasonry) since the late 1700s. At that time they were still a relatively small, although ambitious, banking concern based in Frankfurt, Germany. By cooperating with the secret societies, however, the Rothschilds would be able to expand their banking operations into other European countries, benefiting from the extensive international business and political contacts of Freemasonry, which was already well established throughout the continent. Freemasonry, on the other hand, needed money to finance its efforts to build a New World Order, and the Rothschilds would be able to provide such funds. Thus, each party would benefit from the other.

By the 1820s, the Rothschilds had become the dominant banking family of Europe, controlling the fastest growing banking houses in France, England, Austria, Italy, and Germany. Operations in these countries were overseen by the five Rothschild brothers, each of whom controlled a different country. Those bankers who allied themselves with the Rothschilds and the Masonic Order became wealthy in their own right. Those who didn't would find the going tough.

During the late 1800s, the Rothschilds began to finance various American industrialists as well. They would do so primarily through the Warburgs of Germany who were partners in Kuhn, Loeb, and company of New York. In this fashion, Rothschild/Masonic interests would gain a foothold in the administration of this country's finances. Both the Warburgs and Kuhn Loeb would later become principal stockholders in the Federal Reserve—with Paul Warburg becoming the first chairman of the Federal Reserve Board.*

---

*J.P. Morgan, the famous banker, was a major ally of the New World Order as well. His family had a long history of supporting globalism stretching all the way back to Alexander Hamilton, who was the first U.S. Treasury Secretary and Morgan's distant relative.[3]

Through their U.S. and European agents, the Rothschilds would go on to finance the Rockefeller Standard Oil dynasty, the Carnegie steel empire, as well as the Harriman railroad system.[4] The Rockefellers, who later became intermarried with the Carnegies, would go on to finance many of America's leading capitalists through Chase Manhattan and Citibank, both of which have long been Rockefeller family banks.* Many of these capitalist families would also become intermarried with the Rockefellers so that by 1937 one could trace "an almost unbroken line of biological relationships from the Rockefellers through one-half of the wealthiest sixty families in the nation."[5]

Owing much of their wealth to the Rockefellers, these families have become loyal allies of "the family." The Rockefellers, on the other hand, owing their colossal fortune to the Rothschilds, have for the most part remained loyal to them and their European interests. As a result of this chain, much of America's corporate wealth is ultimately traceable to the old money of Europe and the one-world interests of Freemasonry.

By 1890, Standard Oil of Ohio, owned by John D. Rockefeller, was refining 90 percent of all crude oil in the United States and had already begun its international expansion.[7] Although J.D. and his family were the subject of repeated congressional investigations because of antitrust violations and alleged conspiracy, the investigations had little effect on the family's progress. They always managed to stay a step or two ahead of the federal government.

In 1911, for example, the Supreme Court ruled that Standard Oil of New Jersey was in violation of the Sherman Anti-Trust Law.[8] The holding company was thereupon dissolved and its shares distributed among thirty-three companies in an attempt to break up the monopoly. However, it soon became evident that all of the new companies were owned by the same people (John D. Rockefeller had 25 percent of the stock in each of the firms) "and that there wasn't a shred of competition among any of them."[9] Offshoots of the original Standard Oil Trust included Standard Oil of New Jersey (today Exxon), Standard Oil of New York (today Mobil), Standard Oil of California, Standard Oil of Indiana, Standard Oil of Ohio (Sohio), Marathon, Phillips 66, and Chevron.[10]

In 1966, as a result of congressional investigations headed by

* By the 1970s, the Rockefeller-controlled banks, which by this time included Chemical Bank, accounted for about 25 percent of all the assets of the fifty largest commercial banks in the country and for about 30 percent of all the assets of the fifty largest life insurance companies.[6]

Representative Wright Patman of Texas, it was discovered that four of the world's seven largest oil companies were under the control of the Rockefeller family.[11] According to an earlier *New York Times* report, the largest of these, Standard Oil of New Jersey (Exxon) alone controlled 321 other companies, including Humble Oil and Venezuela's Creole Petroleum, themselves among the largest corporations in the world.[12] By 1975, the Rockefellers had gained control of the single largest block of stock in Atlantic Richfield (ARCO) and were believed to be in control of Texaco as well.[13] It was also discovered that the Rockefellers were operating major joint ventures with Royal Dutch Shell, which was already in the hands of European one-world interests.[14]

Ever since the founding of the Federal Reserve System, consistent efforts have been made by conservative congressional leaders to put a stop to the Fed and the forces behind it, with each decade producing at least one valiant attempt to expose the conspiracy. Congressman Charles Lindbergh, Sr., father of the famous aviator, was among those who fought the passage of the Act and later conducted an investigation into the cartel. His life was made difficult as a result.

At the time the Federal Reserve Act was passed, Lindbergh warned:

> This Act establishes the most gigantic trust on earth. When the President [Wilson] signs this bill the invisible government of the Monetary Power will be legalized . . . the worst legislative crime of the ages is perpetrated by this banking and currency bill. [15]

Lindbergh's efforts to expose the plot were followed by those of Congressman Louis T. McFadden who chaired the House Banking and Currency Committee for ten years during the 1920s and 30s. Three attempts were made on his life. First, he was shot at in Washington, DC. Then his food was poisoned. The third attempt was unfortunately successful. His mysterious death occurred while on a visit to New York City. The cause of death on his death certificate was given as "heart failure," although it was widely believed that he had been poisoned.

During the 1950s, Congressman Carroll Reece of Tennessee headed what became known as the Reece Committee, which conducted a thorough investigation of the major tax-exempt foundations linked to the international money cartel. The investigation centered on those foundations and trusts controlled by the Rockefellers, Fords, and Carnegies, as well as the Guggenheim foundations. The findings regarding the wealth and power of these institutions were so overwhelming that many in Congress found the information difficult to believe.

During the 1960s and early 1970s, Congressman Wright Patman of Texas would also look into manipulation by foundations and the Federal Reserve. Using his influence as Chairman of the House Banking Committee, and later, as Chairman of the Subcommittee on Domestic Monetary Policy, he repeatedly tried to expose the one-world plot by calling for audits of the Federal Reserve and even trying to have the Federal Reserve Act repealed. However, the findings of each of his committees, for some strange reason, were unable to attract any attention from the media. Patman, like those who had gone before him, frequently vented his frustration over this lack of coverage. On one occasion he stated, "Our exposes of the Federal Reserve Board are shocking and scandalous, but they are only printed in the daily Congressional Record, which is read by very few people."[16]

In the 70s and 80s, Congressman Larry P. McDonald would be the one to spearhead efforts against the New World Order. In 1976 he wrote the introduction to *The Rockefeller File*, a book exposing the Rockefellers' financial holdings and secret intentions. The book revealed that the Rockefellers had as many as two hundred trusts and foundations and that the actual number of foundations controlled by the family might number in the thousands. Such control is possible because Rockefeller banks, such as Chase Manhattan, have become the trustees for many other U.S. foundations as well, possessing the right to invest and to vote the stock of these institutions through the bank's trust department. McDonald warned the American public with the following statement:

> *The Rockefeller File* is not fiction. It is a compact, powerful and frightening presentation of what may be the most important story of our lifetime—the drive of the Rockefellers and their allies to create a one-world government combining super-capitalism and Communism under the same tent, all under their control.
>
> For more than one hundred years, since the days when John D. Rockefeller Sr. used every devious strategy he could devise to create a gigantic oil monopoly, enough books have been written about the Rockefellers to fill a library. I have read many of them. And to my knowledge, not one has dared reveal the most vital part of the Rockefeller story: that the Rockefellers and their allies have, for at least fifty years, been carefully following a plan to use their economic power to gain politi-

> cal control of first America, and then the rest of the
> world.
>
> Do I mean conspiracy? Yes I do. I am convinced there
> is such a plot, international in scope, generations old in
> planning, and incredibly evil in intent. [17]

McDonald's warning was written on a congressional letterhead dated November 1975. During the years that followed, frustrated by the media's refusal to report his findings, he began to take his message to the streets by speaking out against these forces publicly throughout the country. McDonald's courageous efforts, however, came to an abrupt end on 31 August 1983 when he was killed aboard the Korean Airlines *007* flight which "accidentally" strayed over Soviet airspace and was "accidentally" shot down.

Media reporting on this event was scant and short-lived; and as a result, the incident was soon forgotten. Even though his activities were widely known among the media and on Capitol Hill, not a single mention was publicly made about the fact that McDonald had been heading a congressional effort to expose what he called a dangerous international conspiracy. Had this fact been made known to the American people, it would have completely altered the way in which we viewed this incident.

The chance of a U.S. congressman being aboard a commercial airliner shot down by the Soviet military is less than one in a million. Depending on the variables entered into the equation, it may be closer to one in a billion. Yet we are expected to believe that it was a pure coincidence; just as we are supposed to believe that the recent deaths of Sen. John Heinz and former Sen. John Tower in two separate plane crashes were a coincidence as well.

Tower had been an outspoken critic of the Eastern Establishment (a term frequently used by conservative lawmakers to describe one-world interests). Although Tower had himself been associated with various one-world organizations, he also had a strong sense of right and wrong, particularly on matters concerning our national security, and was known for bucking the tide. This backfired when certain members of Congress, loyal to the one-world cause, banded together against him in a smear campaign resulting in the denial of Tower's confirmation as U.S. Secretary of Defense. Outraged over the undocumented allegations made to slander his name, Tower set out to write a book telling his side of the story. His controversial book, which heavily criticizes his adversaries in Congress, was published recently. His plane crash on 5 April 1991 came shortly after the book's release.

One day earlier (4 April), Senator John Heinz died in a fiery plane crash near Philadelphia. The plane's landing gear had suddenly malfunctioned. A helicopter was sent up as a result, allegedly to check out the gear, only to end up crashing into the plane itself. Two freak accidents in one—first the landing gear fails, then the rescue aircraft slams into the plane.

Heinz and Tower had both been members of a prominent one-world society known as the Council on Foreign Relations. They had also served on powerful Senate banking and finance committees and knew a great deal about these matters. Could they have known too much? Although accidents do happen, how much longer are we supposed to believe that all of these are mere coincidence?

Since the earlier death of Congressman Larry McDonald, Senator Jesse Helms has led efforts to expose the plot. Thus far, nothing has happened to him. I am sure he would appreciate the prayers of America's Christians for his safety.

The vivid remarks and statements of Senator Helms, like those of his predecessors, have been entered into the Congressional Record without receiving any network coverage. The only attention Helms manages to get is in the form of public ridicule over his conservative voting record.

During the 1960s and 70s, thanks to the efforts of Congressmen Wright Patman, Larry McDonald, and others, the message had begun to reach the American people. Action groups were formed by various citizens in an urgent attempt to get this information into the hands of the public. However, without coverage from the media, their efforts have had only limited results, as these groups have been forced to rely primarily on newsletters, privately published books, and unpublicized speaking engagements to get the word out.

Lt. Col. Archibald Roberts is one individual who has made an impact. As Director of the Committee to Restore the Constitution, he began testifying before state legislatures informing our elected officials at the state level about the deception surrounding the Federal Reserve. His campaign, urging state legislatures to repeal the Federal Reserve Act, was launched on 30 March 1971 when he testified before the Wisconsin House of Representatives. The text of Roberts' address was subsequently entered in the Congressional Record on 19 April 1971 (E3212-E3224) by Louisiana Congressman John Rarick.

As a result of Roberts' work, in which he was assisted by Washington State Senator Jack Metcalf and a number of supporting groups, by the mid-1980s approximately twenty states had taken action to pass legislation calling either for an audit of the Federal Reserve or for the repeal of the Federal Reserve Act. However, there still has been virtually no media coverage and the American public is still largely unaware about the intense battle going on behind-the-scenes.

By the late 1980s, the battle being waged at the state level had once again reached Congress. Representative Henry Gonzales of Texas introduced House Resolution 1469, calling for the abolition of the Open Market Committee of the Federal Reserve System, and then H.R. 1470, calling for the repeal of the Federal Reserve Act of 1913. During the same session, Representative Phil Crane of Illinois introduced H.R. 70, calling for an annual audit of the Federal Reserve. However, all of these efforts, like those of others before them, have failed.

It is difficult to get the public behind a legitimate cause or issue if the media refuse to cover it. This coverage is necessary in order to get the public to put the kind of pressure on Congress that will lead to action. This is particularly true of a Congress in which one-world interests now hold the upper hand.

As I continued my research, I discovered more specifics on how one-world money was being used to influence society.

Each year billions of dollars are "earned" by Class A stockholders of the Federal Reserve. These profits come at the expense of the U.S. government and American citizens paying interest on bank loans, a portion of which ends up going to the Federal Reserve. Much of this money, along with the annual profits stemming from hundreds of corporations and banks owned by these same interests, is then funneled into tax-exempt foundations where it is then re-invested into American and foreign corporations and used to further influence our economy. In this fashion, a small group of people apparently dedicated to the establishment of world government has gained considerable influence over global activity.

It is no coincidence that the forces responsible for the founding of the Federal Reserve were also responsible for the passage of laws permitting the creation of tax-exempt foundations. Private foundations were intended to serve as tax shelters for the enormous wealth generated by the international banking cartel. They have also come in handy for the purpose of funding major think-tanks, which influence virtually every aspect of American life.

The Reece Committee discovered the greatest influence of the Rockefeller-Carnegie-Ford foundations to be in the areas of the social sciences, public education, and international affairs via contributions of huge sums of money to secondary or intermediary foundations which then selected the ultimate recipients of grant money and research funds. Among the secondary foundations investigated by the

Reece Committee and its legal counsel, Rene Wormser, were the National Education Association, the John Dewey Society, the United Nations Association, and the Council on Foreign Relations.

The committee's goal was to find out where the major foundation money was really going. In the area of the social sciences, for example, the committee discovered that the Rockefeller Foundation was financing Dr. Alfred Kinsey's studies on sexual behavior through the National Research Council. Kinsey used these funds to produce his series of unscientific reports promoting sexual freedom (promiscuity).[18] If you attended a college or university, there is a high probability that you took at least one class which espoused the findings and teachings of the Kinsey Institute, presenting them as if they were fact. I know I did!

The field of education is another area that the Rockefeller alliance has attempted to dominate through its foundation money. In fact, few, if any, of the major education associations have escaped the grasp of these international forces. The Reece Committee found that the National Education Association (and numerous other education organizations) was producing and promoting curricula that advocated socialism and globalism with the intent of preparing students for a one-world society. [19] So extensive is foundation control over the field of public education, an entire book could be written just on this one topic.

However, no area has been more influenced by foundation activity than the field of foreign affairs. The cartel has been able to further its global agenda in this area through political think-tanks such as the United Nations Association, the Institute of Pacific Relations, and the Council on Foreign Relations, to name just a few. Rene Wormser of the Reece Committee stated that the influence of the major foundations had "reached far into government, into the policymaking circles of Congress and into the State Department."[20] He went on to explain how this had been accomplished.

> This has been effected through the pressure of public opinion, mobilized by the instruments of the foundations; through the promotion of foundation-favorites as teachers and experts in foreign affairs; through a domination of the learned journals in international affairs; through the frequent appointment of State Department officials to foundation jobs; and through the frequent appointment of foundation officials to State Department jobs.[21]

Wormser also revealed that at least one foreign foundation was allied with the major U.S. foundations in shaping our foreign policy. This institution originated with Cecil Rhodes, the famous British industrialist and globalist. Rhodes, who was a close ally of the Rothschilds and European Freemasonry, made his fortune in the diamond mines of South Africa off the sweat and blood of black slaves. A ruthless tyrant by nature, within a few short years during the 1870s and 80s, he had gained control of nearly all the diamond production in the world. Rhodes used his wealth liberally to advance the cause of world government. Following his death, his colossal fortune would continue to be used to promote globalism through the Rhodes Scholarship Fund.

Wormser summarized the influence of the Rhodes Scholar Program as follows:

> Of a total of 1,372 American Rhodes scholars up to 1953, 431 held or hold positions in teaching and educational administration (among them, 31 college presidents); 113 held government positions; 70 held positions in press and radio; and 14 were executives in other foundations. [22]

At the time of the Reece Committee investigations, the president of the Rockefeller Foundation, the director of the Guggenheim Foundation, and the former president of the Carnegie Foundation were all Rhodes Scholars.

More recently, the Nobel prize has been used in a similar fashion to generate free publicity for one-world darlings. The Nobel Committee has assisted the cartel's efforts by consistently awarding a high percentage of its prizes to people recognized for their globalistic views.

Since the time of these investigations, the influence of one-world foundations in the areas of social science, education, and foreign policy has only accelerated, accomplishing so much because of minimal foundation-supported opposition. Since they were the ones who pushed for the legalization of tax-exempt foundations and were therefore the first to establish them, they were able to get off to a tremendous head start. Even if a sizable foundation-sponsored opposition were to develop, it would only be on a small scale compared to the efforts of the cartel's mega-foundations. The forces of evil, I believe, will always have more power in "this world" because of the devious strategies they are willing to employ to accumulate money and then to manipulate others with it.

Chapter Two
Global Politics

Within months of first learning about these economic manipulations, I would discover that these same forces were promoting their agenda in the political realm as well. My first experience in this regard came during a meeting with a prominent businessman in the Far East. In addition to being a leading entrepreneur, this gentleman was also a member of the Associated Press and the head of a well-known charitable organization. During our luncheon meeting a couple of his country's political leaders stopped by to chat with him.

During the course of the meeting our conversation shifted to the subject of international affairs. At one point, I shared with him my concern over the disturbing trend I had noticed toward a centralized world banking system. He expressed the same concern. Apparently realizing that we held similar political views, he asked me if there was any way I could meet him again on the following evening for dinner, adding that he had something important that he wanted to show me. I checked my itinerary and found the following evening to be free, so I agreed to meet with him. Little did I know the significance of what I was about to learn.

The next day we met at my hotel for dinner, as planned. After we had eaten, the gentleman pulled some papers out of his attache case. Lowering his voice a bit, he began to tell me of what he believed might be an international conspiracy to create a one-world government. The papers he held in his hands contained a list of people from the United States who were believed to be involved in the plot. He handed the papers over to me for my examination.

The list of names read like a who's who of American leaders, including high-level members of the government, private industry, education, the press and media, the military, and high-finance. It included some of the same names I had run across in my research on the Federal Reserve and global economics. There seemed to be a common denominator—everyone on the list was a member of either the Council on Foreign Relations or the Trilateral Commission, with some belonging to both organizations.

For the next few minutes we took turns filling each other in on what we already knew, which admittedly wasn't much at the time. This information provided the tip I needed to lead me to investigate the Council on Foreign Relations and the Trilateral Commission. Although I had run across the names of these organizations before, I had not yet made a concerted effort to look into them.

We finally wrapped up our meeting. On the way back to my hotel room, my head pounded more than before—I was experiencing an information overload!

Had I learned of this information from someone else, I don't know whether I would have taken it seriously. However, considering who this man was, I really had no choice but to at least consider what he had said. Besides, when compared with the data I already had on financial matters, it all made sense. His information supported my own findings.

That night I didn't get much sleep. I kept wondering what all of this meant and how it might affect my future. Why, of all people, did this man share his information with me? Was this meeting just another coincidence, or was God trying to get my attention?

Soon after returning to the states, I began what turned out to be a time-consuming investigation of the Council on Foreign Relations (CFR), the Trilateral Commission, and related organizations, all the while continuing to gather information on global financial matters. During the same year, I would also discover there was a spiritual side to all of this. Soon I was spending most of my free time investigating what I loosely referred to as the one-world movement. The research was exhausting, but I felt driven to do it; inside of me, I knew that this was what God wanted me to do.

After nearly two years of research, I was able to piece together a rough history of the CFR's development and influence on the United States. I hoped to gain an understanding of the organization's real purpose and mission. This history begins with an organization known as the Illuminati.

The Illuminati

The Illuminati was a secret Luciferic order founded in Ingolstadt, Bavaria (Germany) on 1 May 1776 by Adam Weishaupt, a prominent Freemason. The organization was an extension of high, or illuminized, Freemasonry, existing as a special order within an order. Its operations were closely connected with the powerful Grand Orient Masonic Lodge of France. The order's name, meaning "the enlightened ones," signified that its members had been initiated into the secret teachings of Lucifer, the supposed light-bearer or source of enlightenment, according to the doctrines of illuminized Freemasonry.

The Illuminati had been designed for one purpose—to carry out the plans of high Freemasonry to create a New World Order by gaining a foothold in the key policy-making circles of European governments and attempting to influence the decisions of Europe's leaders from within through these advisory positions.

In reference to the various governmental leaders, which the Illuminati had targeted for subversion, Weishaupt remarked:

> It is therefore our duty to surround them with its [the Illuminati's] members, so that the profane may have no access to them. Thus we are able most powerfully to promote its interests. If any person is more disposed to listen to Princes than to the Order, he is not fit for it, and must rise no higher. We must do our utmost to procure the advancement of Illuminati in to all important civil offices.
>
> By this plan we shall direct all mankind. In this manner, and by the simplest means, we shall set all in motion and in flames. The occupations must be so allotted and contrived, that we may, in secret, influence all political transactions.[1]

For the order's strategy to succeed, its activities and the names of its members had to remain confidential. Initiates were therefore sworn to secrecy, taking bloody oaths describing what would happen to them if they ever defected from the order or revealed its plans. As another measure of security, the order's correspondence would be conducted through the use of symbols and pen names. Weishaupt's pseudonym, for example, was Spartacus.

The order was given a tremendous boost at the Masonic Congress of Wilhelmsbad, held on 16 July 1782. This meeting "included representatives of all the Secret Societies—Martinists as well as Freemasons and Illuminati—which now numbered no less than three million members all over the world." [2] It enabled the Illuminists to solidify their control over the lodges of Europe and to become viewed as the undisputed leaders of the one-world movement. Historian Nesta Webster observes:

> What passed at this terrible Congress will never be known to the outside world, for even those men who had been drawn unwittingly into the movement, and now heard for the first time the real designs of the leaders, were under oath to reveal nothing. One such honest Freemason, the Comte de Virieu, a member of a Martiniste lodge at Lyons, returning from the Congres de Wilhelmsbad could not conceal his alarm, and when

questioned on the "tragic secrets" he had brought back
with him, replied: "I will not confide them to you. I can
only tell you that all this is very much more serious than
you think. The conspiracy which is being woven is so
well thought out that it will be, so to speak, impossible
for the Monarchy and the Church to escape from it."
From this time onwards, says his biographer, M. Costa
de Beauregard, "the Comte de Virieu could only speak
of Freemasonry with horror."[3]

It was decided at the Congress that the headquarters of
illuminized Freemasonry should be moved from Bavaria to Frankfurt,
which was already becoming the stronghold of the Rothschilds and
the international financiers.[4] The ensuing cooperation between the
Rothschilds and the Illuminati would prove to be mutually beneficial,
multiplying the influence of both throughout Europe.[5]

After only about ten years in existence, the Illuminati was discovered and exposed by the Bavarian government as a result of tips
received from several of the order's initiates. The leaders of Bavaria
moved quickly to confiscate the order's secret documents. These original writings of the Illuminati were then sent to all the leaders of
Europe to warn them of the plot.[6] However, some of these leaders
had already fallen under the influence of the order. And those who
had not yet succumbed to the Illuminati, found its plans to be so
outrageous they didn't believe something like this possible—they refused to take the warning seriously.

Disbelief remains as the single biggest factor working in
Freemasonry's favor. Decent people tend to find it difficult to believe
that there could be individuals so evil in nature as to actually try to
take control of the world on behalf of Lucifer (Satan). This sounds
like a theme more fitting of a James Bond movie than real life. However, as difficult as it may be to believe, this effort to create a Luciferic
New World Order, I discovered, was, and is, for real.

Although several members of the order were ultimately pros-
ecuted by the Bavarian government, most of the initiates managed
to get away and were taken in by various European leaders.
Weishaupt, for example, took up refuge with the Duke of Saxe-Gotha
where he remained until his death in 1811.[7]

By the time the Illuminati had become exposed, its efforts had
already spread into more than a dozen countries, including the United
States. Since 1776, at least three U.S. presidents have warned the
public of the Illuminati's activities in this country. One of those presidents was George Washington.

I have heard much of the nefarious and dangerous plan
and doctrines of the Illuminati. It was not my intention
to doubt that the doctrine of the Illuminati and the principles of Jacobinism had not spread in the United States.[8]

Washington went on to denounce the order in two separate
letters written in 1798, and would once again warn America against
foreign influence in his farewell address. Concerned that the American people might fall under the sway of these corrupt powers, Washington stated:

Against the insidious wiles of foreign influence (I con-
jure you to believe me fellow citizens), the jealousy of
a free people ought to be constantly awake; since history and experience prove that foreign influence is one
of the most baneful foes of republican government. But
that jealousy, to be useful, must be impartial, else it
becomes the instrument of the very influence to be
avoided, instead of a defense against it. Excessive par-
tiality for one foreign nation and excessive dislike for
another, cause those whom they actuate to see danger
only on one side, and serve to veil and even second the
arts of influence on the other. Real patriots, who may
resist the intrigues of the favorite, are liable to become
suspected and odious; while its tools and dupes usurp
the applause and confidence of the people, to surrender their interests.

The great rule of conduct for us, in regard to foreign nations, is, in extending our commercial relations, to have
with them as little political connection as possible. So
far as we have already formed engagements, let them
be fulfilled with perfect good faith. Here let us stop.[9]

If only America had listened to President Washington's sound
advice!

Although the Illuminati officially ceased to exist after its expo-
sure in the 1780s, the continuation of its efforts would be ensured
through the Grand Orient Lodge of France. Working through the
Grand Orient and the network of illuminized Masonic lodges already
put in place by Weishaupt, high-Freemasonry would continue with
its plans to build a New World Order.

One of the factors working in Freemasonry's favor is that it
rarely, if ever, does anything covert under its own name. In order to
advance its agenda it establishes other organizations, such as the Illuminati, to which it gives special assignments. This way, if anything
goes wrong and the operation gets exposed, Freemasonry remains
relatively unscathed, claiming it had nothing to do with the matter.

Throughout the late 1700s and all of the 1800s, illuminized Freemasonry would continue to operate in this fashion, creating new organizations to carry out the task begun by the Illuminati, often still collectively referred to as the Illuminati by some researchers.

The first major "accomplishment" of illuminized Freemasonry was to incite the French Revolution through the Jacobin Society and Napoleon Bonaparte, who was one of their men. Illuminized Freemasonry would also receive help from Voltaire, Robespierre, Danton and Marat, all of whom were prominent Masons. The Jacobin Society's motives and connections were revealed when it named Weishaupt as its "Grand Patriot."[10]

The U.S. had barely declared its independence when these same European forces began efforts to bring America's young banking system under their control. Alexander Hamilton, believed by some to have been an Illuminist agent, was at the forefront of this drive. President Thomas Jefferson, keenly aware of the plot, argued:

> If the American people ever allow private banks to control the issue of their currency, first by inflation and then by deflation, the banks and the corporations that will grow up around them, will deprive the people of all property until their children wake up homeless on the continent their fathers conquered.[11]

During the mid 1800s, illuminized Freemasonry would be partly responsible for inciting the U.S. Civil War. Charleston, South Carolina, where the Successionist Movement began, also happened to be the American headquarters of Scottish Rite Freemasonry at the time—a little known fact which Freemasonry has successfully kept from the public. The headquarters of the Scottish Rite were later moved to Washington, DC, where they remain to this day.

Abraham Lincoln strongly resisted efforts by Illuminist forces to establish a privately controlled central bank. His foresight and wisdom would prevent the establishment of such a system for another forty-eight years.

Shortly before his assassination, President Lincoln warned:

> As a result of the war, corporations have been enthroned and an era of corruption in high places will follow and the money power of the country will endeavor to prolong its reign by working on the prejudices of the people until wealth is aggregated in the hands of a few and the Republic is destroyed. I feel at this moment more anxiety for the safety of my country than ever before, even in the midst of war.[12]

In 1913, the persistent efforts of illuminized Freemasonry finally paid off with the creation of the Federal Reserve System, ensuring European Illuminists a permanent role in America's finances, along with giving them more money with which to further their cause. Some of this money would eventually go toward financing the Council on Foreign Relations whose formation was influenced by a man named Edward Mandell House.

Colonel House, as he was called, was an Illuminist agent committed to the one-world interests of the Rothschild-Warburg-Rockefeller cartel, serving as their point-man in the White House.*[13] He first gained national prominence in 1912 while working to get Woodrow Wilson nominated as president. After Wilson's election, he became the president's most trusted personal advisor. House was to Wilson what Henry Kissinger would later be to Richard Nixon; he was, without question, the dominant figure in the White House, exerting his influence particularly in the areas of banking and foreign policy.

His accomplishments as Wilson's chief advisor were many. Among other things, he successfully persuaded Woodrow Wilson to support and sign the Federal Reserve Act into law. Later, realizing what he had done, President Wilson remorsefully replied, "I have unwittingly ruined my country."[14]

During World War I, which began within a year after the Act's passage, House would make secret missions to Europe as Wilson's chief foreign diplomat. It didn't take long before he managed to drag the United States into the war (April 1917). As the war came to an end in 1918, House worked diligently to help plan the League of Nations. Funded in part with Rockefeller money, the League was to serve as the first political step toward the forming of a world government.[15]

President Wilson, as a result of House's counsel, would become the leading spokesperson for the League of Nations, publicly viewed as the League's chief architect, in spite of the fact that House was really the one in charge.

However, much to Wilson's dismay and embarrassment, he could not even persuade his own country to join the organization. The American people strongly resisted this move toward globalization, placing heavy pressure on Congress to reject the treaty, thereby keeping the U.S. out of the League.

*House's father, Thomas W. House, was a Rothschild agent who amassed a fortune during the Civil War by supplying the South with essentials from France and England.

The non-entry of the United States into the League of Nations represented a huge setback for Colonel House and the internationalists. There could be no world government without the participation of the world's leading power. The setback, however, proved to be only temporary. The globalists would learn from this experience and would never again underestimate the power of the American people or of Congress. To make sure that a similar incident didn't happen again the second time around, the cartel, working through House and his accomplices, would establish the Council on Foreign Relations.

The Council on Foreign Relations

The Council on Foreign Relations Handbook of 1936 provides the following details concerning the organization's establishment.

> On May 30, 1919, several leading members of the delegations to the Paris Peace Conference met at the Hotel Majestic in Paris to discuss setting up an international group which would advise their respective governments on international affairs. The U.S. was represented by Gen. Tasker H. Bliss (Chief of Staff, U.S. Army), Col. Edward M. House, Whitney H. Shepardson, Dr. James T. Shotwell, and Prof. Archibald Coolidge. Great Britain was unofficially represented by Lord Robert Cecil, Lionel Curtis, Lord Eustace Percy, and Harold Temperley. It was decided at this meeting to call the proposed organization the Institute of International Affairs. At a meeting on June 5, 1919, the planners decided it would be best to have separate organizations cooperating with each other. Consequently, they organized the Council on Foreign Relations, with headquarters in New York, and a sister organization, the Royal Institute of International Affairs, in London, also known as the Chatham House Study Group, to advise the British Government. A subsidiary organization, the Institute of Pacific Relations, was set up to deal exclusively with Far Eastern Affairs. Other organizations were set up in Paris and Hamburg, the Hamburg branch being called the Institut fur Auswartige Politik, and the Paris branch being known as Centre d'Etudes de Politicque Etrangere.... [16]

Baron Edmond de Rothschild of France dominated the Paris Peace Conference, and each of the founders of the Royal Institute ended up being men who met Rothschild's approval.[17] The same was true of the Council on Foreign Relations, which was not officially formed until 29 July 1921.[18]

Money for the founding of the CFR came from J.P. Morgan,

Bernard Baruch, Otto Kahn, Jacob Schiff, Paul Warburg, and John D. Rockefeller, among others.[19] This was the same crowd involved in the forming of the Federal Reserve. The Council's original board of directors included Isaiah Bowman, Archibald Coolidge, John W. Davis, Norman H. Davis, Stephen Duggan, Otto Kahn, William Shepherd, Whitney Shepardson, and Paul Warburg.[20]

Prominent figures who have served as CFR directors since 1921 include Walter Lippmann (1932-37), Adlai Stevenson (1958-62), Cyrus Vance (1968-76, 1981-87), Zbigniew Brzezinski (1972-77), Robert O. Anderson (1974-80), Paul Volcker (1975-79), Theodore M. Hesburgh (1926-85), Lane Kirkland (1976-86), George H.W. Bush (1977-79), Henry Kissinger (1977-81), David Rockefeller (1949-85), George Shultz (1980-88), Alan Greenspan (1982-88), Brent Scowcroft (1983-89), Jeane J. Kirkpatrick (1985-), and Richard B. Cheney (1987-89).[21]

The most powerful man in the CFR during the past two decades has been David Rockefeller, the grandson of John D. Rockefeller. Along with being a Council director for thirty-six years, David served as chairman of the board from 1970-85 and remains as the organization's honorary chairman.[22] During this time, David was also chairman of Chase Manhattan Bank.

The Rockefellers are in no danger of losing control of the CFR any time soon. Another generation of family members are being groomed to continue their tradition. David, Jr.; John D. IV; and Rodman C. Rockefeller are all current members of the Council on Foreign Relations.[23]

As mentioned earlier, the Reece Committee found that the CFR was being financed by both the Rockefeller and Carnegie foundations and investigated it as well as its sister organization, the Institute of Pacific Relations, stating that the CFR "overwhelmingly propagandizes the globalist concept."[24]

More recently, between the years 1987 and 1990, the CFR received matching gifts and special contributions from leading organizations and individuals, including Chemical Bank, Citibank/Citicorp, Morgan Guaranty Trust, John D. and Catherine T. MacArthur Foundation, ARCO Foundation, British Petroleum American, Inc., Mercedes-Benz of North America, Inc., Seagram and Sons, Inc., Newsweek, Inc., Reader's Digest Foundation, Washington Post Company, Rockefeller Brothers Fund, Rockefeller Family and Associates, the Rockefeller Foundation, and David Rockefeller.[25]

During the same period, the CFR received major grants from other major corporations and foundations, including (partial list) the American Express Philanthropic Program, the Asia Foundation, the

Association of Radio and Television News Analysts, the Carnegie Corporation of New York, the Ford Foundation, the General Electric Foundation, the General Motors Corporation, the Hewlett Foundation, the Andrew W. Mellon Foundation, the Rockefeller Foundation, the Alfred P. Sloan Foundation, and the Xerox Foundation.[26]

The Council currently has 2,670 members, of whom 952 reside in New York City, 339 in Boston, and 730 in Washington, DC.[27] Its membership, as we shall see, reads like a *Who's Who* of America, including most of the nation's top leaders in government, business, education, labor, the military, the media, and banking. In addition to its headquarters in New York City, the CFR has thirty-eight affiliated organizations, known as Committees on Foreign Relations, located in major cities throughout the United States.[28]

Rear Admiral Chester Ward, a former CFR member for sixteen years, warned the American people of the organization's intentions.[29]

> The most powerful clique in these elitist groups have one objective in common—they want to bring about the surrender of the sovereignty and the national independence of the United States.
>
> A second clique of international members in the CFR . . . comprises the Wall Street international bankers and their key agents.
>
> Primarily, they want the world banking monopoly from whatever power ends up in the control of global government.[30]

Dan Smoot, a former member of the FBI headquarters staff in Washington and one of the first researchers into the CFR, summarized the organization's purpose as follows: "The ultimate aim of the Council on Foreign Relations . . . is . . . to create a one-world socialist system and make the United States an official part of it."[31] This of course would all be done in the name of democracy.

Congressman John R. Rarick, deeply concerned over the growing influence of the CFR, has been one of the members in Congress making a concerted effort to expose the organization.

Rarick warns:

> The Council on Foreign Relations—dedicated to one-world government, financed by a number of the largest tax-exempt foundations, and wielding such power and influence over our lives in the areas of finance, business, labor, military, education, and mass communication media—should be familiar to every American concerned with good government and with preserving and defending the U.S. Constitution and our free-enter-

prise system.

Yet the Nation's "right-to-know-machinery"—the news media—usually so aggressive in exposures to inform our people, remain conspicuously silent when it comes to the CFR, its members, and their activities. And I find that few university students and graduates have even heard of the Council on Foreign Relations.

The CFR is "the establishment." Not only does it have influence and power in key decision-making positions at the highest levels of government to apply pressure from above, but it also finances and uses individuals and groups to bring pressure from below, to justify the high level decisions for converting the United States from a sovereign Constitutional Republic into a servile member state of a one-world dictatorship.[32]

Any remaining doubts I had over the real intent of the CFR were removed after becoming aware of the statements made over the years by the CFR itself, advocating world government. For example, on 17 February 1950 CFR member James Warburg, testifying before the Senate Foreign Relations Committee, stated, "We shall have world government whether or not you like it—by conquest or consent."[33]

On another occasion, in the April 1974 issue of the CFR journal, *Foreign Affairs* (p. 558), Richard Gardner stated that the New World Order "will have to be built from the bottom up rather than from the top down. It will look like a great 'booming, buzzing confusion,'. . . but an end run around national sovereignty, eroding it piece by piece, will accomplish much more than the old-fashioned frontal assault."[34]

And in Study Number 7, a CFR position paper published on 25 November 1959 the CFR stated that its purpose was to advocate the "building [of] a new international order [which] may be responsible to world aspirations for peace [and] for social and economic change. . . . An international order . . . including states labelling themselves as Socialist [Communist]."[35]

The term New World Order (or New International Order) has been used privately by the CFR since its inception to describe the coming world government. However, since the fall of 1990, CFR members have, for the first time, begun using the term publicly to condition the public for what lies ahead. If the American people hear the term often enough before the world government is formed, it is hoped they will be less likely to resist the effort or feel threatened by it when that day arrives.

The New World Order, it should be explained, is an expression that has been used by illuminized Freemasonry since the days of Weishaupt to signify the coming world government over which the Antichrist would come to rule once it had been built. One of illuminized Freemasonry's secret symbols portraying this message was placed on the back of our dollar bill during the administration of Franklin D. Roosevelt.[36] Roosevelt was himself a thirty-third degree Mason and a close associate of the CFR. This Masonic symbol consists of a pyramid with the all-seeing eye of Osiris or Baal above it. Underneath the pyramid is written "Novus Ordo Seclorum," which means The New Order of the Ages (or The New World Order) in Latin.[37]

U.S. dollar (backside portion, enlarged)

This symbol was designed by Masonic interests and became the official reverse side of the Great Seal of the United States in 1782. What was on the reverse side of the seal, although not a secret, remained largely unknown to the American people for more than 150 years, until it was placed on our one dollar Federal Reserve Note.

At the time the seal was designed, the New World Order was still in the early stages of being built and was not yet complete. This is symbolized by the capstone being separated from the rest of the pyramid. However, once the New World Order has been built and the one-world government is in place, the capstone will be joined to the rest of the pyramid, symbolizing the completion of the task. The hierarchy of Freemasonry and the occult societies, resembling a multilevel pyramid structure, will now be complete, with the Antichrist taking his seat of power atop the pyramid. As I continued my research, I discovered that the CFR had more in common with the Illuminati than a mere use of the same terminology.

One of the reasons we have heard so little about the Council on Foreign Relations is because its rules, like those of the Illuminati, require that important meetings of the membership remain secret. Article II of the organization's bylaws contends that

> it is an express condition of membership in the Council, to which condition every member accedes by virtue of his or her membership, that members will observe such rules and regulations as may be prescribed from time to time by the Board of Directors concerning the conduct of Council meetings or the attribution of statements made therein, and that any disclosure, publication, or other action by a member in contravention thereof may be regarded by the Board of Directors in its sole discretion as ground for termination or suspension of membership pursuant to Article I of the By-Laws.[38]

Page 182 of the CFR's 1990 Annual Report further states that "it would not be in compliance" with the organization's non-attribution rule for a meeting participant

> (i) to publish a speaker's statement in attributed form in a newspaper; (ii) to repeat it on television or radio, or on a speaker's platform, or in a classroom; or (iii) to go beyond a memo of limited circulation, by distributing the attributed statement in a company or government agency newsletter. . . . A meeting participant is forbidden knowingly to transmit the attributed statement to a newspaper reporter or other such person who is likely to publish it in a public medium. The essence of the Rule . . . is simple enough: participants in Council meetings should not pass along an attributed statement in circumstances where there is substantial risk that it will promptly be widely circulated or published.

So much for freedom of the press! What could be so important that secrecy is required if the purpose of the CFR is not to influence U.S. policy in the direction of world government?

. In order to accomplish its mission of leading the American people into a New World Order, the CFR has been using a strategy very similar to that employed by Adam Weishaupt. It would work to surround leaders in high places with members of the Council, targeting especially the key advisory positions in the executive branch of the U.S. government, until the Council's members were in complete control. This tactic would also be applied to the fields of education, the media, the military, and banking, with CFR members eventually becoming the leaders in each of these fields.

The goal of the CFR, quite simply, was to influence all aspects of society in such a way that one day Americans would wake up and find themselves in the midst of a one-world system whether they liked it or not. Their hope was to get Americans to the point where entering a world government would seem as natural and American as baseball and apple pie. This all sounds preposterous until one realizes how far the CFR's plans have already come.

Using illuministic tactics and with backing from the major global foundations, the CFR has been able to advance its agenda rapidly and with relative ease. During the 1920s and 30s the organization made significant strides toward gaining control of the Democratic party and by the 1940s had established a foothold in the Republican party as well.

With the start of World War II the CFR, thanks to the help of Franklin Roosevelt, would gain control of the State Department and, therefore, our foreign policy. Rene Wormser, of the Reece Committee, explains how this happened.

> [The] organization became virtually an agency of the government when World War II broke out. The Rockefeller Foundation had started and financed certain studies known as The War and Peace Studies, manned largely by associates of the Council; the State Department, in due course, took these Studies over, retaining the major personnel which The Council on Foreign Relations had supplied.[39]

The United Nations

CFR control of the State Department would ensure U.S. membership in the United Nations following the war. In fact, the Council on Foreign Relations would act through the State Department to establish the U.N. These details were revealed in 1969 during a debate between Lt. Col. Archibald Roberts and Congressman Richard L. Ottinger, Director, United States Committee on the United Nations. During that debate, Colonel Roberts testified:

> . . . the United Nations was spawned two weeks after Pearl Harbor in the office of Secretary of State, Cordell Hull. In a letter to the President, Franklin D. Roosevelt, date 22 Dec. 1941, Secretary Hull, at the direction of his faceless sponsors . . . recommended the founding of a Presidential Advisory Committee on Post War Foreign Policy. This Post War Foreign Policy Committee was in fact the planning commission for the United Nations and its Charter.[40]

Colonel Roberts went on to identify the people who made up the Committee, besides Secretary of State Hull. The list included various State Department advisors and staff members, CFR officials, and leaders in education, the media, and foreign policy research.[41]

These are the real founders of the United Nations. Altogether, ten of the fourteen Committee members belonged to the CFR. As Roberts pointed out, "Each member of the Committee . . . was without exception, a member of the Council on Foreign Relations, or under the control of the Council on Foreign Relations."[42]

In 1945, at the U.N.'s founding conference, forty-seven members of the CFR were in the United States delegation. Included among these were Edward Stettinius, the new secretary of state; John Foster Dulles; Adlai Stevenson; Nelson Rockefeller; and Alger Hiss, who was the secretary general of the U.N.'s founding conference.[43]

To make sure that the United States would not back out of joining the United Nations as it did with the League of Nations, the international body would this time be located on American soil. This gesture would make the American public less resistant to the move. The land for the United Nations building was "graciously" donated by John D. Rockefeller, Jr.[44]

By getting the United States to join the U.N., which represents a limited form of world government, the Council on Foreign Relations had accomplished its first major objective. Using its influence in public education and the media, the CFR would now proceed to cast a favorable image for the United Nations among the American public, eventually leading step-by-step to U.S. participation in a full-blown system of world government. This, it was realized, would take some time.

Had the CFR tried to bring the U.S. into a world government all at once, the effort would have failed. The American people would have reacted full force against such an attempt. The immediate purpose of the U.N. was therefore merely to warm Americans up to the idea of global government. It was all part of the conditioning.

Since the U.N. was founded in 1945, its leaders have been guilty of an array of outrageous actions. Alger Hiss, for example, was exposed as a Soviet spy. Secretary General U Thant praised Lenin as a leader whose "ideals of peace and peaceful coexistence among states have won widespread international acceptance and they are in line with the aims of the U.N. Charter." And Secretary General Kurt Waldheim was discovered to be a Nazi foot soldier during World War II.[45] Yet, in spite of these revelations, most Americans today view the United Nations as a "good organization." It is amazing what a little favorable publicity from the media can accomplish!

Along with being responsible for the United Nations, the Council on Foreign Relations would go on to serve as a mainspring for numerous spin-off groups, such as the Bilderbergers, the Club of Rome, and the Trilateral Commission, each of which was designed to carry out a specific task within the broader mission of establishing a New World Order. The creation of these new organizations would represent a mere restructuring of the one-world political hierarchy, which is always changing, revising, and adapting itself to current situations in a way that will most effectively further its agenda.

The hierarchy, among other things, had called for world government to be achieved in stages through the forming of world administrative regions. This was in accordance with the U.N. Charter, which encourages the implementation and administration of world government on a regional basis. [According to chapter 8, Articles 52 (2-3) and 53 (1) of the Charter, under "Regional Arrangements."][46] The strategy was simple. The countries of the world would first be merged into several regions. This would serve to break down concepts of national sovereignty, then, these regions would be merged into a system of world government.

However, it was soon realized that regionalized world government would be next to impossible to achieve politically because of resistance to the idea from the world's people. So the powers-that-be decided to divide the world into economic regions first, hoping to pave the way for later political unions based on these same geographical boundaries. In order to accomplish this feat, several special task organizations were established to oversee the creation of regional trade associations. The society responsible for Europe's economic integration would be the Bilderberg Group, better known as the Bilderbergers.

The Bilderbergers

The public name for the group was derived from the Bilderberg Hotel in Oosterbeek, Holland, the site of the association's first meeting in 1954.[47] The group consists of approximately one hundred power-elite from the member nations of NATO (North Atlantic Treaty Organization).[48] Its leadership is interlocked with that of the Council on Foreign Relations, and may therefore be accurately categorized as a CFR sister organization.

Funded by a number of major one-world institutions, including the Rockefeller and Ford foundations, the express purpose of the Bilderberger Group was to regionalize Europe.[49] This goal was revealed by Giovanni Agnelli, the head of Fiat and one of the leaders of the Bilderbergers. Agnelli stated, "European integration is our goal and where the politicians have failed we industrialists hope to succeed."[50]

George McGhee, the former U.S. ambassador to West Germany, revealed that "the Treaty of Rome which brought the Common Market into being was nurtured at the Bilderberg meetings."[51] In other words, today's European Economic Community which is soon to become a political union (on 31 December 1992) is a product of the Bilderberg Group.

The overriding purpose of the Bilderbergers like that of its sister organizations—the Council on Foreign Relations and the United Nations—is the establishment of a world government. This philosophy of the Bilderbergers was clearly explained by the group's first chairman, Prince Bernhard of the Netherlands (whose family is a principal owner of Royal Dutch Shell Oil Company). Bernhard wrote:

> Here comes our greatest difficulty. For the governments
> of the free nations are elected by the people, and if they
> do something the people don't like they are thrown out.
> It is difficult to reeducate the people who have been
> brought up on nationalism to the idea of relinquishing
> part of their sovereignty to a supernational body. . . .
> This is the tragedy.[52]

Prominent American Bilderbergers have included David and Nelson Rockefeller; Thomas Hughes of the Carnegie Endowment; Winston Lord, former director of planning and coordination for the State Department; Henry Kissinger; Zbigniew Brzezinski; Cyrus Vance; Robert McNamara, former president of the World Bank; Donald Rumsfeld; George Ball, former undersecretary of state and director of Lehman Brothers; Robert Anderson, president of ARCO and associated with the Aspen Institute; President Gerald Ford; Henry Grunwald, Managing Editor of *TIME*; Henry J. Heinz II, chairman of the board, H.J. Heinz Company; Father Theodore M. Hesburgh, former president of Notre Dame University; and Shepard Stone of The Aspen Institute for Humanistic Studies.*[53]

Virtually every one of the American Bilderbergers is a current or former member of the CFR. European participants have included prime ministers, foreign ministers, and financial leaders such as Helmut Schmidt of West Germany; Rumor of Italy; Baron Edmond de

---

* The Aspen Institute is also a sister organization of the CFR and the Bilderbergers, and like both of these organizations, is heavily funded by the Ford and Rockefeller Foundations. It has been described as "a training and orientation school for prospective world government administrators."[54]

Rothschild and Giscard d'Estaing of France; and Sir Eric Roll, chairman of Warburg & Co. in England; to name just a few.[55]

The Club of Rome

Another organization that has drawn a high percentage of its members from the Council on Foreign Relations is the Club of Rome. The Club of Rome (COR) claims to be an informal organization of less than one hundred people who are, in their own words, " . . . scientists, educators, economists, humanists, industrialists, and national and international civil servants. . . ."[56] Included among these have been members of the Rockefeller family.[57] Altogether, there are approximately twenty-five CFR members who belong to the American Association for the Club of Rome.[58]

The Club had its beginnings in April of 1968, when leaders from ten different countries gathered in Rome at the invitation of Aurelio Peccei, a prominent Italian industrialist with close ties to the Fiat and Olivetti Corporations.[59] The organization claims to have the solutions for world peace and prosperity. However, these solutions always seem to promote the concept of world government at the expense of national sovereignty.

The Club of Rome has been charged with the task of overseeing the regionalization and unification of the entire world; the Club could therefore be said to be one step above the Bilderbergers in the one-world hierarchy. (COR's founder, Peccei, has been a close associate of the Bilderbergers.)[60] As far as I have been able to determine, most of the directives for the planning of the world government are presently coming from the Club of Rome.

The Club's findings and recommendations are published from time to time in special, highly confidential reports, which are sent to the power-elite to be implemented. On 17 September 1973 the Club released one such report, entitled *Regionalized and Adaptive Model of the Global World System*, prepared by COR members Mihajlo Mesarovic and Eduard Pestel.[61]

The document reveals that the Club has divided the world into ten political/economic regions, which it refers to as "kingdoms." (This sounds to me like a fulfillment of Daniel 7:15-28 and Revelation 13 in the making.) While these "kingdoms" are not set in concrete and changes could still occur, it gives us an idea of what lies ahead.*

Referring to the Mesarovic-Pestel study, Aurelio Peccei, the

*During the Nixon Administration the United States was further divided into ten federal sub-regions for the alleged purpose of "emergency management" and the "decentralization of the Executive Branch."

Club's founder, states:

> Their world model, based on new developments of the
> multilevel hierarchical systems theory, divides the world
> into ten interdependent and mutually interacting regions
> of political, economic or environmental coherence. . . .
> It will be recognized of course that these are still pro-
> totype models. Mesarovic and Pestel have assumed a
> Herculean task. The full implementation of their work
> will take many years.[62]

In 1974, only a year after the report's distribution to Club members, Mesarovic and Pestel released their "findings" in a book entitled *Mankind at the Turning Point*, which was intended for public consumption. On pages 161-164 of this book, the authors display the same ten regions; only this time the word "kingdoms" has been omitted. They obviously didn't want the public to know the true nature of the Club's political ambitions.

What is particularly disturbing about all of this is that the Club of Rome is being spiritually driven—spiritually as in occultism. On pages 151 and 152 of *Mankind at the Turning Point*, Aurelio Peccei reveals his pantheistic/New Age beliefs, talking about man's communion with nature and the transcendent and using the term "noosphere" in referring to the collective field of intelligence of the human race. This uncommon expression cannot be found in a dictionary. By use of the term "noosphere" Peccei gives himself away as a student of Pierre Teilhard de Chardin, a French Jesuit priest (now deceased) whose occult ideas and writings, I would later discover, have had a deep impact on the New Age movement. In fact, Chardin is one of the most frequently quoted writers by leading New Age occultists.

At the conclusion of the book, Peccei remarks: "Philosophers have, from ancient times, stressed the unity of existence and the interconnection of all the elements of nature, man and thought. However, their teaching has seldom been reflected in political or social behavior."[63] The Club of Rome and its network of affiliated organizations would like to change all of that.

COR's New Age slant is reflected in its American Association membership, which included the late Norman Cousins, the long-time honorary chairman of Planetary Citizens and possibly the best-known and respected name at the forefront of the New Age movement. Other members are John Naisbitt, author of *Megatrends*; Amory Lovins, speaker at John Denver's New Age center (Windstar, in Snowmass, Colorado); Betty Friedan, the founding president of the National Organization for Women; and Jean Houston and Hazel Henderson, well-

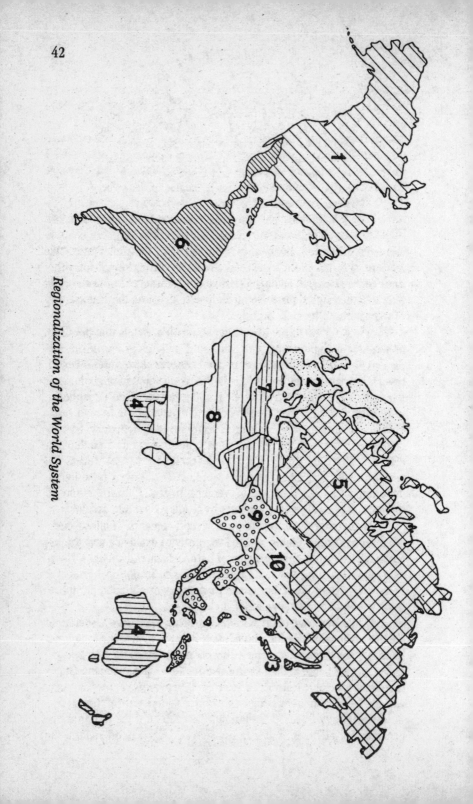

Regionalization of the World System

known authors and speakers at New Age centers and conferences. Robert O. Anderson and Harlan B. Cleveland are also members. Both men belong to the CFR and have been closely associated with the Aspen Institute for Humanistic Studies. Four of our U.S. congressmen are members, along with representatives of Planned Parenthood, officials of the United Nations, and people connected to the Carnegie and Rockefeller foundations.[64]

These are more of the people who are at the forefront of establishing the New World Order! There can be no mistaking the fact that they have political intentions. On page 193 of *The Limits to Growth* (COR's first book, published in 1972), the Club states, "We believe in fact that the need will quickly become evident for social innovation to match technical change, for radical reform of the institutions and political processes at all levels, including the highest, that of world polity."

The Executive Committee of the Club of Rome concludes the book with the following:

> We believe that an unexpectedly large number of men and women of all ages and conditions will readily respond to the challenge and will be eager to discuss not "if" but "how" we can create this new future.
>
> The Club of Rome plans to support such activity in many ways. . . . And, since intellectual enlightenment is without effect if it is not also political, The Club of Rome also will encourage the creation of a world forum where statesmen, policy-makers, and scientists can discuss the dangers and hopes for the future global system without the constraints of formal intergovernmental negotiation.[65]

In *Mankind at the Turning Point*, the Club is no less blatant about its intentions. Referring to the problems of economic control, food shortages, and the environment, the authors state:

> "The solution of these crises can be developed only in a global context" with full and explicit recognition of the emerging world system and on a long-term basis. This would necessitate, among other changes, a new world economic order and a global resources allocation system. . . . A "world consciousness" must be developed through which every individual realizes his role as a member of the world community. . . . It must become part of the consciousness of every individual that "the basic unit of human cooperation and hence survival is moving from the national to the global level."[66]

The book closes with a commentary by COR Directors Aurelio Peccei and Alexander King, who state:

> The winds of change have begun to blow. A keen and anxious awareness is evolving to suggest that fundamental changes will have to take place in the world order and its power structures, in the distribution of wealth and income, in our own outlook and behavior. Perhaps only a new and enlightened humanism can permit mankind to negotiate this transition without irreparable lacerations.[67]

The Trilateral Commission

During the 1950s and 60s, the same congressional leaders who had been actively campaigning against the Federal Reserve System began to expose the Council on Foreign Relations. They received considerable help from citizens' action groups who recognized the threat and responded accordingly. As a result of these efforts and, particularly, the congressional investigations of the late 60s and early 70s, the truth was beginning to reach the American people in significant numbers, in spite of the media's lack of coverage. For the first time, a large number of Americans were aware of the fact that major segments of U.S. industries were falling under the control of just a few establishments.

Global planners realized that something had to be done in order to avoid losing all the ground they had gained over the past fifty years. Their strategy would involve funneling American and European consumer money to Japanese industrialists and Arab oil magnates who would promptly use it to acquire Western companies and real estate. This way, if the American people were to blame anyone for their difficult times, it would be the Japanese and the Arabs—not the Rockefellers and their allies, who were really the ones responsible.

Even though Arab leaders had never been able to get along before, they suddenly, almost overnight, came together to impose an effective oil embargo in 1973. One possible catalyst for cooperation could have been their commonly held Islamic religion. However, this had never prevented them from quarreling in the past. The only other common denominator between Arab countries was oil, which was being explored, drilled, and marketed for them by the American and European oil cartel. All that Arab leaders had to do was sit back and watch as their silent partners made them rich. The fact was, and continues to be, that the Arab princes owe most of their wealth to the Rockefellers and their allies.

Some of this oil money was immediately funneled back into

American and European superbanks, such as Chase Manhattan, with a few of the Arab sheiks actually becoming vice-presidents of these same banks. Much of the rest of the money was reinvested into American industry and real estate.

The OPEC energy crisis would also have the effect of turning Japan into an industrial giant. Japan had the compact cars ready to go. American consumers, forced to cut back their energy consumption, flocked to purchase these inexpensive, fuel-efficient cars. Japanese auto manufacturers could hardly keep up with the demand. All of these activities would be protected under our liberal free-trade laws. In the meantime, the U.S. auto industry was plunged into a deep recession from which it has never fully recovered.

Japanese industrialists would invest their fortunes in other budding Japanese industries. Before long the U.S. was being flooded by inexpensive imported products, ranging from consumer electronics to industrial robots. A good part of the money from these profits, like the Arab oil money, has been used to buy real estate in the United States and throughout the rest of the world.

As it turned out, the oil crisis would serve to build the New World Order at a rate even faster than insiders could have hoped for. By working through Japanese and Arab partners, the globalists would be able to advance their agenda with little suspicion. The redistribution of the world's wealth would simply be used to foster a new era of "global economic interdependence," a concept that would prove useful in laying the groundwork for world government. To accommodate these efforts, David Rockefeller formed the Trilateral Commission in 1973.[68]

The purpose of the Trilateral Commission would be to promote world government by encouraging economic interdependence among the superpowers. Steering the economies of the member nations into a position where they would be completely intertwined, the Trilateral Commission augments the regionalization efforts of its sister organizations, the Bilderbergers and the Club of Rome. Rockefeller's main accomplice in this endeavor would be Zbigniew Brzezinski, who drafted the Commission's charter and went on to become the organization's first director (1973-1976).[69]

Brzezinski, who would later become Jimmy Carter's National Security Advisor, wrote several books detailing his worldview. In one of these books, entitled *Between Two Ages*, written in 1970, Brzezinski calls for a new international monetary system and prepares the reader for the acceptance of a global taxation system.[70] He also reveals (on pg. 72) his views about the philosophies of Karl Marx.

> Marxism represents a further vital and creative stage in
> the maturing of man's universal vision. Marxism is si-
> multaneously a victory of the external, active man over
> the inner, passive man and a victory of reason over
> belief: it stresses man's capacity to shape his material
> destiny—finite and defined as man's only reality.

Like his fellow collaborator, Aurelio Peccei, of the Club of Rome,
Brzezinski favored the writings of the French Jesuit priest, Teilhard
de Chardin.

> Marxism has served as a mechanism of human
> "progress," even if its practice has often fallen short of
> its ideals. Teilhard de Chardin notes at one point that
> "monstrous as it is, is not modern totalitarianism really
> the distortion of something magnificent, and thus quite
> near to the truth?" (pg. 73).

Brzezinski continues:

> Marxism, disseminated on the popular level in the form
> of communism, represented a major advance in man's
> ability to conceptualize his relationship to his world (pg.
> 83).

Guided by these illuministic beliefs, the Trilateral Commission
has become a virtual carbon copy of the Council on Foreign Relations.
It is led by many of the same people, espouses the same philosophies,
and is funded by the same sources, with the Ford Foundation having
been the Trilateral Commission's largest contributor.[71] In fact, all eight
American representatives to the founding meeting of the Commission,
held at David Rockefeller's estate, were members of the CFR.[72]

Like the CFR, the Commission is headquartered in New York
City. However, unlike the CFR, whose membership is drawn only from
the United States, the Trilateral Commission is composed of leaders
from the world's three economic superpowers—North America, Western Europe, and Japan. Hence, the term "trilateral." (It is worth not-
ing that these are also the first three economic regions [kingdoms]
listed on the Club of Rome's global model.)

Another difference is that the Trilateral Commission is much
smaller than the CFR. Unlike its sister organization, which has over
2,500 members, the Commission has only 325 members, of which
98 are from N. America, 146 from Europe, and 81 from Japan. On a
per capita basis, Japan has by far the greatest number of members of
any nation. At least one director of nearly every major Japanese corporation is represented.

The Commission's North American chairman continues to be
David Rockefeller; the European chairman is Georges Berthoin, hon-

orary chairman of the European movement, and the Japanese industrialist, Isamu Yamashita, is the Commission's chairman for Japan. It
is worth mentioning that most, if not all of the important Frenchmen
who are members of the Commission, belong to the Grand Orient
Lodge of Freemasonry.[73]

By the late 1970s and early 80s, the growing influence of the
CFR and Trilateral Commission in our governmental affairs had become difficult to ignore. And the number of congressmen who were
willing to take a stand against these organizations was increasing.
Congressman Larry McDonald took the matter before Congress on 4
February 1981 calling for a comprehensive congressional investigation of the CFR and the Trilateral Commission, following up Resolution 773 of the American Legion, which urged Congress to investigate these organizations to determine their influence on U.S. policy.

In spite of getting no coverage on this matter from the media
and having only limited results in Congress, McDonald refused to give
up. He did everything humanly possible to expose the plot right up
until his death aboard the Korean Airliner in 1983.

The *007* "accident" backfired on the establishment as it set off
a wave of repulsion at the state level. Infuriated by McDonald's death
and the failure of the media to even mention the fact that he had
been exposing a conspiracy, those aware of the battle being waged
behind-the-scenes began to apply pressure on Congress to take action.
One of the states at the forefront of this effort was Indiana where
Resolution 773 had originated. (Indianapolis is the national headquarters of the American Legion.)

On 3 April 1985 the Indiana House of Representatives introduced Resolution No. 19 calling for a comprehensive investigation of
the Trilateral Commission and the Council on Foreign Relations, pur-
suant to the efforts of Larry McDonald. However, like other calls for
congressional investigations, this too would go unanswered, largely
because of a lack of public pressure on Congress—which was in part
the result of NO MEDIA COVERAGE.*

McDonald's death gave other congressional leaders courage to
continue the fight. Though spearheading the effort, McDonald was not

* It is no coincidence that Indiana native Dan Quayle, who is not a member of
the CFR or the TC, has been the focus of so much ridicule and criticism by the
media. Nor was it a coincidence that Bush chose Quayle as his running mate. With
one of the most conservative voting records in Congress and coming from a state
that has long been viewed as a bastion of conservatism, his appeal was
obvious.Making Dan Quayle vice president, I believe, was a superficial attempt
by George Bush to appease the conservative wing of the Republican party, which

the only congressman trying to expose the plot to create a world government. While some congressmen decided to back off as a result of the Korean Airline incident, other leaders, such as Senator Jesse Helms, would only intensify their efforts.

Since McDonald's death, Helms has become the most outspoken critic of these organizations in Congress, repeatedly taking a stand against the establishment. Speaking before the Senate on 15 December 1987 Senator Helms launched into a detailed discussion of these matters in an urgent appeal to his colleagues. Here are a few excerpts from his important speech:

> This campaign against the American people—against traditional American culture and values—is systematic psychological warfare. It is orchestrated by a vast array of interests comprising not only the Eastern establishment but also the radical left. Among this group we find the Department of State, the Department of Commerce, the money center banks and multinational corporations, the media, the educational establishment, the entertainment industry, and the large tax-exempt foundations.
>
> Mr. President, a careful examination of what is happening behind the scenes reveals that all of these interests are working in concert with the masters of the Kremlin in order to create what some refer to as a new world order. Private organizations such as the Council on Foreign Relations, the Royal Institute of International Affairs, the Trilateral Commission, the Dartmouth Conference, the Aspen Institute for Humanistic Studies, the Atlantic Institute, and the Bilderberger Group serve to disseminate and to coordinate the plans for this so-called new world order in powerful business, financial, academic, and official circles. . . .
>
> The psychological campaign that I am describing, as I have said, is the work of groups within the Eastern establishment, that amorphous amalgam of wealth and social connections whose power resides in its control over our financial system and over a large portion of our industrial sector. The principal instrument of this

did not trust him. The ensuing assault upon the vice president by the media only served to give Bush the opportunity to "prove" himself to conservatives by sticking it out with Quayle. This strategy worked. Many conservatives ended up voting for Bush because of Quayle and because of the fact that if they didn't elect Bush, Dukakis would become president. After the job the media has done on Dan Quayle, few would now blame Bush if he dropped the former Indiana senator in favor of another running mate in 1992. It will be interesting to see what happens.

control over the American economy and money is the Federal Reserve System. The policies of the industrial sectors, primarily the multinational corporations, are influenced by the money center banks through debt financing and through the large blocks of stock controlled by the trust departments of the money center banks.

Anyone familiar with American history, and particularly American economic history, cannot fail to notice the control over the Department of State and the Central Intelligence Agency which Wall Street seems to exercise. . . .

The influence of establishment insiders over our foreign policy has become a fact of life in our time. This pervasive influence runs contrary to the real long-term national security of our Nation. It is an influence which, if unchecked, could ultimately subvert our constitutional order.

The viewpoint of the establishment today is called globalism. Not so long ago, this viewpoint was called the "one-world" view by its critics. The phrase is no longer fashionable among sophisticates; yet, the phrase "one-world" is still apt because nothing has changed in the minds and actions of those promoting policies consistent with its fundamental tenets.

Mr. President, in the globalist point of view, nation-states and national boundaries do not count for anything. Political philosophies and political principles seem to become simply relative. Indeed, even constitutions are irrelevant to the exercise of power. Liberty and tyranny are viewed as neither necessarily good nor evil, and certainly not a component of policy.

In this point of view, the activities of international financial and industrial forces should be oriented to bringing this one-world design—with a convergence of the Soviet and American systems as its centerpiece—into being. . . . All that matters to this club is the maximization of profits resulting from the practice of what can be described as finance capitalism, a system which rests upon the twin pillars of debt and monopoly. This isn't real capitalism. It is the road to economic concentration and to political slavery.[74]

I was about to discover just how far down this road we had already come!

Stepping Stones to Global Government

Founding Date	Organization	Location
1913	Federal Reserve System	Washington, DC (Headquarters for the Board of Directors)
1920	League of Nations	Geneva
1920-1921	Royal Institute of International Affairs	London
	Council on Foreign Relations	New York
	Branch Organizations:	
	Institute for Pacific Relations	New York
	Centre d'Etudes de Politicque Etrangere	Paris
	Institut fur Auswartige Politik	Hamburg
1945	United Nations	New York
1954	The Bilderberger Group	Oosterbeek, The Netherlands (Meeting sites vary.)
1968	Club of Rome	Rome
1973	Trilateral Commission	New York

Chapter 3
America's Shadow Government

After being on the CFR and Trilateral Commission mailing lists for several years, and receiving their annual reports and literature, I was prepared to do an analysis of the membership to see for myself what control these institutions exercised over American politics. I knew they were powerful, but I had no idea how far things had gone.

For the first time, I realized that I, as well as most Americans, had been living in a "false reality." We thought that because we had the right to vote and choose candidates that we, the people, were somehow in control. But the fact is, we aren't!

From the time of Franklin D. Roosevelt, the influence of the Council on Foreign Relations in the executive branch of government has continued to grow. By the Nixon administration, at least 115 CFR members held positions within the executive branch. And during the Carter years, more than a dozen Trilateralists were appointed to top positions in the administration. Those who weren't TC members were often members of the CFR, while many were members of both organizations. Each of the seven men on Carter's National Security Council, including Carter himself, currently or previously belonged to at least one of the two groups (e.g., Walter Mondale, vice president, CFR/TC; Zbigniew Brzezinski, national security advisor, CFR/TC; Cyrus Vance, secretary of state, CFR/TC; Harold Brown, secretary of defense, CFR/TC; Gen. David Jones, chairman of the Joint Chiefs of Staff, CFR; and Stansfield Turner, director, CIA, CFR).

(It is common practice for Trilateralists to resign from the Commission shortly before running for public office. The same holds true for the CFR. However, these outward political gestures do not mean that former members are no longer influenced by these organizations.)

The tradition continued during the Reagan years. Even though Reagan had campaigned against the two groups; once elected, he appointed no less than seventy-five CFR and Trilateral Commission members to key posts. The Bush administration, however, would shatter all previous records, as more than 350 CFR and TC members currently hold positions within the executive branch. Top-level Bush officials who are past or present members of the Council on Foreign Relations and/or the Trilateral Commission include George Bush, president, CFR/TC; Brent Scowcroft, national security advisor, CFR/TC; Richard Cheney, secretary of defense, CFR; Dick Thornburgh, attorney general, CFR; Colin Powell, chairman of the Joint Chiefs of Staff, CFR; and Carla Hills, U.S. trade representative, TC.

Given the subtlety of the Council on Foreign Relations and the Trilateral Commission, I believe it is possible for a person to belong to these organizations for a short period of time without recognizing the danger or understanding their purpose. Some may simply join for the prestige or to further their careers; while others are invited in for "window dressing." However, someone naive enough to join and remain in such organizations exercises very poor judgment and does not deserve to hold a position of leadership in the United States government.

All of the executive departments, I would discover, are dominated by establishment insiders. This has been the case for some time. The State Department, which was penetrated by globalists during World War II, has been particularly hard hit. Although Secretary of State James Baker is not a member of the Council on Foreign Relations or the Trilateral Commission, just about everyone else of importance is, including Deputy Secretary Lawrence S. Eagleburger, and numerous U.S. ambassadors.

The Treasury Department is another division of the executive branch, which has been dominated by the CFR and the TC, led by past and present secretaries such as Nicholas F. Brady and Donald Regan.

Globalists within the Treasury Department have been assisted by the efforts of their comrades at the Federal Reserve, including Federal Reserve Chairman Alan Greenspan, CFR/TC; Harold Anderson, CFR; Cyrus R. Vance, CFR/TC; and Paul Volcker, CFR/TC.

Through the Treasury Department and the Federal Reserve System, the Rockefellers and their allies have been able to direct America's fiscal and monetary policies, making U.S. economic policies synonymous with their own.

In addition to the areas of foreign affairs and economic policy, the establishment has had a lock on the key positions dealing with our national security. Since the Eisenhower administration, numerous CFR/TC members have served as national security advisors, including Walt Rostow, CFR; Henry Kissinger, CFR/TC; Brent Scowcroft, CFR/TC; Zbigniew Brzezinski, CFR/TC; Robert McFarlane, CFR; Frank

Carlucci, CFR/TC; and Colin Powell, CFR.

Our national defense has been dominated by insiders as well. Every U.S. defense secretary of the past thirty-five years, with the exception of Clark Clifford (1968-69), has belonged either to the Council on Foreign Relations or the Trilateral Commission.

The same group has supplemented its efforts in the Defense Department with the control of other strategic military posts. For example, every Supreme Allied Commander in Europe has been a member of the CFR or the TC.

Every U.S. ambassador to NATO has been a member of the CFR or TC as well. And the Central Intelligence Agency (CIA), which is so critical to our national defense, has also been dominated by establishment insiders, with nine of its thirteen directors having been CFR members.

The list goes on and on, with virtually every area of the military being dominated by members of the CFR. I was somewhat relieved to discover that Gen. Norman Schwarzkopf was not among the military leaders belonging to the CFR. However, this provides little comfort when viewed against the background of the preceding facts.

The four executive positions that have most frequently been filled by CFR/TC members are probably also the most influential positions in the U.S. government, apart from the presidency itself—the secretary of the treasury, secretary of state, national security advisor, and secretary of defense.

Altogether, since 1920, fifteen of twenty-one treasury secretaries have been members of the CFR. Another twelve of our last fourteen secretaries of state (since 1944) have been members. And since the Eisenhower years, ten of thirteen national security advisors have belonged to the CFR. During this same period of time the U.S. had twelve defense secretaries, eleven of whom were CFR members.

Of the sixty people who have held these strategic positions during the years specified, forty-eight have been members of the Council on Foreign Relations. This represents a total of 80 percent.

If this isn't disturbing enough, consider the fact that every U.S. president since World War II, with the possible exceptions of John F. Kennedy and Ronald Reagan, has been either a Freemason, a member of the CFR, or a member of the Trilateral Commission. George Bush is perhaps the most prominent insider ever to have attained the position of president. In addition to belonging to the Skull and Bones, a secret society at Yale University, he has served as a Director of the Council on Foreign Relations from 1977 to 1979 and is listed by the Trilateral Commission as a "Former Member in Public Service."

The following is a list of our last nine presidents along with their past or present organizational affiliations.

Franklin D. Roosevelt—Masonic Lodge
Harry S. Truman—Masonic Lodge
*John F. Kennedy—CFR
Lyndon B. Johnson—Masonic Lodge
Richard M. Nixon—CFR
**Gerald R. Ford, Jr.—Masonic Lodge/CFR
***James E. Carter, Jr.—CFR/TC
****Ronald W. Reagan—Masonic Lodge
*****George H.W. Bush—SB/CFR/TC

Not only have our presidents belonged to these organizations, but the candidates running on the opposing tickets have, almost without exception, been members as well. A typical example of this came during the 1980 presidential campaign when the establishment put up John Anderson (CFR/TC), Howard Baker (CFR), George Bush (CFR/TC/SB), Jimmy Carter (CFR/TC), and Ted Kennedy (CFR—Boston Affiliate) as candidates.

Only Ronald Reagan was not a member of one of these groups at the time of the election. He won the race partially as a result of this fact. He had openly campaigned against the CFR and the Trilat-

---

* One source lists JFK as having been a CFR member. However, the Council's historical membership roster does not include him. One possible explanation for this discrepancy is that John F. Kennedy may at one time have belonged to a CFR affiliate like his brother, Ted, who is a member of Boston's Committee on Foreign Relations.

** Although Gerald Ford is a current member of the CFR, he did not belong to the organization at the time of his presidency. He was, however, one of this nation's highest ranking Freemasons and had attended meetings of the Bilderberger organization.

***Jimmy Carter was a member of the Trilateral Commission prior to his presidency, but did not become a CFR member until 1983.

**** Ronald Reagan was made an honorary Freemason near the end of his second term in office. Reagan turned down two previous opportunities to receive this award before finally accepting it after a third invitation. However, controversy surrounded the legitimacy of the award as Reagan apparently did not meet the specified requirements for receiving the honorary degree. Therefore, while unofficially being an Honorary Freemason, officially, Reagan is not.

***** Although Bush is not officially a Freemason, he is a member of a powerful secret society with Masonic overtones known as the Skull and Bones. Ron Rosenbaum, a writer for *Esquire* magazine, revealed in a 1977 article that the S and B is linked to the Illuminati. The skull and bones also happens to be one of the secret symbols of Freemasonry.

eral Commission in the southern states, promising there would be changes if he was elected. But for some reason (possibly the presence of V.P. George Bush) these changes never occurred.

Other losing presidential candidates include 1952, 1956 Adlai Stevenson (CFR); 1964 Barry Goldwater (* M); 1972 George McGovern (** M/CFR/TC); and 1988 Michael Dukakis (** CFR). Membership in these organizations doesn't guarantee victory, it only guarantees you the right to run!

This trend of stacking the ticket is likely to continue in the elections of 1992 and beyond. If you've been wondering why everything continues to head in the same direction regardless of who gets elected, now you know why! It is not unfair to say that the Council on Foreign Relations and the Trilateral Commission run our government. In fact, any statement to the contrary, given the preceding information, would be inaccurate. As we have seen, membership in these organizations has become a prerequisite of running for the presidency or for being appointed to a significant position in the executive branch. This represents a complete breakdown in our political process.

Even if the CFR and the Trilateral Commission were acting in the best interests of the American people, would such concentration of power be justified? Such a centralized political system cannot fairly represent the public. Regardless of who gets elected, the same agenda moves forward, because candidates from both parties are consistently drawn from the same school of thought espousing universalism. We aren't being presented with any real alternatives. This isn't democracy. This is political manipulation!

If these same leadership positions were held by evangelical Christians belonging to a particular church denomination, we could rest assured that the media would cry conspiracy every day until something was done to correct the situation. Yet the chances of 80 percent of our leaders consistently coming from a single church denomination without the manipulation of the political process are far greater than these same leaders coming from the Council on Foreign Relations and the Trilateral Commission—since many church denominations have hundreds of thousands, or even millions of members, while the CFR and TC together have less than three thousand members. In fact, the chances of a majority of our leaders consistently

---

* Although Goldwater is a Mason, he has consistently taken stands opposing the one-world movement. He, like many other Masons, might not be aware of the true nature of their order.

** Joined the CFR some time after the election and is a current member.

coming from such a small group of people as a matter of coincidence are so remote as to not even warrant serious consideration. So why has the media not informed us about these important matters? The answer to this question would become clear as I continued to study the membership lists.

Help from the Media

Walter Cronkite, the former "CBS News" anchor and long-time Rockefeller admirer, once stated, "The Rockefellers are the epitome of the nation's permanent Establishment: governments change, economics fluctuate, foreign alliances shift—the Rockefellers prevail."[1] This statement certainly holds true for the media.

Although I knew that certain members of the information industry had fallen under the influence of the Rockefeller establishment, I was once again surprised by the extent of this control. I found that each of the three major networks were almost completely dominated by CFR/TC members. The list of media personalities belonging to these organizations was so comprehensive that my driving question was no longer "Who is involved in them?" but rather, "Who is not involved in them?" The following is a partial list of past and present members: CBS William Paley (CFR), Dan Rather (CFR), Harry Reasoner (CFR), and Bill Moyers (CFR); from NBC/RCA Tom Brokaw (CFR), John Chancellor (CFR), Marvin Kalb (CFR), and Irving R. Levine (CFR); from ABC David Brinkley (CFR), John Scali (CFR), and Barbara Walters (CFR); from Cable News Network (CNN) Daniel Schorr (CFR); and from the Public Broadcast Service Robert McNeil (CFR), Jim Lehrer (CFR), and Hodding Carter III (CFR).

In addition to most of the major media personalities belonging to the Rockefeller controlled CFR or TC, the television networks are influenced by the Rockefeller's family bank. A July 1968 report, issued by a House Banking subcommittee, revealed that Chase Manhattan Bank alone controlled 5.9 percent of the stock in CBS and that it had gained interlocking directorates with ABC.[2]

A later report issued by Congress in 1974 indicated that Chase Manhattan's stake in CBS had risen to 14.1 percent, and that it had made major inroads toward control of NBC by purchasing 4.5 percent of RCA Corporation, the parent of NBC. The same report disclosed that Chase held stocks in twenty-eight broadcasting firms. The report, entitled "Disclosure of Corporate Ownership," was the result of more than two years of investigation and was published by the Senate subcommittee on intergovernmental relations.[3] Shortly after the release of these findings, yet another study revealed that Chase had gained control of 6.7 percent of ABC's stock as well.[4]

It should be pointed out that the preceding statistics were the result of investigations in the 60s and 70s. The Rockefeller's share in the three major networks was increasing rapidly at the time. Their holdings today could be several times higher. Also, these statistics reveal only Chase Manhattan's stake in the networks. The holdings of other Rockefeller banks and companies, which may own additional shares in the same networks are not included. Nor do these findings reveal the percentage of stock that Rockefeller allies might have in the networks. When one considers that 5 percent ownership of the stock of a widely-held corporation is usually enough to assure minority control of that firm, the influence of just one family in the television industry is truly mind-boggling.

The Rockefeller controlled Council on Foreign Relations has also made significant strides toward gaining control of the wire services, which supply much of our news. For example, wire service officials Katharine Graham of the Associated Press, H.L. Stevenson of U.P.I., and Michael Posner of Reuters are past or present members of the CFR.

I am glad that the Associated Press member who tipped me off about these organizations did not belong to them. It just goes to show that there are still a few good reporters out there.

Independent newspapers have also been the target of establishment takeovers and mergers. In 1983, the Congressional Research Service reported that only 531 of the nation's 1,700 dailies were still independently owned. (Most of these were small town papers, which have only a limited impact on shaping the nation's views.) This figure was down from 1,381 independent daily newspapers that existed in 1945.[5] Some of the major newspapers influenced by the CFR include the New York Times Company with the largest number of past or present CFR and/or TC members, Newsweek/Washington Post including numerous leading syndicated columnists and owner Katharine Graham, Dow Jones & Co. (*Wall Street Journal*) with a number of past or present CFR and/or TC members, and representation from the *Boston Globe*, the *Baltimore Sun*, the *Chicago Sun Times*, the *L.A. Times* Syndicate, the *Houston Post*, and the *Minneapolis Star/Tribune*.

Other major newspapers with CFR interlocks are: the *Arkansas Gazette*, *Des Moines Register & Tribune*, Gannett Co. (publisher of *USA Today* and newspapers in more than forty cities from New York to Hawaii), the *Denver Post*, and the *Louisville Courier*. The CFR further influences the press through its thirty-eight affiliated Committees on Foreign Relations, whose members staff scores of additional newspapers all around the country.

Major magazines in the CFR orbit include: *Fortune, Time, Life, Money, People,* and *Sports Illustrated* (all of which are under the umbrella of Time, Inc.), *Newsweek, Business Week, U.S. News & World Report, Saturday Review, Reader's Digest, Atlantic Monthly, McCall's,* and *Harper's Magazine.*

These publications have also been influenced by a growing number of establishment banks and corporations whose advertisements generate huge revenues for the magazines, such as Citicorp, Chase Manhattan Corporation, Chemical Bank, Bankers Trust New York, Manufacturers Hanover, Morgan Guaranty, Exxon, Mobil, Atlantic Richfield/ARCO, Texaco, IBM, AT & T, General Electric, General Motors Corporation, Ford Motor Company, and Chrysler Corporation.

Rockefeller-owned or -influenced oil companies, banks, and blue-chip corporations are not the only buyers of advertising space. One must include in this list the major department store chains, which are probably the largest advertisers. R.H. Macy and Company, Federated Department Stores, Gimbel Brothers, Sears, Roebuck and Company, J.C. Penney Company, the May Department Stores Company, and Allied Stores Corporation have all had on the board of directors members of the CFR or partners from the CFR interlocked international banking firms.[6] To this list must be added the hundreds of additional corporations directly owned by the Rockefeller banks, oil companies, and foundations who must also put their advertising money somewhere.

Along with controlling the major networks, newspapers, and magazines, the Rockefeller establishment has a lock on book publishing as well. The following publishers have been represented on the Council on Foreign Relations: MacMillan, Random House, Simon & Schuster, McGraw-Hill, Harper Brothers, IBM Publishing and Printing, Xerox Corp., Yale University Press, Little Brown and Company, Viking Press, Cowles Publishing, and Harper and Row. Many of these specialize in publishing textbooks—which brings us to an important point.

If the mass communication industry is dominated by individuals and organizations committed to the advancement of global government, then the only public medium left to warn us about this danger is public education. But how can this be accomplished if the major textbook publishers are owned or influenced by establishment insiders?

Discovering this hidden influence prompted me to take a closer look at the field of public education to see what the establishment was up to there. What I discovered was even more disillusioning than the situation concerning the media. Although I knew that public education was going through troubled times, I didn't realize that much of this was due to the fact that it was one of the first areas targeted for subversion. I finally understand why our schools are such a mess.

Using Public Education

John D. Rockefeller made his first move on education in 1902 when he formed the General Education Board (GEB).[7] To ensure control of this tax-exempt organization he put his assistant, Frederick T. Gates, in charge as chairman.[8] Gates revealed the Rockefeller philosophy on education in the board's "Occasional Letter, No.1."

> In our dreams we have limitless resources and the people yield themselves with perfect docility to our moulding hands. The present educational conventions fade from our minds, and unhampered by tradition, we work our own good will upon a grateful and responsive rural folk.[9]

The General Education Board would later expand its activities to include the city folk as well.

Between 1902 and 1907, John, Sr., would give a total of $43 million to the GEB. And from 1917 to 1919 he and his son, John D., Jr., gave a combined total of $200 million to the GEB, the Rockefeller Foundation, and the Laura Spelman Rockefeller Memorial.[10] The total amount of Rockefeller funds given to influence education from 1902 to 1930, in today's money, would be equivalent to more than $2 billion. This is an incredible sum of money going to promote globalism and socialism within education, particularly when one considers that there was little, if any, foundation-sponsored opposition during this same period of time.

According to Gary Allen, who wrote *The Rockefeller File*,

> the foundations (principally Carnegie and Rockefeller) stimulated two-thirds of the total endowment funding of all institutions of higher learning in America during the first third of this century. During this period the Carnegie-Rockefeller complex supplied twenty percent of the total income of colleges and universities and became in fact, if not in name, a sort of U.S. Ministry of Education.[11]

(It should be noted that the Rockefeller and Carnegie foundations often had interlocking directorates and frequently acted in unison. This is still the case today.)

These same foundations began in the early thirties to back John

Dewey's Socialist philosophy with large amounts of money.[12] Dewey, who became known as the "father of progressive education" went on to influence the thinking of American educators more than any other individual. What few people today realize about Dewey is that he was one of America's leading atheists. He wrote:

> There is no God and no soul. Hence, there are no needs for the props of traditional religion. With dogma and creed excluded, then immutable (unchangeable) truth is also dead and buried. There is no room for fixed, natural law or permanent moral absolutes.[13]

One can see the results of Dewey's philosophy in the state of chaos existing in our public school system today.

Dewey's association with the Rockefeller family went back a long way as he taught four of the five Rockefeller brothers, including David and Nelson. He started his educational career in 1894 at the University of Chicago, which was one of the first schools to receive Rockefeller money.[14] Dewey worked there until 1904, when he resigned and moved to the Teacher's College at Columbia University. He would spend the rest of his life teaching teachers. "Today, twenty percent of all American school superintendents and forty percent of all teacher college heads have advanced degrees from Columbia where Dewey spent many years as the Department head."[15]

As Gary Allen explains:

> Since America's public school system was decentralized, the foundations had concentrated on influencing schools of education (particularly Columbia, the spawning ground for Deweyism), and on financing the writing of textbooks which were subsequently adopted nationwide.[16]

The Reece Committee realized this strategy and focused much of its energy on investigating foundation control over teacher training schools. Rene Wormser, Counsel for the Committee, observed:

> Research and experimental stations were established at selected universities, notably Columbia, Stanford, and Chicago. Here some of the worst mischief in recent education was born. In these Rockefeller-and-Carnegie-established vineyards worked many of the principal characters in the story of the suborning of American education. Here foundations nurtured some of the most ardent academic advocates of upsetting the American system and supplanting it with a Socialist state.[17]

Traditionalist teachers, who had strongly resisted Deweyism, were swamped by education propagandists backed with millions of

Rockefeller-Carnegie dollars. The National Education Association (NEA), the country's chief education lobby, was also being financed largely by the Rockefeller and Carnegie foundations.[18] By 1934, the NEA adopted John Dewey's philosophy of humanism, socialism, and globalism, and incorporated it into the classroom.[19] It was interesting to learn that while all of this was going on, Dewey managed to slip away to Russia for a time to help organize the Marxist educational system there.[20]

The Rockefellers not only used their money to seize control of America's centers of teacher training, they also spent millions of dollars on rewriting history books and creating textbooks that undermined patriotism and free enterprise.[21] Among the series of public school textbooks produced by Rockefeller grants was one called *Building America*. These books promoted Marxist propaganda to the extent that the California legislature refused to appropriate money for them.[22] Rene Wormser concluded:

> It is difficult to believe that The Rockefeller Foundation and the National Education Association could have supported these textbooks. But the fact is that Rockefeller financed them and the NEA promoted them very widely.[23]

The Rockefeller foundations have also worked through the secondary foundations and think-tanks to influence education and to shape public opinion by financing the production of hundreds of reports and studies that subtly promote a globalistic and socialistic view of society. These "findings" are then quoted in textbooks and identified by the media as fact, though in reality, most think-tanks are little more than propaganda divisions of the Rockefeller establishment, generating tainted data.

According to Shoup's "Imperial Brain Trust," as of 1969, the Council on Foreign Relations had in its membership twenty-two trustees of the Brookings Institute, twenty-nine officials from Rand Corporation, fourteen from the Hudson Institute, and thirty-three from the Middle East Institute. Among the major foundations, the CFR boasted fourteen of nineteen trustees at the Rockefeller Foundation, ten of seventeen at the Carnegie Foundation and seven of sixteen at the Ford Foundation.[24]

The establishment's influence in our schools has continued to grow during the past few decades. Today its lock on public education is nearly complete. This fact is evidenced in the numbers of teacher college heads who belong to the Council on Foreign Relations, including Michael I. Sovern, Columbia University (CFR); Frank H.T. Rhodes,

Cornell University (CFR); John Brademus, New York University (CFR); Alice S. Ilchman, Sarah Lawrence College (CFR); Theodore M. Hesburgh, Notre Dame University (recently resigned) (CFR/TC); Donald Kennedy, Stanford University (CFR); Benno C. Schmidt, Jr., Yale University (CFR); Hannah Holborn Gray, University of Chicago (CFR); Steven Muller, Johns Hopkins University (CFR); Howard R. Swearer, Brown University (CFR); Donna E. Shalala, University of Wisconsin (CFR); and John D. Wilson, Washington and Lee University (CFR).*[25]

With these prestigious teacher training centers under the influence of globalists, regaining control of public education has become a next to impossible task.

America's Role

After first learning about the establishment's lock on our political system, I was outraged. My intelligence had been insulted. I didn't see how I could have gone as long as I did without knowing anything about these matters. Until a few years ago, I had never even heard of the Council on Foreign Relations or the Trilateral Commission!

After finding out about the establishment's control of mass communication, I was even more appalled, but now, at least, I understood why I hadn't learned about the conspiracy any earlier. The Rockefellers controlled every facet of the information industry, from television to public education. Therefore, unless a person comes across one of the citizen's groups trying to expose the conspiracy, or stumbles onto some aspect of it, as I did, there is no way to find out about it.

As I continued to investigate the one-world movement, the question that kept recurring in my mind was, "Where does America fit into the plans of the hierarchy? What role has it been destined to play?"

Reflecting on this matter, I am convinced that America's purpose in the overall plan was to lay the necessary groundwork for the world government; and then, having accomplished this mission, to lead humanity to the threshold, if not actually into, the New World Order. Only America, with its record of integrity and leadership (as the hero of World Wars I and II and as the world's policeman in the area of human rights) could accomplish such a feat. President Bush made this point clear in his State of the Union address on 29 January 1991. Consider the following excerpts from his speech:

---

*As a further example of establishment dominance over the major training schools, there are a total of sixty-nine CFR members on the faculty at the University of Chicago, fifty-eight at Princeton, and thirty at Harvard.[26]

For two centuries, America has served the world as an
inspiring example of freedom and democracy. For generations, America has led the struggle to preserve and
extend the blessings of liberty. And today, in a rapidly
changing world, American leadership is indispensable.
Americans know that leadership brings burdens and
sacrifices.

But we also [know] why the hopes of humanity turn to
us. We are Americans; we have a unique responsibility
to do the hard work of freedom.

We can find meaning and reward by serving some
higher purpose than ourselves—a shining purpose, the
illumination of a thousand points of light.

Referring to the Persian Gulf War, Bush went on to reveal what
this "higher purpose" was.

We know why we're there. We are Americans: part of
something larger than ourselves . . .

What is at stake is more than one small country; it is a
big idea: a new world order, where diverse nations are
drawn together in common cause to achieve the universal aspirations of mankind . . .

With few exceptions, the world now stands as one . . .
for the first time since World War II, the international
community is united. The leadership of the United Nations, once only a hoped-for ideal, is now confirming its
founders' vision. . . .

The world can therefore seize this opportunity to fulfill the long-held promise of a new world order. . . . Yes,
the United States bears a major share of the leadership
in this effort. Among the nations of the world, only the
United States of America has had both the moral standing and the means to back it up. We are the only nation on this Earth that could assemble the forces of
peace. This is the burden of leadership. . . .

The winds of change are with us now. The forces of freedom are together and united. And we move toward the
next century more confident than ever that we have the
will at home and abroad to do what must be done—the
hard work of freedom.[27]

. . . A New World Order—all in the name of freedom and democracy! Who would have believed it possible even a generation ago?

As Congressman McDonald pointed out, if the hidden forces
were to have any hope of establishing a one-world government, they
would first have to gain control of the United States, and use its eco-

nomic influence to lead the rest of the nations into the new order.

Only America, with its vast resources, was capable of putting the final pieces for a global system into place. It was the New York-based international banks and American computer companies who made this automation and centralization of global banking possible; and it was our telecommunications companies who built the satellites needed to enforce a system of global government.

Only America was capable of producing the economic wealth necessary for the super-capitalists to buy up the world. Many countries and foreign merchants have become rich off of the enormous wealth of the United States, becoming loyal allies of the establishment that made this possible. As a result of this wealth, English has become the world's business language, and the U.S. dollar is the closest thing to a world currency.

A one-world government could not be accomplished through a perceived dictatorship. In order to be accepted, the New World Order would have to ride in on the back of what appeared to be a trusted democracy. America filled this description, being viewed as the world's greatest bastion of freedom—the last great hope of mankind. Furthermore, America is the world's largest cosmopolitan nation—virtually everyone in the world has at least one relative or friend living in the United States. This goes a long way in alleviating distrust and building a favorable image for the New World Order.

The Gulf War, I believe, was only the latest tactic used by insiders to accomplish their goal. As one who had a nephew on the front lines during the war, I had mixed feelings about America's involvement. On the one hand I wanted to be supportive of our sons and daughters who were putting their lives on the line. At the same time, I felt in my heart that the war had been contrived by those in high places to move us closer toward their objective.

The war would accomplish several purposes. It would serve as an excuse for hiking up oil prices, thereby generating billions of dollars of additional revenue for the establishment's oil companies. But more importantly, it would unite the nations of the world against a common enemy—which was necessary to take humanity the final step into a one-world system. Hussein played the role of the perfect villain who all decent people like to hate (like Hitler).

The war would also establish America as the undisputed leader of the world and the enforcer of the New World Order, showing other countries what they would encounter if they opposed the emerging world system. It would make true patriots who opposed the concept of a New World Order appear to be unpatriotic, while making

globalists who supported the U.N. appear as patriots, essentially turning the tables upside down.

I have nothing against American leadership in the world if it is
the kind of leadership that espouses godly principles and virtues, and
sets a noble example for other nations to follow. I would like to be a
patriot of the America envisioned by the Pilgrims, by Abraham Lincoln, Louis T. McFadden, Larry McDonald, and other leaders from our
past. However, their vision did not include an America of material-
ism, corruption, and godlessness, which has become a stronghold for
the secret societies; nor did it include a nation that manipulates other
nations for the purpose of achieving a world government. I believe
that a great many Americans would agree with me on this.

Having gained some idea of America's role in building the New
World Order, the only remaining question I had was "What will happen to the U.S. once it has fulfilled its mission?" There is some disagreement among researchers on this question. Some believe that
once we have entered the New World Order, Europe will be made
the headquarters of the world government. Others believe that the
seat of power for the world government will be in the United States,
specifically in New York City.

As things currently stand, New York would be the logical choice
to be the world's capitol, given the fact that it is the most powerful
and influential city in the world and that the United Nations, the
Council on Foreign Relations, and the Trilateral Commission are all
headquartered there. However, the secret hierarchy of Europe, which
is still ultimately in charge, might have different plans. If they intend
to locate the world capitol in Europe, they will find a way to do so.
Such a decision, however, would probably involve either the economic
devastation or physical destruction of New York City. This could be
accomplished in several ways—economically, through a planned collapse of the stock market or a severe depression resulting from our
excessive national debt; or physically, as an act of terrorism, as a
nuclear "accident," or through a limited nuclear war. Whatever
method would be selected, the European hierarchy, I believe, would
be capable of carrying it out (if God allows it).

Is New York destined for destruction? I don't know the answer
to this question, nor do I wish such a fate upon the people of that
city. However, the parallels between New York and the great, but
wicked, city described as Mystery Babylon in Revelation 17 and 18
are difficult to ignore. I can only hope these passages are describing
something else.

Chapter 4
The New Age Movement

Early on, I had become aware of the fact that the political and economic efforts to create a world government were being undergirded by a network of spiritually motivated organizations that have collectively become known as the New Age movement. My first experience in this regard came during a business trip to a nearby city where I met with officials from a small, but profitable, manufacturing concern. After the meeting, I joined the company's representatives for lunch at a restaurant.

When our food arrived, I noticed that my hosts quietly bowed their heads to pray over the meal. Being a Christian myself, I was glad to be in the presence of other believers—something that didn't happen very often in my business. Subsequently, during the luncheon conversation, one of the officers shared the following incident, which had just happened at their company.

Their corporation, known for its charity, had recently been approached by a local "good works" organization to inquire whether they could use the company's boardroom to house their monthly meetings. They approved the request. As part of the arrangement, a member of the company's staff was going to assume the office of secretary to take the minutes at the meetings of this newly formed organization.

It did not take long for the company to figure out what was happening. According to the secretary's testimony, the organization was planning ways in which they could infiltrate and influence the community with their "New Age" ideas and activities. It was all in the name of peace and unity while meeting the needs of the community. On the surface, it sounded very humanitarian. Had it not been for the fact that the secretary was herself a Christian, and that she shared her experiences with a fiance who was perceptive about such matters, she would not have seen through the deception.

The company had not screened the organization very carefully and, therefore, did not realize that the group was New Age. Even if they had, it would have meant little to them since they had never heard of the New Age movement. (This was in the early 1980s when a limited number of outsiders knew about such a network.)

After discussing the matter, the corporate officials asked their employee to continue as secretary for the organization's meetings in order to gather more information. In the meantime, the company had organized its own mini-conference for the purpose of gaining an understanding of this so-called New Age. They told me that they had asked a Christian gentleman who knew more about this subject to come and give a presentation. Learning about my interest, they invited me to attend this private session. Ironically, this meeting to expose the movement would be held in the same boardroom that was used by the New Age organization.

Prior to this, I had never heard about the New Age and did not see the reason for all of the alarm. However, I was intrigued enough by the secretary's reports to make the two hour drive back to attend the meeting later that week.

I was unprepared for the heaviness of the conference. I am not sure what I expected; but by the time the presentation was over, my head was reeling with questions. The speaker, however, was articulate and patient and was able to provide intelligent answers to my questions. I realized, both from what he said and from the documentation that he shared, that he had insight into this subject. It appeared that this "New Age movement" was real and that it presented a growing threat to our society. Little did I know at the time that this gentleman and I would become the best of friends and would later work together as partners in researching this movement.

The amazing thing about all of this was that my experiences dealing with the new currency, the global societies and the New Age movement all took place within an eight month period. It took these three experiences to knock me out of my complacency. I believe this was God's way of getting my attention. My life has never been the same since. I was now prepared to do some serious investigation.

Within a few months, I was up to my ears in New Age research material. Along with getting more information about the global political societies and doing some research on economic matters, I had begun to visit various health food stores in our community. My new friend—the lecturer—had informed me that the New Age movement frequently used health food stores as fronts to distribute their literature and to propagate their ideas. He recommended I visit a few of them and browse around; I decided to give it a try.

My friend was right. The first health food store I walked into, less than two miles from our home, carried everything from the *New*

Age Journal to *Mother Earth News*. The owner of the store was so
excited to see my interest that she decided to throw in a few old copies
of the *New Age Journal* free of charge.

The next visit to a health food store was even worse. The store
carried a variety of blatant occult material. On its bulletin board was
pinned a flier with information on how one could join WICCA, the
national organization for witches. Beneath the invitation was written Serious Students Only! I could hardly believe my eyes. I should
mention that I did find a few good old-fashioned health stores that
were not peddling occult material, but they were in a minority.

After a few Saturdays of such legwork, I had accumulated a small
pile of New Age books, newsletters, and magazines. Using various alias
names, I got myself placed on several mailing lists by responding to
some of the advertisements in these New Age publications. By doing
so, I would be able to determine who was in contact with whom and
which organizations were networking with each other—at least to the
point of sharing mailing lists.

In just six months of doing this, I was getting New Age literature from all around the country; within a year, I was no longer able
to even scan through all the material I was receiving. Several large
boxes full of New Age/occult literature were piling up in my house.

I had gotten pretty good at playing the role of a New Ager and
would carry on extended conversations with the owners and manag-
ers of New Age bookstores. My goal was simply to determine where
they were coming from and why they believed as they did. Additionally, I benefited from the research of my friend and several of his
friends. Before long, we had our own little network through which
we exchanged information and kept each other current. We were all
drawn together by our mutual love for Christ and our commitment
to exposing the works of darkness.

After nearly two years of studying the New Age, I felt that I had
a grasp of the movement and its inner workings, and I believed that
I had accomplished my purpose in this area. I did not want to dwell
on the New Age writings any more than I had to. The material was
so dark and oppressive that I always felt weighed down after reading it. I believed God had called me to expose the movement, otherwise I would have stopped researching it much earlier. I do not rec-
ommend that anyone do this type of research unless they are absolutely certain it is God's will for them. Then, they should offset anything they read by reading the Bible at least the same amount of time.

Satan isn't called the master deceiver for nothing. While some
New Age writings are so blatantly satanic that they pose little threat

to a grounded Christian, other writings are so subtle and deceptive that they are capable of derailing even the most committed believer. Therefore, I cannot be overly insistent that readers not take these matters lightly.

It is impossible to cover the entire New Age movement within the scope of this book. There are numerous outstanding books on the market which delve more extensively into the evil crevices of the New Age movement. But, in a nutshell, here is what I learned.

New Age Mysticism

The religion of the New Age, simply put, is pantheism—the belief that God is the sum total of all that exists. According to pantheists, there is no personal God, instead their concept of God consists of what they refer to as a god-force (or life-force). They teach that this energy, or god-force, flows through all living things—plants, animals—and human beings. Since this god-force flows through all of us, they rationalize, we must therefore be gods or, at least, part of God.

Because of this belief, most pantheists will automatically support the concept of a one-world government since global unity is essential to the proper flow of the god-force. Humanity will then, presumably, take a "quantum leap" to a higher level of existence. The result will be that all humans will suddenly receive mystical powers to do what they could never do before. A new age of enlightenment— a New World Order—will be born.

Pantheism also teaches that we will never die, and therefore, we must face no personal judgement by God. We just keep coming back in different life forms (reincarnation)—an acceptable concept to pantheists since they believe that we are all "one with nature" anyway.

It is amazing that man has fallen for these deceptive teachings since pantheism is clearly based on the two oldest lies of Satan—the same lies that tripped up Adam and Eve. The serpent lured the first couple into sin by promising them that if they ate of the forbidden fruit 1) they would never die, and 2) they would become like God.

But man, it seems, is willing to do just about anything to escape accountability and submission to a higher authority. The belief that there is no accountability to a personal God, I believe, is the main appeal of pantheism. People would rather believe a delusive lie and be their own authority than to accept the truth and draw near to their loving Creator.

Another thing that I discovered was that occult practices emanate from pantheistic beliefs, best illustrated in the area of witchcraft. Contrary to popular belief, many (perhaps most) witches do not be-

lieve in Satan; nor do they see themselves as practicing satanic rituals. Most witches and sorcerers believe that witchcraft consists merely
of manipulating the forces of nature, or the god-force (pantheism).

Pantheism is Satan's religion. Although direct Satan worship
(satanism) has drawn some followers, most people will not embroil
themselves in it because of its blatantly evil overtones. Instead, something more subtle—such as pantheism—developed to draw in the
masses.

If occult practices emanate from pantheistic beliefs, it only follows that the leaders of the Eastern pantheistic religions must also
be the leading occult experts in the world. I found that hard-core New
Agers, those who were heavily involved in the occult, considered the
Eastern religious leaders to be the leading authorities on the occult—
subsequently Indian swamis and yogis have been able to attract large
followings in the West. However, the most revered gurus among New
Agers are the Tibetan monks, resided over by their spiritual master,
the Dalai Lama. Many of the personalities, such as Alice Bailey and
Helena Petrovna Blavatsky of the Theosophical Society, whose writings have had the most influence on the New Age movement of today, studied for a time under the occult masters of the Far East.

One of the misconceptions that has thrown people off track and
prevented them from making the connection between pantheism and
the occult is a misunderstanding of the word *mystic* or *mysticism*—
at least in its modern usage. New Agers, I found, used the terms *mysticism* and *occultism* interchangeably. In fact, the most popular dictionary among New Agers is Nevill Drury's *Dictionary of Mysticism
and the Occult*. Time and time again in my research, I found these
words being used together or synonymously. I finally decided to look
up the word *mystic* in *Webster's New Collegiate Dictionary* to see
what it really meant. One of the definitions is "of or relating to mysteries or esoteric rites: occult."[1]

Mysticism, as it turns out, is simply a kinder, gentler way of
saying occultism. What has thrown people even further off track is
the term "new age," which is even more pleasant sounding but has
come to be synonymous with mysticism and the occult. In modern
language, being a New Ager, a mystic, or occultist all means the same
thing.

Because of these subtleties, many people involved on the fringes
of the New Age movement are not aware of the fact that they are
embracing occult concepts. They do, eventually, discover that they are
practicing occultism; however, by then they have become so hooked
on their new beliefs and practices that they are often unwilling to

turn around and go back. The occult is seductive and incredibly addictive, possibly as much as, or more than, mind-altering drugs.

Perhaps the most addictive and dangerous aspect of occultism is entering into, or inducing, an altered state of consciousness. I found that achieving altered states was one of the chief unifying factors among New Agers.

I believe that God created us with a type of protective dome to shield us from the realm of the occult. However, if we choose to disobey God and His warnings, it is possible to break through this invisible shield to tap directly into the occult and to communicate with the powers of darkness (demons). This can be achieved in many ways, using a variety of concentration and meditation techniques—most of which have the effect of inducing an altered state of consciousness.*

Some people who go into altered (or trance) states do not have a "significant experience" for some time; others have occult experiences on the very first try. These phenomena include such things as out-of-body travel (also referred to by New Agers as astral projection or space travel); use of hypnosis to travel back into their "past lives" (past life regression); distinct visions about future events (forms of divination); or direct interaction with spirit beings (usually referred to as spirit guides, or simply guides).

Going into an altered state is extremely dangerous. In fact, there are New Age books available about techniques that will supposedly protect against having bad experiences. Gurus in India take precautionary measures as they delve deeper and deeper into meditative states. They are horrified at the casualness of amateur practitioners in the West.

The fact that most Christians don't realize what this is all about has only added to the problem. Few preachers, due to a lack of understanding or courage (or both), have been willing to tackle such issues from the pulpit. As a result, apart from the warnings of the Bible against occultism and spiritism, the public has been left open for Satan's deception.

What few people realize is that going into an altered state could give Satan a license to influence our thinking. It is possible that these altered states break down our defense mechanisms. Some psycholo-

---

*Occult meditation is not to be confused with biblical meditation which we are encouraged to participate in. Unlike occult meditation, which involves going into a trance state, biblical meditation, as referred to by David in the Psalms, is an active process. To meditate upon God's Word, for example, means to think about, or to reflect upon the principles and truths of the Bible and how they relate to our lives.

gists believe that in a trance state, a person has little power to reason or to screen out falsehood or deception. Satan is no fool. He understands this. Is it possible that in this state a person has little sense of right or wrong and is more likely to accept whatever the spirit (or the hypnotist) says?

For example, if under a deep hypnosis you were told that you rode a tricycle down the main street of your city yesterday, you might believe it. It could become a fact in your mind. This dangerous power of the occult is demonstrated in the following incident.

A few years ago an expert on hypnosis was invited to my niece's high school to demonstrate "the art." He asked for volunteers to come up to the platform, after which he succeeded at placing several of these students into trances. Two years later when he came back to the same school, he demonstrated that his power was still in effect over those who had been hypnotized. He simply spoke a "trigger" word and the sound of his voice allegedly put the previously hypnotized students back into a trance. This spooked a number of the students . . . as well it should!

While this particular hypnotist appears to have been benevolent up to this point, his practices are nevertheless cultish and should be avoided. There is no such thing as good occultism or good (white) magic. Both are of Satan. What appears to be good in the realm of the occult only appears that way until the moment that Satan decides to use it for his evil intentions. No one should allow themselves to be fooled into thinking that they can use or manipulate occult powers to harmlessly accomplish good "positive changes." If they do, it is they who are being manipulated, not the spirit world.

Something else I discovered while researching this subject was that mind-altering drugs have been used for thousands of years to accomplish this same purpose of inducing altered states. In fact, author Nevill Drury contends that the philosophers of ancient Greece were known to use a drug very similar to LSD to place themselves into trances. This drug was made from the ergot that grew on the cereal crops in nearby fields and was frequently used before initiates partook in the occult rituals of the Greek mysteries. Some of the philosophers were particularly heavy into the occult and drugs and had been initiated into the Mysteries of Eleusis.[2]

It is no coincidence that the use of drugs and the practice of occultism in this country exploded at the same time during the 1960s. The two go hand-in-hand. Mind-altering drugs, such as LSD and heroin, are merely the lazy man's way of achieving an altered-state, or taking a trip, which is really an occult experience. This is only one of the reasons why drugs are so addictive. I know of one person who gave up drugs after finding out that he could have the same experiences by practicing occult meditation. It was less expensive and less damaging to his body . . . so he believed!

Some people, who regularly put themselves into trances may eventually be directly approached by spirit beings during their trance. Some theologians believe that these spirits, which are actually demons, can take on any form they choose, depending on what that particular person believes. For example, a New Ager who has embraced pantheism along with its inherent belief in reincarnation, may, while in a trance, encounter a spirit which approaches under the guise of being a more highly evolved being. This being, or "ascended master," has gone through several incarnations, and is allegedly therefore able to communicate in ways that less evolved humans cannot.

Those in the fields of philosophy and psychology who have delved into the occult, such as Carl Jung, have had similar experiences—only they refer to these beings as archetypal images or "Ideal Forms." Strict humanists, on the other hand, who do not believe in the existence of a spirit realm, are more commonly approached by beings posing as extraterrestrials who claim that they are higher forms of life from other worlds and are able to communicate in ways that humans have not yet discovered.

In short, demons will tell people whatever they want to hear and are willing to accept. It is amazing that so many people, who refuse to believe in the existence of a God are not only willing, but eager, to accept such lies. Not much has changed over the years. It was the same way during the Old Testament era.

It was interesting to discover that all of the ancient mystery religions from the Bible era were pantheistic. Pantheism originated in the ancient city of Babylon in Mesopotamia and from there spread rapidly in all directions to cover the face of the earth. Hinduism is one of the off-shoots of the original Babylonian pantheism (via the Aryans of ancient Persia). And Buddhism is an off-shoot of Hinduism. All of the Eastern religions of today are ultimately traceable to ancient Babylon, where the post-flood rebellion against God began.

The nation of Israel was completely surrounded by these occult societies. To the west were the Egyptian Mysteries (also known as the Mysteries of Osiris), out of which God had delivered the Israelites. To the south were the Arabian Mysteries; to the east were the Babylonian and Persian Mysteries (respectively known as the Mysteries of Semiramis and the Mithraic Mysteries, or Zoroastrianism). To the north were the Assyrian and Phoenician Mysteries (including Baal worship) and later on the Mysteries of Greece and Rome (referred to as the Mysteries of Eleusis, Dionysus, Bacchus, etc.). All of these pantheistic religions (at their base) were the same and were traceable to ancient Babylon and the time of Nimrod.

God scattered the people from Babylon at the building of the Tower of Babel, but this did not put an end to occultism, it merely broke it up and slowed its spread for a time. As new civilizations arose in Egypt, Persia, India, etc., the occult practices of old were revived. The people, as it turned out, had merely taken their beliefs and practices with them.

Although some changes and modifications took place in these "new" mysteries to suit the developing cultures of the various language groups, the basic tenets and practices remained the same. All of the ancient mysteries, for example, had an occult priesthood, which ruled the country or empire in association with the appointed priest-king. In order to enter the priesthood, one always had to go through a series of secret occult rituals and initiations. When an initiate reached the highest level (or inner circle) of the priesthood, the secret doctrine was revealed. It always included the worship of Lucifer, more frequently referred to in the mysteries as the God of Hades, or the God of the Underworld and usually symbolized by the serpent or dragon. This should have sent a clear message to the people of the day that their religions were satanically inspired.

The highest priests took their orders directly from Satan or his demon messengers in altered states of consciousness. The techniques for achieving these states were once the deepest, best kept, secrets of the high priests. Later, they would be kept alive and carried forward by the secret societies. Within the past generation, however, these same techniques (or variations of these techniques) have made it into the mainstream of Western society.

The demonic spirits with whom the priests communicated became the gods and goddesses of the mystery religions. I further believe that the idols worshipped in these religions, in many instances, were formed in the actual images of the demons as they appeared to the priests. If this is true, the masses were worshipping more than mere pieces of stone, clay, or metal; they were actually praying to the demons portrayed by the images. This is why God was so adamant in his commandments to Moses that the Israelites worship no other gods.

And God spoke all these words:

I am the Lord your God, who brought you out of Egypt,
out of the land of slavery. You shall have no other gods

before me. You shall not make for yourself an idol in
the form of anything in heaven above or on the earth
beneath or in the waters below. You shall not bow down
to them or worship them; for I, the Lord your God, am
a jealous God. (Ex. 20:1-5a)

God further warned the Israelites through Moses:

When you enter the land the Lord your God is giving
you, do not learn to imitate the detestable ways of the
nations there. Let no one be found among you who
sacrifices his son or daughter in the fire, who practices
divination or sorcery, interprets omens, engages in
witchcraft, or casts spells, or who is a medium or spirit-
ist or who consults the dead. Anyone who does these
things is detestable to the Lord, and because of these
detestable practices the Lord your God will drive out
those nations before you. (Deut. 18:9-12)

In pursuing occult phenomena, such as altered states, a person
is playing with fire. He is breaking through the supernatural barrier,
which has been placed there by God for his protection. This is why
the Bible repeatedly warns us to steer clear of these practices. Additional passages, which deal specifically with this topic, include
Jeremiah 29:8-9; Zechariah 10:2; Isaiah 47:13-15; Leviticus 19:4, 26,
31 and 20:6.

Through willing or naive vessels who practice occult meditation, Satan is able to orchestrate his worldwide drive for a New World
Order. Using secret occult hierarchies, he has systematically advanced
his plans with the only serious threat to his efforts coming from knowl-
edgeable, obedient Christians who stand in his path. Much of "the
plan" is revealed piece-by-piece to individuals throughout the world
who are in regular contact with Satan's agents through altered states.
Not everyone practicing occult meditation actually comes into contact with spirit entities; however, a great many do and these encoun-
ters are far more prevalent than most people realize or care to admit.

While it is impossible to know the exact number of individuals
in the United States who are involved in the occult, it is fair to say
that they have multiplied by the thousands during the past three
decades. This movement has its recognized leaders and authorities,
and it generates huge volumes of books and occult writings, which
are faithfully read by its followers. If I had to, I believe that I could
come up with a list of at least a thousand New Age organizations that
exist in this country alone. Some of these groups are as small as a
few dozen people whose reach is limited to a small community. Other

organizations, particularly those built around major publications, have tens of thousands on their mailing lists.

Many of the leaders of the New Age movement, I am convinced, know exactly what they are doing and who they are in touch with (demonic spirits). Many of the occult initiates directly under these leaders, on the other hand, might not be aware of the actual Lucifer worship going on at the top. They must, however, realize that the techniques and rituals, which they are practicing, relate to the occult.

A majority of New Agers, I believe, fall into neither of these categories. They operate along the fringes of the movement, naively unaware of what they are involved in. Such individuals may have become associated with the movement because of one or more shared beliefs or practices such as an obsession with the environment, holistic health, world peace, the practice of Transcendental Meditation, yoga, or other forms of occult meditation. I sympathize with these people, as they have been drawn into the movement unwittingly.

Traditionally, the Theosophical Society has been at the forefront of the movement, playing an important role in conditioning humanity to accept the New World Order. The organization has produced many of the most widely read occult classics, such as *The Destiny of the Nations*, *The Reappearance of the Christ*, *Discipleship of the New Age*, and *The Secret Doctrine*, written by the society's founder, Helena Petrovna Blavatsky.

On page 53 of *The Secret Doctrine*, Blavatsky quotes Milton's *Paradise Lost* in reference to the "Fallen One" or Satan, stating, "Better to reign in hell than serve in heaven!" On the same page, she declares, "Better be man, the crown of terrestrial production, and king over its opus operatum, than be lost among the will-less Spiritual Hosts in Heaven."[3]

On page 76 of *The Secret Doctrine*, Blavatsky, referring to Lucifer, states, ". . . it is this grandest of Ideals, this ever-living symbol—nay apotheosis—of self-sacrifice for the intellectual independence of humanity . . ." She continues in the same section by approvingly quoting Eliphas Levi as follows:

> It (Satan) is that Angel who was proud enough to believe himself God; brave enough to buy his independence at the price of eternal suffering and torture; beautiful enough to have adored himself in full divine light; strong enough to still reign in darkness amidst agony, and to have made himself a throne out of this inextinguishable pyre . . . the prince of anarchy, served by a hierarchy of pure spirits.[4]

I could continue, but it gets even worse. Some of the results of *The Secret Doctrine* have already been witnessed, as the book strongly influenced Hitler.[5] Blavatsky clearly understood that there is a God and had clearly chosen to rebel against Him, taking the side of Lucifer. Her position was again confirmed when she decided to publish a magazine entitled *Lucifer*, which was in circulation for a short time before succumbing to public pressure and shutting down.[6]

Another leader of the Theosophical Society, Alice Bailey, would establish The Lucifer Press for the purpose of printing and distributing the society's literature. (This was around 1920.) Due to public outrage, however, the name was soon changed to Lucis Press, Ltd. Until a couple of years ago, Lucis Trust, the parent organization, was appropriately headquartered at United Nations Plaza in New York. It has over six thousand members and is among the many foundations sponsoring the one-world movement.[7]

Some of the Luciferic organizations established by the Theosophical network of Bailey and Lucis Trust include the Arcane Schools (of New York, London, Geneva, and Buenos Aires); the Triangles; and World Goodwill—all founded during the 1920s and 30s.

The Arcane Schools are special training centers that place a person on the fast track for service within the high level network of the New Age movement. Lucis Trust's Triangles program is another way in which the organization helps to promote the New World Order. The Triangles consist of hundreds of meditation groups of three people who simultaneously imagine triangles of light as they recite the Great Invocation for the return of "the Christ" (the Antichrist).[8]

World Goodwill, on the other hand, is composed of individuals who are collectively referred to as the "New Group of World Servers," founded in 1933 and purposed to distribute literature worldwide promoting theosophy's Luciferic views. In 1961, this group was joined with another occult organization calling itself World Union[9], which is today heavily involved in the politics of planning and implementing the world government.

A number of the most powerful New Age organizations, such as Lucis Trust and World Union, are well connected with the one-world political societies and feed directly into the World Constitution and Parliament Association, the organization charged with the task of actually bringing us into the New World Order.

The World Constitution and Parliament Association

The World Constitution and Parliament Association (WCPA) was founded in 1959 in Lakewood, Colorado, near Denver. The main figure behind the organization's establishment and development has been Philip Isely, who, since 1966, has served as the WCPA's secretary general. Under Isely's direction, as part of its role of putting the final pieces into place, the association has assembled a Provisional World Parliament. Three sessions of the Parliament have already been held since 1982, and a number of World Legislative Acts have been adopted at these meetings. The fourth session of the Provisional World Parliament will be held in the near future. A total of five sessions were originally planned leading up to the New World Order.

At the third session, held in 1987, a Provisional World Presidium and World Cabinet were appointed to serve as the equivalent of an executive branch for the emerging world government. In addition to these activities the WCPA has found time to oversee the drafting of a world constitution and lobbying to get this constitution ratified by national parliaments and governments, many of which are already dominated or strongly influenced by members of these same groups.

The final ratification campaign was officially launched in the spring of 1991 at the meeting of the World Constituent Assembly in Portugal. The amount of time it will take for this drive to gain acceptance depends largely on how many people can be warned about the WCPA's plans in advance. To say that the matter is extremely urgent is not an overstatement. When one considers everyone who is involved in this plot and the fact that the WCPA is composed of a global *Who's Who*, one is forced to take this threat seriously.

The strategy of the WCPA and its affiliated organizations has been to quietly put as many pieces into place as possible, with no more people knowing about their plans than was necessary to accomplish the task. Then, once most of the groundwork had been laid, the WCPA and its large New Age support network would rush forward as quickly as possible, implementing the world government before people really have had a chance to think about what is happening or are able to form an effective opposition.

The WCPA does not like the word "conspiracy." Instead, it chooses to use the words "collaborating" or "networking for change" to describe its efforts. Though it has done all of its planning and scheming of the past thirty years behind the backs of the American people, it has the audacity to claim that it is acting in the interests of democracy. It has even gone so far as to have its legislative acts and its world constitution copyrighted, seeking to protect its activities under the U.S. Constitution—the very document that it is trying to replace.

Not too many years ago, people such as these would have been tried for treason and hung in a public square. But after more than three generations of seductive and cleverly planned global propaganda, people have been conditioned to the point where the WCPA now believes that it can go public and gain acceptance among a majority of the world's inhabitants.

The WCPA's plan, which includes a ten region world government, has been taken straight out of the Club of Rome's handbook. For example, among the WCPA's plans is a proposal calling for a new international monetary system, referred to as the "New World Economic Order"—the exact wording used by the Club of Rome to describe the same. The WCPA is also using the environment as its chief argument for why a world government is required, similar to COR's strategies and proposals.

I first became aware of the World Constitution and Parliament Association in the spring of 1987 through a friend in our network of researchers who had penetrated the organization by posing as a New Ager. This friend had been invited by the WCPA to attend the 3d session of the Provisional World Parliament, which was scheduled to convene in June of that year in Miami Beach. My friend invited me to attend the meeting, so that I too could get an inside look at the organization. I proceeded to fill out my application form, trying to portray myself as a globalist with New Age leanings. My International Trade Specialist job and Yugoslav-German parents made it easy for me to cast this international image. I was exactly the kind of person they wanted in their network, and my registration was approved.

However, after making all the arrangements to attend the session, I had to back out at the last moment due to my mother-in-law's sudden death from a rapid form of cancer.

In spite of the fact that I cancelled my reservations, I continued to receive literature from the WCPA. I was startled by the blatant nature of the documents, which clearly stated the organization's intent to form a world government. Reproductions of some of these letters are found in the Exhibits in the back of this book.

You will notice in Exhibit B that Isely went out of his way to create the impression that these meetings were normal and natural as can be. Special functions were even planned for the delegates' children, whom they were encouraged to bring along. One of these events was called the "Children's Peace Circle" and was organized and resided over by Yogi Shanti Swaroop of India, who is the WCPA's official "Spiritual Liaison."

The spiritual motivation behind the WCPA was once again demonstrated in a letter revealing the list of speakers at the Provisional World Parliament (Exhibit C). At the bottom of the page, under "World

Spiritual Leaders," you will notice that the "spiritual leaders" who were to speak at the conference were all yogis or swamis from the Far East. Listed on the same page with these occult masters was the Reverend Jesse Jackson, leader of the Rainbow Coalition and a presidential candidate at the time. Jackson is also a current member of the Council on Foreign Relations.[10] He is one of the few African-Americans (from a percentage standpoint) who is involved in this scheme. Ramsey Clark, former U.S. attorney general, was another of the recognized American leaders who was to speak at the Parliament session. He is also one of the vice presidents of the WCPA as well as being a former member of the Council on Foreign Relations.

One indication that Isely was completely comfortable in what he was doing was demonstrated in the fact that he encouraged delegates to publicize the event. The fact that he felt sufficiently covered by globalists in high government positions or safe enough to begin operating out in the open with little or no fear shows how far things have come.

After the Miami Beach session, I continued to receive information on a regular basis. I did whatever I could to keep Isely from becoming suspicious by playing the part of a New Ager. During 1989 and the first part of 1990, however, I heard very little from the WCPA and wondered if something was wrong. So on 14 March 1990 I contacted Isely to keep the lines of communication open and to make sure he was still convinced that I was "one of them."

We chatted for some time, and I felt that everything was alright—I did not sense any suspicion on his part. For the first time, however, I felt sorry for the man and had a real burden in my heart to share the message of Christ with him. But I realized that this would pose too great of a risk. I could not allow my cover to be blown—at least, not yet.

Isely went on to bring me up-to-date, sharing that a major meeting of the World Constituent Assembly would be held later that year to launch the final ratification campaign for the world constitution. It was clear from his standpoint that he expected the final pieces to fall into place fairly quickly (within a few years) once this meeting had been held. The site of the World Constituent Assembly would be Alexandria, Egypt.

Isely agreed to keep me posted. Several months passed without hearing anything. So in November, I decided to call him again to see where things stood. He informed me that the dates of the meeting had been pushed back until sometime in the spring of 1991. He was not yet certain of the exact dates.

By this time I had a sense of urgency that I had never had before. After much prayer, I believed that this was God's appointed time for me to come forward with the organization and its plans. It was during this time that I approached Huntington House Publishers with my information. Things fell into place rapidly, and by the end of January, I had already begun work on this book.

In the meantime, I received what would be my last personal letter from Isely. Along with the letter, he sent me everything I would need to effectively expose the conspiracy. He encouraged me to study everything carefully in preparation for the upcoming session of the World Constituent Assembly. Study carefully . . . this I would do, but not for the purpose of participating in the meeting!

The results of my study are presented in Part 2 of this book, which has been devoted entirely to exposing the World Constitution and Parliament Association. Parts of the organization's plans and documents have been reproduced in that section. If you have been a skeptic, wondering whether a plot to create an occult New World Order really exists, this section is for you!

During the winter of 1991, I still planned to attend the World Constituent Assembly to gather additional information. This is one of the reasons I started out writing this book under a pseudonym—I did not know how soon the book would be completed, and I did not want my cover blown before attending the meeting.

However, the last week in February I received a general letter from the WCPA (Exhibit F), sent out to everyone in its network, explaining that the site of the meetings had been changed to a location near Lisbon, Portugal.

In reviewing the information packet, I also realized for the first time that there were stringent conditions attached to my participation in the World Constituent Assembly, specifically to "prove myself" by personally promoting the Assembly and its call for a world government. This could be done in several ways: 1) by getting the signatures of seven hundred or more people on election petitions approved by the Preparatory Committee, 2) by publishing advertisements that promoted the event in periodicals with a combined circulation of twenty-five thousand or more, or 3) by getting an organization of five thousand or more members to ratify the Call to the 1991 World Constituent Assembly and to accept the Constitution for the Federation of the Earth.

There were other ways of attending the convention as well, but all of them were designed so that one would personally have to promote the world government in some way. I had known of the fact that I would have to obtain signatures to attend the Assembly even before receiving this letter, but I did not realize the large numbers involved. Up to this point, I had figured that I could get the necessary signatures from friends who, knowing what they were doing, would be willing to play along. However, in order to get the large number of signatures that the WCPA required, I would now have to go beyond my circle of friends. This was something I could not do. I was not willing to compromise my faith by actually promoting these activities and possibly being responsible for dragging someone else into supporting this Luciferic effort.

I still wanted to attend the meetings; however, I finally yielded to God. The line had been clearly drawn and I could not step across it. I realized that I had gone as far as I could go.

Realizing that I had been a Christian spy, I reflected upon the lives of other spies who had been used by God in previous ages. I wanted to see how they responded in similar predicaments. I did not want to tell Isely outright lies as to why I was not attending the convention, even though they may have been justified in this circumstance. But, if I told him the truth—that I would not be attending the meeting because my conscience did not allow it and because I would be busy writing a book to expose his organization—I probably would not live to get this message out. Whatever I did, I could not give Isely even a hint of what my real intentions were. After much thought and prayer, I finally drafted a letter on 25 March.

Additionally, to Philip Isely, I wish to say this ". . . I have nothing against you individually. Perhaps you have even convinced yourself that you are doing the right thing. However, what you have undertaken is extremely dangerous and will result in threatening not only the physical existence, but also the spiritual existence of those you influence. Your endeavor is built upon a faulty foundation, one that is based upon the occult and the supporting religions of pantheism. This new age of enlightenment that you are seeking to usher in, will in the end only bring chaos and destruction. Furthermore, you have set yourself against God and disregarded all the warnings of His Scripture against such an endeavor. For this reason your effort will ultimately fail. Won't you please reconsider your position?"

I encourage everyone reading this book to draft their own personal letter, addressed to Philip Isely and the executive cabinet of the WCPA, urging them to cease their activities and explaining why you are opposed to what they are doing. The WCPA's address appears on letterheads in the Exhibits, along with the organization's fax and telephone numbers. If you are fearful of giving out your name, it is not necessary that you attach your name or address to the letter. The message will get through just the same. But please write your letter in a tactful fashion, just as Christ leads you. Perhaps if these people hear from enough concerned Christians and realize the size of the opposition, there is still a chance that they will see the light and cease or delay their activities. Even if they do not, however, at least they will know and understand why we are against such an endeavor, and will have been warned about what is wrong with it.

My reasons for exposing this deception are that I earnestly believe that God has called me to do so, and because I do take this threat seriously. One reason I waited as long as I did before going public with this information was that I wanted to be absolutely certain that the WCPA was not some kind of fluke organized by a group of mere wishful thinkers. If this were the case, there would be no reason for alarm. However, after thoroughly examining the connections between the World Constitution and Parliament Association and other powerful global societies who are working for a one-world government as well, I had no choice but to believe that this is in fact the beginning of the final push to usher in the New World Order. After considering the following information, and reviewing the material in the Exhibits of this book, I believe the reader will agree.

Connections

The organization that has figured most prominently in the WCPA's leadership is World Union. According to the letterhead of February-April 1987, presented in Exhibit D, the general secretary of World Union, Sri A.B. Patel, is the WCPA's honorary president for life. Mr. N.S. Rao, the chairman of World Union, on the other hand, is listed as one of the WCPA's two co-presidents. According to *Who's Who in the World*, Philip Isely is a member of World Union as well, although the letterhead does not reveal this information.[11] And another letter I received indicates that the new general secretary of World Union, Samar Basu, is also an official of the WCPA.

As mentioned earlier, World Union joined with World Goodwill—a creation of Lucis Trust—in 1961. Lucis (or Lucifer) Trust is an offshoot of the Theosophical Society, which is plugged into the highest levels of Freemasonry. Past and present members of Lucis Trust include: Robert McNamara, Donald Regan, Henry Kissinger, David Rockefeller, Paul Volcker, and George Shultz[12]—the same crowd that runs the Council on Foreign Relations and the Trilateral Commission.

Besides the CFR/WCPA connection existing through Lucis Trust and World Union, the WCPA has at least four CFR members directly in its ranks. They include current CFR members Gerard Piel, Dr. Kenneth B. Clark, and Dr. Glenn T. Seaborg, who are all WCPA honorary sponsors; and Ramsey Clark who is a former CFR member.[13] Jesse Jackson's affiliation with the two groups must also be considered. In addition to this, one must not forget that the CFR is the real power behind the United Nations, having conceived the organization. More than 20 percent of the WCPA's honorary sponsors are identified with that organization.

Another organization collaborating with Isely's World Constitution and Parliament Association is the World Council of Churches. Cynthia Wedel, the WCC's president since 1975, is an honorary sponsor of the Provisional World Parliament. This is perhaps the most blatant evidence yet of the WCC's hidden agenda. This organization has come to represent the leadership of most of the mainline Protestant church denominations in America and has privately been pushing for unification with the Church of Rome. But it appears that the WCC is only trying to "unite" Christianity in order to bring it into the New World Order. This also makes it easier to understand why the Council has been so active in promoting interfaithism—the merging of all the world's major religions under one umbrella. This false unity was all necessary in order to bring humanity into a world government.

One can get an idea of the extent of the WCPA's network by reviewing the list of organizations to which its director belongs. In addition to being a member of World Union, Isely is a member of the International Association of Educators for World Peace, World Federalist Association, Amnesty International, American Civil Liberties Union (ACLU), American Academy of Political and Social Science, Global Education Associates, Friends of the Earth, Sierra Club, Audubon Society, the Wilderness Society, American Humanist Association, SANE, Planetary Society, Worldwatch Institute, Planetary Citizens, and the Global Futures Network (partial listing). Given his busy schedule, it is difficult to imagine how he finds time to eat or sleep, or to run for Congress—something he did in 1958.[14]

The greatest number of connections with the WCPA comes through the World Future Society of which Isely is also a member. From all appearances, the World Future Society has become that "world forum," called for in the Club of Rome's 1972 book, *The Limits to Growth*. In that book, the Club's Executive Committee stated:

> Since intellectual enlightenment is without effect if it is
> not also political, The Club of Rome also will encourage
> the creation of a world forum where statesmen, policy-
> makers, and scientists can discuss the dangers and hopes

for the future global system *without the constraints of formal inter-governmental negotiation*[15] (emphasis added).

The World Future Society is where the political, economic, and spiritual aspects of the one-world government all come together. It seems to be a type of common ground or clearinghouse for all of the global societies. According to a World Future Society advertisement from several years ago, the organization's directors include Arnold Barach (Editor, Special Projects, The Kiplinger Washington Editors, Inc.), John W. Gardner (Chairman, Independent Sector, formerly U.S. Secretary of Health, Education, and Welfare), Barbara Marx Hubbard (President, Futures Network), Robert S. McNamara (Former President, World Bank), and Glenn T. Seaborg (Professor of Chemistry, University of California, formerly Chairman, U.S. Atomic Energy Commission), among others.

Clearly, the World Future Society is an organization that must be reckoned with.

The Society sponsors an annual symposium that is attended by the leading movers and shakers of the New Age/one-world movement. Since 1980 these meetings have focused on such issues as: Global Community Networking; The Aquarian Conspiracy; The Future of International Governance; and Thinking Globally, Acting Locally.[16] Perhaps the most important symposium to date, however, was Worldview 84 (held in 1984), which was nothing less than a world government planning session.

The World Constitution and Parliament Association emerged from this meeting with the lead role for ushering in the New World Order. It had already held the first of its Provisional World Parliament sessions prior to Worldview 84 and was in the process of planning its second session. However, this conference helped to solidify the WCPA's position.

The WCPA endeavored to appear as a grassroots movement so that the public would not become alarmed. For this reason, many of the other better known organizations who are involved in the plot have taken a temporary backseat so as not to blow the WCPA's cover as a peoples' movement. Every impression had to be created that "We, the People" are really the ones in control of this historic move for "world peace and unity."

Hundreds of organizations were represented at Worldview 84 and would therefore have to be aware of the WCPA's plans. Some of the more important institutions include the American Humanist Association, Baha'i, the Brookings Institute, Club of Rome, Council on

Foreign Relations, Fellowship of Inner Light, Global 2000 Project, International Association of Educators for World Peace, National Organization for Women (N.O.W.), Planetary Initiative, The Hunger Project, The International Monetary Fund, The World Bank, Trilateral Commission, World Future Society, and Y.E.S.[17]

It would be impossible to attend this meeting without understanding the fact that a world government was being planned. Therefore, if all of these organizations came away from the symposium supportive of the World Future Society, we know that they are also involved in advancing the cause of global government and are privately supportive of the WCPA.

I believe the same can be said about the leaders of those corporations who sponsor the World Future Society and its planning sessions, such as AT&T, General Electric Corporation, General Motors Incorporated, IBM Limited, Ortho Pharmaceutical Corporation, and Xerox Corporation, among others.[18]

(GE, GM and Xerox are among those that also support David Rockefeller's Trilateral Commission.[19])

From the looks of who was present at Worldview 84 and who funds the World Future Society's efforts, one is forced to take the World Constitution and Parliament Association seriously, since Isely and his organization, as stated, emerged from the session with the lead role. The preceding have been just a few of the WCPA's interconnections. Believe it or not, these represent just the tip of the iceberg; there are hundreds of organizations involved in the plot.

Chapter Five
Freemasonry—The Hidden Catalyst

A New Age Link

More than two years before learning about the WCPA, I discovered that the Theosophical Society and its sister organizations were playing important roles in laying the groundwork for the New Age movement—certainly no secret among New Age researchers. However, it was not until the fall of 1985 that I first began to suspect the existence of an even higher center of direction, serving as the main coordinator between the economic, political, and spiritual elements of the one-world government. This suspicion resulted from a phone call I received from Don Boyer, Director of Marketing and Public Relations for Sandi Patti Helvering, the popular Christian song artist.

Don was an old college friend and had first learned about the New Age movement earlier in the year. He explained how earlier that summer he had conducted research in advertising and asked his assistant to contact a number of magazines to obtain their advertising "rate cards." Most of the publications were the likes of *Better Homes and Gardens*, *Reader's Digest*, etc. However, unbeknownest to Don, his assistant had also included the *New Age Magazine*, believing he was simply inquiring about a health magazine.

In response to his assistant's request for information, Don received the letter shown on the following page. He was surprised to see the Masonic reference on the letterhead of the *New Age Magazine*, and for reasons he could not explain, he said that just holding the letter gave him chills. He added that he sensed something very unsettling, especially about the expressions "Mother Supreme Council of the World" and "The Supreme Council of the Thirty-Third and Last Degree." This is when he called me, wondering about the Freemasons' involvement in the New Age movement.*

*Due to unwanted adverse publicity, Masonic leaders recently changed the name of this magazine to *The Scottish Rite Journal*.

MOTHER SUPREME COUNCIL OF THE WORLD

THE SUPREME COUNCIL
OF THE THIRTY-THIRD AND LAST DEGREE

ANCIENT AND ACCEPTED SCOTTISH RITE OF FREEMASONRY
SOUTHERN JURISDICTION, U. S. A.

1733 SIXTEENTH STREET, N. W.   WASHINGTON, D. C. 20009
TELEPHONE 202-232-3579   CABLE SCSJUSA

THE NEW AGE
MAGAZINE

AEMIL POULER, 33°, G∴C∴
MANAGING EDITOR

CHRIS A. POULER, PH. D.,33°
ASSISTANT MANAGING EDITOR

August 12, 1985

Mr. Don E. Boyer
Director of Public Relations
The Helvering Agency
530 Grand Avenue
Anderson, Indiana 46012

Dear Mr. Boyer:

    Thank you for your letter of inquiry and interest in The New Age. Because we do not carry advertising I am unable to comply with your request.

    With every good wish,

Sincerely,

Chris A. Pouler
Assistant Managing Editor

CAP/akp

Letter from Supreme Council to Don Boyer

As I had not previously been aware of any connection between the New Age movement and Freemasonry, I began what turned out to be several months of research on the topic. I realized the possibility of the magazine's name being just a coincidence, in which case there would be no link between the two; but statements appearing in a Lucis Trust publication entitled *Thirty Year's Work* would prove to the contrary. *Thirty Year's Work* summarizes the books written by Alice Bailey, former head of the Theosophical Society and the founder of Lucis Trust and the Arcane Schools. According to this publication, Alice Bailey received frequent instructions on Freemasonry through her spirit guide, Djwhal Khul, referred to as the Tibetan master. It states:

> The books written by Alice Bailey with the Tibetan contain many references to the Masonic Craft; to its origins, the course of its history over the centuries, and to the significant part a revitalised and re-spiritualised Masonry can and will play in the future in carrying the light and

the energy of the Mystery teachings through the Aquarian era.[1]

Alice Bailey offers a more revealing personal account of Free-masonry (or simply Masonry) in her book, *The Externalisation of the Hierarchy*. On page 511 she writes:

> The Masonic Movement when it can be divorced from politics and social ends and from its present paralysing condition of inertia, will meet the need of those who can, and should, wield power. It is the custodian of the law; it is the home of the Mysteries and the seat of initiation. It holds in its symbolism the ritual of Diety, and the way of salvation is pictorially preserved in its work. The methods of Diety are demonstrated in its Temples, and under the All-seeing Eye the work can go forward. It is a far more occult organisation than can be realised, and is intended to be the training school for the coming advanced occultists. In its ceremonials lies hid the wielding of the forces connected with the growth and life of the kingdoms of nature and the unfoldment of the divine aspects of man.[2]

Foster Bailey, the husband of Alice, was also involved with Free-masonry and even wrote a book on the organization entitled *The Spirit of Masonry*. In that book appears the text of a lecture delivered by Foster Bailey to a lodge in New Jersey. Also appearing in the book is the text of an article by Alice Bailey first published in the *Master Mason Magazine*.[3]

As I continued my investigation I learned that Bailey's forerunners, Madame Blavatsky, founder of the Theosophical Society as well as her successor, Annie Besant, were both heavily involved with Free-masonry. Cardinal Caro y Rodriguez, archbishop of Santiago, Chile, in his book, *The Mystery of Freemasonry Unveiled*, examines these relationships. He states:

> Madame Blavatsky, the promoter or founder of Theosophy in Europe, was also a member of the Masonic Lodges*; her successor, Annie Besant, President of the Theosophical Society in 1911 was Vice President and

---

* Historically, with the exception of the Grand Orient Lodge, the Masonic Order had been exclusively male. However in 1893, the French Lodge, "Freethinkers," reversed the trend by adding the special feature of admitting women. This Lodge became known as "The Great X Symbolic Lodge of France," or "Lodge of Human Rights," and was the beginning of what is today known as Co-Masonry or adoptive Masonry. This lodge is headquartered in Paris and has hundreds of affiliated lodges throughout Europe and the Americas.[5]

great Teacher of the Supreme Council of the International Order of Co-Masonry . . . and among us, in our
city, the brother masons are the ones that contribute
mostly to spread the Theosophical Society.[4]

Apparently, the leaders of illuminized Freemasonry decided that
it would create less suspicion if the most visible roles for preparing
the way for the New Age went to the women Masonic leaders of the
Theosophical Society (Blavatsky, Besant and Bailey). Since Freemasonry was viewed as a predominantly male organization, this would
prevent people from suspecting it as the center of direction.

According to Rodriguez:

The inner circle [of the Theosophical Society], known
as the Esoteric Section, or rather the Eastern School of
Theosophy usually referred to as E.S., is in reality a secret society, consisting in its turn of three further circles,
the innermost composed of the Mahatmas or Masters of
the White Lodge, the second of the Accepted Pupils or
Initiates, and the third of the Learners or ordinary members. The E.S. and Co-Masonry thus compose two secret
societies within the open door controlled by people who
are frequently members of both.[6]

Cardinal Rodriguez summarizes his research on Co-Masonry as
follows:

It is understood: The theosophical doctrines on the nature of God and the soul and the relationship between
God and the soul, are the same doctrines as taught in
masonry. It is enough to read the books dealing with
the history of Theosophy to see that each theosophical
center is founded, almost without a doubt by members
of the Lodge.[7]

Organizational Structure

Convinced of the fact that Freemasonry was closely connected
with Theosophy and therefore with the New Age movement, I set out
to learn more about the Masonic institution itself, studying its origin,
purpose, and beliefs. To gain insight on these matters I interviewed
a number of current as well as former Masons, eight of whom had
reached the level of either Thirty-Second or Thirty-Third degree.

What I learned from these conversations was that most Masons
initially joined the Lodge either out of peer pressure or for the sake
of camaraderie. Many also join because they feel it enhances their
social stature and helps them advance in their careers, since most
prominent businessmen and government officials, they explained,
were Masons. The Order enables them to rub elbows with society's

elite. On these points, present and past members agreed. But the similarities ended there.

The testimonies of current Masons differed drastically from those of Masons who had left the Order. Current members expressed no knowledge whatsoever of any higher religious aims of the Order. They were fiercely loyal to the lodge and told me that Freemasonry was nothing more than an international secret fraternity based on good works.

Former Masons, on the other hand, offered views that could not have been more opposite from those of their counterparts. They told me that the organization was anti-Christ and that it was dangerous, particularly in its higher levels, citing the previous as their main reason for leaving, adding that it was Luciferically-inspired. I could not understand how such huge discrepancies could exist between the experiences of past and present Masons. I concluded that current members either would not reveal what they knew because of the oaths of secrecy they had taken or else they truly were unaware of these things, not yet having reached a level where they were exposed to the underlying purpose of their Order.

Possibly the biggest factor working in Freemasonry's favor is that a majority of its three million-plus members in this country think of it as a noble and virtuous society. While they should know better than to join a secret society to whom they must swear blind allegiance, they are usually unaware of the hidden agenda of the Order.

Men wishing to become Masons typically apply for membership through a friend who is already a member. The new member first joins the Blue Lodge, the basic organization of Masonry, which consists of three degrees: 1) Entered Apprentice, 2) Fellowcraft, and 3) Master Mason.[8] Initiates are instructed that each degree teaches moral lessons. In order to earn the degree, they must learn the lessons and participate in a ritual that illustrates them.

Once a member acquires the third degree, he may proceed in either or both of the two branches of advanced Masonry, the Scottish Rite and the York Rite. The Scottish Rite includes a total of twenty-nine degrees ranging from the fourth through the thirty-third degree and is probably the more powerful of the two branches.[9]

Unlike the other degrees in the Scottish Rite, the thirty-third degree cannot be earned; it can only be bestowed upon a member by the Supreme Council. In this fashion, the Council chooses who becomes part of its inner circle. According to the Supreme Council of the Northern Jurisdiction, this degree is conferred upon a member "because of outstanding service to the Fraternity or for service to others which reflects credit upon the Order."[10]

If a Mason chooses to advance in the York Rite, he may receive a total of ten additional degrees, structured as follows: Degrees of the Chapter include 4) Mark Master, 5) Past Master, 6) Most Excellent Master, and 7) Royal Arch; Degrees of the Council include 8) Royal Master, 9) Select Master, and 10) Super-Excellent Master; and Degrees of the Commandery include 11) Knight of the Red Cross, 12) Knight of Malta, and 13) Knight Templar.

Those Masons who have reached at least the thirty-second degree in the Scottish Rite or the degree of Knight Templar in the York Rite have the option of joining the Shrine, officially known as The Ancient Arabic Order of Nobles of the Mystic Shrine.[11]

Other Masonic affiliates include the Grotto (formally, the Mystic Order of Veiled Prophets of the Enchanted Realm) and the Tall Cedars of Lebanon.[12] Women's groups include the Order of the Eastern Star, the Order of the Amaranth, and the Order of the True Kindred.[13] Boys may join the Order of DeMolay and the Order of Builders. Girls may join the Order of Job's Daughters and the Order of Rainbow.[14] I also found that many, perhaps most, of the world's secret societies view Freemasonry as their mother organization from which their ceremonies, rituals, and beliefs emanate. *World Book Encyclopedia* supports this conclusion stating that "more than a hundred fraternal organizations have a relationship with Masonry. . . ."[15]

The former Masons, whom I had interviewed, recommended that I read certain Masonic books such as *Morals and Dogma* and *Mackey's Encyclopedia of Freemasonry*. These books, they said, would give me a glimpse of what Freemasonry was all about. In spite of efforts to do so, I was unable to locate these books at the time.

However, a friend called my attention to a Masonic work entitled *Freemasonry and the Ancient Gods*, which was most revealing. Here are some excerpts from this book first published in 1921.

> Freemasonry, to me, is the most wonderful thing in the world. In it there is a spiritual vitality which has enabled it to survive its worst enemies. . . . Despite ignorance, despite deliberate attempts to destroy some of her most glorious treasures, she yet survives, and, waxing in wisdom, strength, and beauty, spreads her branches over the whole earth.

> The plain man, who never studied the ancient wisdom, and laughs at the message of the stars, can see the writing on the wall; but those who are grounded in the ancient wisdom and the cosmic lore know full well that this is the age of Mars, the Destroyer. In days of old the

Christ came when the point of the vernal equinox was in the new sign Pisces, and that sign ushered in the new dispensation and our modern world.

Today Pisces is fallen from his high estate, and a new sign draws nigh. It is Aquarius, the sign of the perfected man. Under his rule we may look to see a great awakening of the spiritual in man, an uplifting of man towards the Godhead in place of the descent of the Godhead into man. This means a new dispensation, a new type of religious outlook. . . . We are moving towards a better, a more spiritual world, but before us lie darkness, difficulties, and danger, it may even be the Valley of the Shadow of Death, for Mars still has his work to do ere the moon shines forth and proclaims the time of change and is succeeded by the sun in all his glory, and the reign of the new era is established.

One thing I know will survive, as it has previously survived the wreck, not merely of mighty empires, but of civilisations themselves—Freemasonry.

In the new age which is passing through the long-drawn travail of its birth, Freemasonry will be there, as of old, to lay the broad foundations on which the new religion will be built.[16]

(The author of this book, J.S.M. Ward, was a very prominent Mason. Eight full lines in the title page are devoted to listing the important positions he held within Freemasonry.)

It seemed as if I was reading straight out of a new age manual. In addition to the obvious references to the coming one-world religion of the Antichrist toward which Freemasonry is working, these statements and other similar elaborations existing in other Masonic writings indicated that Freemasonry deified man (exalted man to the position of God) and was deeply involved in astrology, a form of occult divination strictly forbidden in the Bible. I renewed my efforts to dig deeper into the history of Freemasonry.

Masonic Origins

After months of getting nowhere, a door finally opened. One Sunday evening in 1986 while sharing at a church in northern Indiana, I met an elderly lady who introduced herself to me at the close of the service. She inquired whether I knew anything about Freemasonry and its influence on the New Age. I told her I was aware of its involvement but that I still did not understand exactly what role the Masonic Order played in the overall scheme of things.

She went on to share that she had been researching the Ma-

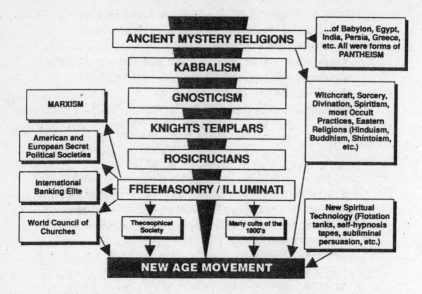

History of Occultism and One-World Movement

sonic movement for the past twenty years and had quite a collection of materials on the Order (much of which she had obtained from widows of deceased Masons who were unaware of the significance of the Order and its literature). She would make her materials available to me if I wanted them and explained that she had been un-successful at getting anyone to listen to her because of her age and the lack of a fancy job title. We ended up meeting several times at her home to sort through her materials on Freemasonry. Whatever this elderly saint did not have, it seemed she knew where to get.

In the months that followed, I received quite an education while combing through the major Masonic reference works. I found a re-peated mention of such orders as the Illuminati, the Knights Templars, and the Rosicrucians, along with other cultish groups, which I had previously thought to be only myths. But I soon became convinced to the contrary, not only learning that they existed, but that Freemasonry was a modern-day continuation of Gnosticism and of the ancient mystery religions.

While most sources placed the official birth of Freemasonry at 1717, Masonic references clearly indicated that the organization's history went back much further than this. The above diagram, based on my research in both Masonic and non-Masonic sources, depicts the roots of the Order along with its historical and modern-day lines of influence.

(A number of other false religions and subversive movements have also had an influence on the Masonic Order. However, those depicted above are the main sects and religions to which the existence of Freemasonry and the New Age movement may be attributed. The names have changed, but the beliefs, tactics, and designs of the groups have remained essentially the same.)

The history of Freemasonry, I discovered, was also the history of the secret societies, and the history of the secret societies is the history of organized occultism—particularly in the Western world. Perhaps the most complete history of organized occultism has been provided by Albert Pike in his 861 page occult classic entitled *Morals and Dogma of the Ancient and Accepted Scottish Rite of Freemasonry* (more commonly referred to by Masons as simply *Morals and Dogma*). Drawing from the sources available to him as the long-time leader of Freemasonry (1859-1891), Pike was able to trace the chronological growth and spread of the Mysteries over the face of the earth from ancient Babylon down to the present-day Masonic Order.

In reference to the esoteric doctrines of the Mysteries, Pike states:

> The communication of this knowledge and other secrets, some of which are perhaps lost, constituted, under other names, what we now call *Masonry*, or *Free*, or *Frank-Masonry* .... The present name of the Order, and its titles, and the names of the Degrees now in use, were not then known. ... But, by whatever *name* it was known in this or the other country, Masonry existed as it now exists, the same in spirit and at heart ... before even the first colonies emigrated into Southern India, Persia, and Egypt, from the cradle of the human race [ancient Babylon].[17]

Pike goes on to remark, "We reproduce the speculations of the Philosophers, the Kabalists, the Mystagogues and the Gnostics."[18] Dozens of supporting statements are scattered throughout the same volume, leaving no doubt that Pike meant what he said. Other Masonic reference works provide a similar account of the Order's roots. *The Freemason's Monitor*, for example, explains:

> Our records inform us, that the usages and customs of Masons have ever corresponded with those of the Egyptian philosophers, to which they bear a near affinity. Unwilling to expose their mysteries to vulgar eyes, they concealed their particular tenets, and principles of polity, under hieroglyphical figures; and expressed their notions of government by signs and symbols, which they

communicated to their Magi alone, who were bound by
oath not to reveal them.[19]

I discovered that historical documents pertaining to the beginnings of Freemasonry and the spread of organized occultism had been
preserved in a number of Masonic libraries throughout the world. In
Europe, for example, a sizeable collection can be found in Freemason's
Hall located on Great Queen Street in the heart of London. In the
United States, on the other hand, a large depository of Masonic writings is located at the Grand Lodge of Iowa in Cedar Rapids. The most
extensive collection by far, however, can be found at the House of
the Temple in Washington, DC.

Along with serving as the headquarters for the Mother Supreme
Council of the World (the governing body of Freemasonry) and containing a vast, exquisite Masonic shrine, the House of the Temple also
houses a universally renowned Masonic library. Henry C. Clausen, the
former Sovereign Grand Commander of the Scottish Rite referred to
this library in his book, *Masons Who Helped Shape Our Nation*,
written in 1976.

> A priceless treasure of The Supreme Council is its Li-
> brary. One-third of the 175,000 volumes which it con-
> tains deal with Freemasonry in all its branches, form-
> ing one of the most comprehensive collections on this
> subject in the entire world.
>
> The Archives in the House of the Temple supplement the
> Library. More than two-and-a-half million papers, giving
> details of the history of Masonry and of the Scottish Rite
> are carefully filed and indexed.[20]

Another prominent Masonic writer, H.L. Haywood, confirms
these figures, claiming the existence of "fifty or sixty thousand Masonic books."[21]

If Freemasonry were nothing more than a social organization,
as it publicly claims to be, then how could one account for the in-
credible number of books existing on the Order? What kind of social
organization would possess an archives of two-and-a-half million documents along with a library of sixty thousand books containing its
history? The mere existence of such a collection suggested that Freemasonry was more than a large group of citizens organized for community service.

As a result of my research, I finally came to conclude that a
careful history of the occult had been maintained by the ancient priests
wherever the mysteries were practiced. This information was probably initially passed along chiefly by word of mouth and possibly as-

sisted by the use of hieroglyphics and other forms of primitive writing developed among the ancient civilizations. However, as time progressed, this knowledge consisting of the secret rituals, beliefs and practices of the occult priesthood, was put into writing on manuscripts, providing a permanent record of these Luciferic activities.

Much of this ancient knowledge was allegedly first recorded by some of the Greek and Roman philosophers, whose philosophical societies existed as special extensions of the occult priesthood. According to Masonic sources, this information has been meticulously preserved ever since, having been passed from one generation to the next through an unbroken line of occult priests. The Masonic Order claims to be the latest in a succession of occult orders who have served as the guardians of this ancient knowledge.

Many specifics of the Order's diabolical legacy have been revealed in the works of Masonic historians such as Pike, Mackey, Haywood, M.P. Hall, and others who have provided summaries of Masonic/occult history. While some discrepancies exist among the various accounts, there is, nevertheless, a remarkable degree of uniformity and consistency considering the complexity of the subject. However, to understand the Masonic Order's complete role and where it fits in, a bit of world history is required.

A Historical Perspective

By the days of Noah the world had become completely saturated with the occult to the point where only one righteous family was left. As a result, God, who was grieved by man's sin and wickedness, judged the world by sending a flood. After the flood, however, it took only a few generations before man had once again begun to embrace the occult. This was evidenced at the building of the Tower of Babel, which is believed to have been the first ziggurat—an ancient occult worship tower with a shrine at the top. Under the umbrella of pantheism, the ancient occult mysteries began to take hold and spread. By the time of Abraham and Lot, the human state, at least in their part of the world, had once again gotten out of control. Those were the days of Sodom and Gomorrah when perversion and immorality were taken to new heights.

Although Abraham was himself not perfect, he was a man who sought to do right in the eyes of God. Because he and his family were the only righteous ones left who were willing to acknowledge Him, God would honor Abraham's faith by choosing to create a nation from his seed. God would work through this nation, Israel, to keep His truth and the way of righteousness alive in the midst of a dark, occult-ravaged world. After a few hundred years when Abraham's seed had sufficiently multiplied, there were enough Israelites to constitute a physical nation. At that time, God led His people out of Egypt through His servant Moses.

The history of Israel would be one of ups and downs. When the Israelites were obedient to God, they prospered; and none of their pantheistic neighbors could stand against them. However, when the Israelites themselves began to fall for the spiritual lies of the surrounding nations, they were oppressed by these same powers. God sent a steady stream of holy prophets to teach Israel His ways and to warn them of what would happen if they did not obey. Much like the relationship between a loving father and his child, while longing for his child (Israel) to be good and loving, there were times when that child was rebellious and needed to be disciplined before something much worse happened.

The Israelites, through Moses, had been instructed to bring regular animal offerings or sacrifices before God. These sacrifices symbolized the payment for their sins, reminding them that sin does not come without a penalty. These offerings were also symbolic of the coming supreme sacrifice of Jesus Christ, who would pay the penalty for the sins of the entire world at the appointed time.

After the proper groundwork had been laid, God sent His Son. The message of forgiveness and the promise of eternal life to those who believe in Christ would be carried forward from Israel to all nations. Although this gospel (the good news) spread in all directions, it would not be equally accepted by all peoples and would meet with more resistance in some places than in others. Those missionaries, for example, who carried the message into Babylon, Persia, and India were violently rejected; and only a small number of people believed and received the truth there. Similarly, today, in spite of nearly twenty centuries of missionary efforts in the Far East, with the exception of a few areas, the message of Christ has been overwhelmingly rejected.

The hold of Satan on these countries was so complete and established that, to this day, only a small percent of the orient believes in Christ. Hinduism—the oldest surviving pantheistic religion is still being practiced by a majority of India's inhabitants.

The story would be different in the Mediterranean where the gospel was accepted in large numbers, in spite of fierce persecution against those who believed. Within a few generations there were so many Christians in this region that the high priests of the Mysteries of Greece, Rome, and Egypt began to loose their control. The teachings of Christ went head-to-head against the pantheistic beliefs and occult practices of the priests, exposing them for what they were. The more the believers were persecuted, the larger their numbers grew, until finally the occult priests were forced to go underground in order to keep their secret knowledge and traditions alive.

These occult teachings have been handed down from generation to generation ever since, kept alive in the Western world by the secret societies, which are little more than a continuation of ancient occult priesthoods. Satan's plan was to keep his priesthood and secret doctrines alive until, being sufficient in number and power, the priesthood could once again seize control over his lost territories. Gnosticism, the most effective and widely accepted form of pantheism, was more deceptive and clever than the others, developing the occult's only major counter explanation to the message and person of Christ. The Gnostics were the chief adversaries of the Apostle Paul and the early Church, relentlessly pursuing Christians wherever they went, long before the mystery religions even began to crumble.

According to Albert Pike, Gnosticism was an offshoot of Kabalism, an oral occult tradition, which was adhered to by a minority of the Jews. At some point, which remains uncertain, these occult teachings were reduced to writing, and the Kabalah was born. On page 626 of *Morals and Dogma*, Pike states, "The Kabalah is the key of the occult sciences; and the Gnostics were born of the Kabalists."

Kabalism was merely a unique version of the ancient mysteries specifically designed to deceive God's chosen people. Unlike the other mysteries, its teachings dealt specifically with Israel, offering occult counter-explanations to the revelations of the prophets, complete with a cleverly disguised occult interpretation of the history of Israel. Moses, for example, rather than being the righteous prophet of God who led the Israelites out of Egypt, was made out to be an occult figure whose purpose was to initiate the Israelites into the enlightened and more advanced teachings of Egypt.

If Kabalism could be viewed as the occult counter-explanation of the Old Testament, Gnosticism, existing as a further development of Kabalism and taking into account Satan's "new problem" posed by the risen Christ, would serve as the main occult counterattack against the New Testament. Thus, Kabalism and Gnosticism combined, composed a type of occult parallel to the Old and New Testaments.

Gnosticism, although originally composed of Jewish occultists, rapidly gained Gentile followers until it soon became predominantly Gentile. As the priesthoods were forced to take on new forms, Gnosticism became a magnet for these occult adepts. Branches of Gnosticism represented the first significant secret societies of the post-resurrection era, with various degrees or levels of initiation and the inner circle of initiates worshipping Lucifer.

Gnosticism

A significant amount of space has been devoted to the discussion of Gnosticism in Masonic reference works. *Morals and Dogma*, for example, has allotted more than forty pages to Gnosticism and its connection with Freemasonry. Albert Pike, the book's author, offers the following explanation of Gnosticism:

> The Gnostics derived their leading doctrines and ideas from Plato and Philo, the Zend-avesta and the Kabalah, and the Sacred books of India and Egypt; and thus introduced into the bosom of Christianity the cosmological and theosophical speculations, which had formed the larger portion of the ancient religions of the Orient, joined to those of the Egyptian, Greek, and Jewish doctrines, which the New-Platonists had equally adopted in the Occident.[22]

Gnosticism flourished through various offshoots such as the Manicheans of the third century, the Euchites of the fourth century, the Paulicians of the seventh century, and the Bogomils of the ninth century.[23] It is not possible within the scope of this book to identify and define each branch of Gnosticism that has existed over the centuries, but the following teaching of the Bogomils will give us an idea of what beliefs the Knights Templars embraced before passing them on to Freemasonry.

> God, the Supreme Father, has two sons, the elder Satanael, the younger Jesus. To Satanael, who sat on the right hand of God, belonged the right of governing the celestial world, but, filled with pride, he rebelled against his Father and fell from Heaven. Then, aided by the companions of his fall, he created the visible world, image of the celestial, having like the other its sun, moon, and stars, and last he created man and the serpent which became his minister. Later Christ came to earth in order to show men the way to Heaven, but His death was ineffectual, for even by descending into Hell He could not wrest the power from Satanael, i.e., Satan. This belief in the impotence of Christ and the necessity therefore for placating Satan, not only "the Prince of this world," but its creator, led to the further doctrine that Satan, being all-powerful, should be adored.[24]

At the base of each form of Gnosticism existed this adoration or worship of Satan, as well as a profound hatred for Christ and his teachings. It was perversions such as these, handed down in an unbroken tradition from the earliest Gnostics, that were eventually embraced by the Knights of the Temple (Knights Templars) in the twelfth century.

Knights Templars

The Knights Templars were a military and religious order first established in AD 1118 in Jerusalem by nine French knights under the leadership of Hugues de Payens of Champagne and Godefroi de Saint-Omer.[25] Their stated mission was to protect pilgrims on their way to the Holy Land during the crusades.[26] They also fought in various battles of the crusades and became famous for their bravery.[27] "Baldwin II, King of Jerusalem, gave the Knights Templars quarters in his palace, built on the site of Solomon's Temple."[28] From this, the order derived its name—Knights of the Temple.

Membership in the Knights Templars was originally limited to nobles.[29] However, later on, the order opened its ranks to other men who it felt could be used to further its aims. The order grew rapidly and in the year 1128 was taken under the special protection of the pope.[30]

During the Crusades, the Knights Templars established local offices in all the Christian countries to encourage enlistment in the crusading armies and to take care of funds for the pilgrims.[31] (The pilgrims gave donations to the Order—which existed as a tax-exempt organization—in exchange for protection to and from Jerusalem.) The Templars, being composed mostly of nobles, were also granted favors by many European rulers and gained possession of property throughout the continent.[32] Through gifts of land and money, the Templars became extremely wealthy and powerful.[33]

After the fall of Jerusalem to Saladin in 1187, the order established its headquarters in Acre. The Templars were forced to relocate once again in 1291 when Acre fell to the Muslims. This time their headquarters were moved to the island of Cyprus.[34] However, by then

> the Templars, through their enormous wealth and widespread organization, had become the bankers of Europe, and the order was no longer primarily a military one. It was especially influential in Spain, France, and England, where commanderies of knights, men-at-arms, and chaplains were organized, each under its own superior, subordinate to the Grand Master of the order.[35]

Morals and Dogma adds, "Their watchword was, to become wealthy in order to buy the world. They became so, and in 1312 they possessed in Europe alone more than nine thousand seignories."[36] (A seignory refers to the estate or dominion of a noble or feudal lord.[37])

The Knights Templars were probably corrupt from the beginning. But whether the order started out degenerate or became this way later, it is certain that the Templars had, during their exploits in the Middle East, become strongly influenced by both the Gnostics and the Assassins (a ruthless Arabic military order). It is a fact that several of the founders of the Knights Templars were initiates in the sect of the Assassins.[38] The Templars, while adopting the religious beliefs of the Gnostics, received many of their organizational and political traits from the Assassins. The Templars represented the first wide-scale attempt to organize and mobilize the forces of occultism for the purpose of gaining control of the world.

Occult historian Edith Starr Miller summarizes the demise of the Templars as follows:

> Having embraced Gnosticism while in Palestine, and in touch with the sect of the Assassins, the Templar order degenerated, and some of its members, under the influence of that sect, were said to practice Phallicism or sex-worship and Satanism and to venerate "The Baphomet," the idol of the Luciferians. The crime of Sodomy was a rite of Templar initiation.[39]

"In 1307 the Templars were charged with heresy and immorality by a former member of the order."[40] As a result, Philip IV of France launched an investigation looking into the alleged misdeeds of the organization.[41] On 13 October 1307 the king had the Templars of France arrested and brought before the Inquisitor for France by whom they were examined.[42] The knights confessed to a variety of notorious crimes and admitted to taking blasphemous oaths against Jesus Christ upon admission into the order.

> [T]hey said, they had been shown the cross on which was the figure of Christ, and had been asked whether they believed in Him; when they answered yes, they were told in some cases that this was wrong (*dixit sibi quod male credebat*), because He was not God, He was a false prophet (*quia falsus propheta erat, nec erat Deus*). Some added that they were then shown an idol or a bearded head which they were told to worship; one added that this was of such "a terrible aspect that it seemed to him to be the face of some devil, called in French, *"un maufe,"* and that whenever he saw it he was so overcome with fear that he could hardly look at it without fear and trembling." All who confessed declared that they had been ordered to spit on the crucifix, and very many that they had received the injunction to com-

mit obscenities and to practise unnatural vice. Some said
that on their refusal to carry out these orders they had
been threatened with imprisonment, even perpetual imprisonment; a few said they had actually been incarcer-
ated; one declared that he had been terrorized, seized
by the throat, and threatened with death.[43]

Pope Clement V, however, refused to respond to the charges
and confessions of the Templars.

Clement V, deeply resenting the King's interference with
an Order which existed entirely under papal jurisdiction,
wrote in the strongest terms of remonstrance to Philippe
le Bel urging their release, and even after their trial,
neither the confessions of the Knights nor the angry
expostulations of the King could persuade him to believe
in their guilt.[44]

The pope was not only slow to respond to the confessions but
actually did what he could to protect the order. Later on, however,
he gave the following reasons for his actions (in his own words):

Because it did not seem likely nor credible that men of
such religion who were believed often to shed their
blood and frequently expose their persons to the peril
of death for Christ's name, and who showed such great
and many signs of devotion both in divine offices as well
as in fasts, as in other devotional observances, should
be so forgetful of their salvation as to do these things,
we were unwilling . . . to give ear to this kind of insinu-
ation . . . (*hujusmodi insinuacioni ac delacioni
ipsorum . . . aurem noluimus inclinare*).[45]

Due to mounting pressure from a suspicious public and because
a number of the confessions before Philip IV were allegedly made
under torture, the pope finally decided to mount his own investigation, consenting to receive in private audience "a certain Knight of
the Order, of great nobility and held by the same Order in no slight
esteem."[46] Upon being questioned by the pope, the Knight "testified
to the abominations that took place on the reception of the Brethren, the spitting on the cross, and other things which were not law-
ful nor, humanly speaking, decent."[47]

Pope Clement V then decided to examine seventy-two other
French Knights at Poictiers in order to discover whether their earlier confessions before the Inquisitor for France were true. These hear-
ings were conducted without torture, with the witnesses taking an
oath promising "the full and pure truth." The Templars' Grand Master, Jacques de Molay and the French leaders of the order were likewise questioned in the presence of three Cardinals, four public nota-

ries and many others.[48] Before these many witnesses the Templars admitted their crimes as previously confessed during the trials of King Philip IV.[49] The Knights Templars, as it turned out, had been masters of deception, experts in duplicity, appearing to serve Christ on the surface while worshipping Lucifer within their inner rites. *Morals and Dogma* confirms this character.

> The templars, like all other Secret Orders and Associations, had two doctrines, one concealed and reserved for the Masters . . . the other public. . . . Thus they deceived the adversaries whom they sought to supplant.[50]

"The Pope, however, still refused to take action against the whole Order merely because the Master and Brethren around him had 'gravely sinned.'"[51] Instead, he decided to hold a papal commission in Paris which took place in November 1309.[52] But by then, the word about the Templars was out and the public had become outraged. In addition to Italy and France, "Templars in England, Germany, Spain, and Portugal also stood trials, but most were acquitted."[53]

Philip IV of France, more than any other monarch, pursued the members of the Order and sentenced many of them to death, charging them with conspiracy and Satan worship. On 12 May 1310 he had fifty-four French Templars burned alive in Paris.[54] In 1312, Pope Clement V was finally persuaded to abolish the Order.[55] And on 18 March 1314 the Grand Master, Jacques de Molay, along with three of his highest ranking officers, were burned at the stake.[56] It is this diabolical knight after whom today's Masonic Order of De Molay, reserved for young men, was named.

Following the death of De Molay, the Templars found refuge in Portugal under King Dinis II who became their protector.[57] The Order suffered a temporary setback resulting from the confiscation of most of its property; but it remained influential, continuing to operate underground. *Morals and Dogma* attests to the survival of the Knights Templars stating that De Molay, prior to his execution,

> created four Metropolitan Lodges, at Naples for the East, at Edinburg for the West, at Stockholm for the North, and at Paris for the South. [The initials of his name . . . found in the same order in the first three Degrees, are but one of the many internal and cogent proofs that such was the origin of modern Free-Masonry . . .][58]

In a continued reference to the Templar order, *Morals and Dogma* adds:

> . . . it lived, under other names and governed by unknown Chiefs, revealing itself only to those who, in

passing through a series of Degrees, had proven themselves worthy to be entrusted with the dangerous Secret.[59]

The Rosicrucians

Evidence suggests that the surviving Knights Templars either founded or merged with an existing secret order in the early 1300s, later referred to as the Order of the Rose-Croix (the Rosicrucians). Very few details are known about its actual beginnings due to this order's ability to conceal its activities.

Morals and Dogma however, establishes a definite link between the Rosicrucians and the Templar Order.

> The Successors of the Ancient Adepts Rose-Croix, abandoning by degrees the austere and hierarchial Science of their Ancestors in initiation, became a Mystic Sect, uniting with many of the Templars, the dogmas of the two intermingling . . . [60]

By the early 1600s, more than three hundred years had passed since the Templars had been abolished. As a result, the secret order decided to test the waters to see how the public would respond to its occult philosophies. For obvious reasons, the Order could not share its real history linking it to the Templars, so it devised an allegory of its history around a mythical character by the name of Christian Rosenkreuz.

This tale was published in a document known as the "Fama Fraternitatis," which the Order circulated throughout Europe. The story elaborates how Rosenkreuz traveled to Syria and then Egypt to study the occult. After learning from all of the great masters of occult philosophy in the Middle East and Northern Africa, he returned to Europe to spread his "enlightenment" throughout that continent. But he was unfavorably received and therefore, returned home to Germany where he hoped to establish a society based on his teachings.[61] This fictitious life of Christian Rosenkreuz symbolically conveyed the story of the Templars.

According to *Mackey's Encyclopedia of Freemasonry*, " . . . the fiction was readily accepted as a truth by most people, and the invisible society of Rosenkreuz was sought for with avidity by many who wished to unite with it."[62] However, the Order only wanted to test the reaction it would prompt and did not respond. (A number of societies sprang up claiming to possess the occult secrets of Rosenkreuz; but these aberrations were not the real Rosicrucian Order.)

This well calculated move by the secret Order allowed them to monitor Europe's openness to the occult without revealing the true identity of the Order or the names of its members. It also created a renewed interest in the occult throughout the Continent. But nearly another century would pass before the Order would begin to expand by publicly enlisting initiates.

Some contemporary leaders of the Masonic movement have denied any connections between their Order and the Knights Templars and Rosicrucians. However, enough evidence exists, which, if considered along with earlier statements from *Morals and Dogma*, clearly reveals that modern-day Freemasonry is a continuation of the preceding Orders. One outstanding example is in the names of the last three degrees of the York Rite—the Knight of the Red Cross, Knight of Malta and Knight Templar—and the eighteenth degree of the Scottish Rite—Sovereign Prince of Rose-Croix, which together with the seventeenth degree is known as the Chapter of Rose Croix.

The Birth of Freemasonry

If the Rosicrucians were to progress toward their goal of establishing a New World Order, they would eventually have to go public to enlist the support of more people to carry out their task. In the tradition of the Templars, they decided to take on the outer appearance of a benevolent organization of good works in order to continue their occult traditions within. They merged with and finally took over the stone mason guilds of Europe, retaining many of their symbols from the building trade. The stone masons became referred to as Operative Masons, as they were actually employed in the building profession; unlike the occult adepts who took over their guilds, who became known as Speculative Masons.

The builders' guilds had become a natural target for the takeover, since the Templars, centuries before, had themselves been great builders. With their enormous wealth, they constructed scores of castles and princely estates of their own pleasure and as monuments to their success and viewed themselves as great builders. They were even known to conceal themselves at times under the name of "Brethren Masons."[63]

With the construction of cathedrals on the decline, the operative guilds were shrinking in size and were in danger of going under. If they wanted to keep their traditions alive, they would have to open up their ranks to outsiders. Thus, with the two groups in need of each other, the marriage was sealed. The operative guilds, in time, became known as speculative guilds as they were flooded by esoteric occultists.

This transition from Operative to Speculative Masonry took several decades to complete. The move, which began as early as the

1640s, culminated in the forming of the world's first Grand Lodge in London in 1717. By way of this gradual takeover, the torch was passed to the Masonic order, with the Rosicrucians embedding themselves deep within its structure and hierarchy to become the Adepts, or the Princes of Freemasonry.

The "new" Order expanded rapidly. By the late 1700s, it had become firmly established as an organization known for its good works, and was, for the most part, viewed favorably by the public. With the groundwork successfully laid, the Adepts were once again free to pursue their age-old ambition of re-establishing the Luciferic World Order. *Morals and Dogma* states:

> The Initiates, in fact, thought in the eighteenth century that their time had arrived, some to found a new Hierarchy, others to overturn all authority, and to press down all the Social Order under the level of Equality.[64]

Toward this end, a new ultra-secret society was formed, enlisting in its ranks members from the highest degrees of the Masonic Order. This Order within an Order would come to be known as the Illuminati.

The Illuminati

The Masonic historian, Albert G. Mackey, describes the Illuminati as a "secret society, founded on May 1, 1776, by Adam Weishaupt, who was professor of canon law at the University of Ingolstadt."[65] In his biographical sketch of Weishaupt, Mackey opens with the following words, "He is *celebrated in the history of Masonry* as the founder of the Order of Illuminati of Bavaria"[66] (italics mine). Mackey later adds, "His ambition was, I think, a virtuous one; that it failed was his, and perhaps the world's misfortune."[67]

Any lingering doubts I had over whether the Order was Masonically inspired were removed when I discovered that H.L. Haywood, another highly esteemed Masonic historian, also included Weishaupt's biography in his book *Famous Masons and Masonic Presidents*. Weishaupt's esteemed summary is one of only one hundred biographical sketches appearing in the book, indicating that he had to have been a very prominent Mason.[68]

John Robison, an eighteenth century historian and a prominent Mason, was entrusted with some of the original documents and correspondence of the Illuminati. In his book, *Proofs of a Conspiracy*, written in 1798, he reproduced major segments of the Illuminati's original writings. Robison stated, "the express aim of the Order was to abolish Christianity, and overturn all civil government."[69] He went on to quote Weishaupt as stating that the plan for a New World Order can succeed "in no other way but by secret associations, which will by degrees, and in silence, possess themselves of the government of the States, and make use of those means for this purpose. . . ."[70]

Using deception and intrigue, Weishaupt and his inner circle of adepts succeeded at gaining the support of Germany's Masonic lodges. "All these branches were controlled by the twelve leading adepts headed by Weishaupt, who at the lodge in Munich held in his hands the threads of the whole conspiracy."[71] Mackey admits to the initial success of the Illuminati, commenting:

> The Order was at first very popular, and enrolled no less than two thousand names upon its registers, among whom were some of the most distinguished men of Germany. It extended rapidly into other countries, and its Lodges were to be found in France, Belgium, Holland, Denmark, Sweden, Poland, Hungary, and Italy.[72]

In 1782, at the Masonic Congress of Wilhelmsbad, Weishaupt's Illuminati solidified its position among Europe's secret societies as the undisputed leader of the occult one-world movement. Around the same time, Weishaupt also succeeded at forging an alliance between illuminized Freemasonry and the growing Rothschild banking network, thereby giving the Order the financial means to begin to carry out its plans.[73]

As a result of this alliance with the international financiers, the Freemasons regained the banking prominence once held by the Templars, and the Illuminati gained momentum. H.L. Haywood observes, "It took root, it grew, it flourished, it gathered into itself more men of royal and noble titles than were possessed by the Hohenzollern family; even the Jesuits joined it."[74]

Although Weishaupt's Illuminati was exposed within ten years, he had accomplished more to further "the plan" during this time than all of Freemasonry's efforts of the previous fifty years combined. One reason for his success was that he had gotten many Christian leaders to join the Order by convincing them that the Illuminati was a Christian organization purposed to unify the world for the sake of Christ. Robison states, "In this scheme of Masonic Christianity, Spartacus [Weishaupt] and Philo [Baron Von Knigge] laboured seriously together. Spartacus sent him the materials, and Philo worked them up."[75] This apostate teaching, which was presented to Christian initiates, was explained by Von Knigge.

> Jesus Christ established no new Religion; he would only set Religion and Reason in their ancient rights. For this purpose he would unite men in a common bond. He

would fit them for this by spreading a just morality, by enlightening the understanding, and by assisting the mind to shake off all prejudices. He would teach all men, in the first place, to govern themselves. Rulers would then be needless, and equality and liberty would take place without any revolution, by the natural and gentle operation of reason and expediency. This great Teacher allows himself to explain every part of the Bible in conformity to these purposes; and he forbids all wrangling among his scholars, because every man may there find a reasonable application to his peculiar doctrines. Let this be true or false, it does not signify. This was a simple Religion, and it was so far inspired; but the minds of his hearers were not fitted for receiving doctrines. I told you, say he, but you could not bear it. Many therefore were called, but few were chosen. To these elect were entrusted the most important secrets; and even among them there were degrees of information. There was a seventy, and a twelve. All this was in the natural order of things, and according to the habits of the Jews, and indeed of all antiquity. The Jewish Theosophy was a mystery; like the Eleusinian, or the Pythagorean, unfit for the vulgar, and thus the doctrines of Christianity were committed to the Adepti, in a *Disciplina Arcani*. By these they were maintained, like the Vestal Fire. They were kept up, only in hidden societies, who handed them down to posterity; and they are now possessed by the genuine Free Masons.[76]

Using this cover of working for worldwide Christian unity, Weishaupt was able to gain the backing of numerous credulous leaders who thought they were working for a noble cause. In fact their every move was designed by Weishaupt to nudge the Illuminists one step closer to world domination.[77] I can think of more than a few Christian leaders who could learn a lesson from this. Christian unity is not something that can be organized; it comes naturally among those who share a common love for Christ. The false ecumenical/interfaith unity being promoted today by the World Council of Churches—an organization that is strongly influenced by Freemasonry—is nothing new. It has been used for centuries to try to further the cause of world government. As long as Christians do not unite with the peoples of other religions, there can be no world government. This unwillingness of Christians to compromise their faith has been the chief obstacle for the conspirators.

Weishaupt received a special thrill out of being able to deceive

Christians in this fashion. On one occasion, after having persuaded a Protestant leader to join his "unification effort," he wrote:

> You can't imagine what respect and curiosity my priest-degree has raised; and, which is wonderful, a famous Protestant divine, who is now of the Order, is persuaded that the religion contained in it is the true sense of Christianity. O MAN, MAN! TO WHAT MAY'ST THOU NOT BE PERSUADED. Who would imagine that I was to be the founder of a new religion.[78]

Although the Illuminati's efforts officially ceased in the 1780s, unofficially its agenda continued to move forward through the network of illuminized Masonic lodges that had already been set in place. The main catalyst for this continued drive seemed to come from the Grand Orient Lodge of France, and later on, from the Masonic leaders of Italy and the United States.

On American Soil

Already dominating the political affairs of Europe, the Masonic Order had made significant progress in the United States by the late 1700s. In fact, many of this country's political founding fathers were Masons. Most of them, like George Washington, were decent men who knew of no higher aims of the Order and who even spoke out against the activities of the Illuminati. However, with the Masonic lodges having gained acceptance in America, the Illuminati finally had in place the network through which it could recruit members and carry on its work. As a result, the first Supreme Council of Scottish Rite Freemasonry was established in Charleston, South Carolina, in 1801.

According to a Masonic publication entitled *Facts of Scottish Rite*, "all other regular Supreme Councils throughout the world are descended from it."*[79] The tremendous potential of the United States somehow had to be harnessed and brought under control if the plan for a New World Order was ever to succeed. Therefore, during the 1800s, as the U.S. emerged as a world power, the Illuminati gradually shifted its attention from Europe to the United States.

Freemasonry experienced tremendous growth during the nineteenth century, particularly during the second half of the century when Freemasonry flourished as never before. This was also a time of rapid

---

*In 1813, the Northern Supreme Council was established as an extension of the Charleston group. The Northern Jurisdiction today consists of fifteen states and is headquartered in Boston. The Southern Jurisdiction, whose headquarters have been relocated from Charleston to Washington, DC, covers the remaining thirty-five states, the District of Columbia, and U.S. territories and possessions. It is today the Mother Supreme Council of the World.[80]

growth for Masonically inspired religious cults. In addition to founding the Theosophical Society, Freemasonry participated in the rise and spread of Christian Science and Unitarianism; and Masons Rutherford and Russell founded the Jehovah's Witnesses. All of these cults have served to subtly direct people away from the truth of Christ. The largest of these religious offshoots, however, would be the Mormon Church, which was founded by Joseph Smith, another high ranking Mason.

Smith was already heavily into the occult prior to becoming a Mason and had published his Book of Mormon in 1830, some twelve years before joining the Order. However, on 15 March 1842 Smith received his first degree in Freemasonry, and he was raised to the level of Sublime Master of the Royal Secret on the very next day, something virtually unheard of.[81] "Six weeks later, on May 2, 1842, Smith was teaching these Masonic secrets as his own 'revelations' to Mormon leaders as the temple Endowment."[82] "Into the fabric of Freemasonry he wove his own peculiar brand of occultism, claiming it to be 'revelation' from on high."[83] Brigham Young, the other significant early Mormon leader, was also a Mason and contributed to the rise of this occult hierarchy.[84]

Several books have been written during the past few years by former Mormons, exposing the connection between Mormonism and Freemasonry. Included among these are *What's Going On in There?*, by Chuck Sackett; and *The God Makers*, by Ed Decker, co-authored with Dave Hunt, a non-Mormon. These books reveal how Mormonism's Masonic heritage is reflected in everything from its symbols to its rituals and secret doctrines.

Mormonism today has over four million members, and is, per capita the wealthiest "church" in the world. "Its influence politically and otherwise is enormous."[85]

The New Super-Rite

During this same period of time, the Masonic Order was making major inroads in American politics and economics. By the late 1800s, Freemasonry had grown so large that it had become inefficient and difficult to manage. Its many divisions, sects, and rites lacked a sense of unity and direction. Thus, in an effort to centralize the authority of Universal Freemasonry a new ultra-secret governing body was established on 20 September 1870.[86] This represented the first major restructuring (or perestroika) of illuminized Freemasonry. At the center of this creation was Albert Pike, who stated:

> The blind Force of the people is a Force that must be
> economized, and also managed.... It must be regulated

by Intellect.*. . . When all these Forces are combined,
and guided by the Intellect, and regulated by the RULE
of Right, and Justice . . . the great revolution prepared
for by the ages will begin to march. It is because Force
is ill regulated that revolutions prove failures.[87]

Pike would end up doing more than any other figure of the
nineteenth century to prepare the way for this "great" revolution of
which he spoke.

Pike was born in Boston in 1809.[88] He eventually settled in Little
Rock, Arkansas, where he became a Mason in 1850.[89] He "lived and
talked Indian, taught a backwoods school, studied law, got admitted
to the bar, [and] joined the Confederate Army," where he served as
Brigadier-General.[90] Following the war "he located in Washington, D.C.,
uniting with ex-Senator Robert Johnson in the profession of the law."[91]

In *Famous Masons and Masonic Presidents*, H.L. Haywood describes Pike as "a powerful orator of the antique type who could hold
an audience for four hours at a stretch."[92] Haywood continues, "He
taught himself ancient languages; made a specialty of Zoroastrianism
and its *'Zend Avesta'*; read continually but never read anything below the greatest."[93] Pike was a literary genius with the ability to read
and write in sixteen ancient languages.[94] Mackey says of Pike, "His
standing as a Masonic author and historian, and withal as a poet, was
most distinguished, and his untiring zeal was without a parallel."[95]

Pike was also "a great student of the Cabala and the occult."[96]
His literary achievements in this area were numerous, including *Ariel*,
The Sephar H. Debarim, *Book of the Word*, *Legenda Magistralia*,
Ritual of the New and Reformed Palladium (4 grades out of 5), *The
Ritual of Elect Magus*, and *The Book of Apadno*, which "contains the
prophecies concerning the reign of the Anti-Christ from the Satanic
point of view."[97] Some of these went on to take their place among
the notorious classics of Freemasonry, but no other work of Pike
would gain the prominence of his 861 page book—*Morals and Dogma
of the Ancient and Accepted Scottish Rite of Freemasonry*—written
in 1871, which Haywood describes as "the Scottish Rite Bible."[98]

When Albert G. Mackey became the secretary general of the
Supreme Council in Charleston, he persuaded Pike to join the circle.
According to Haywood, "Pike soon became so captivated by the pos-
sibilities he saw stretching before it that he set aside his other voca-
tions and avocations, became Sovereign Grand Inspector General, and
devoted himself to the Rite until his death."[99]

*Intellect here is a reference to the Illuminati or the highest adepts of
Freemasonry.

Pike was placed in power in 1859 when, according to Mackey, he was elected to the position of Sovereign Grand Commander of the Southern Supreme Council.[100] He remained the leader of Scottish Rite Freemasonry until his death in 1891. In the 1860s, Giuseppe Mazzini, the Italian revolutionary leader and the worldwide director of illuminized Freemasonry from 1834 to 1872, established relations with Pike making him the head of the Illuminati's activities in the United States.[101] Finally, on 20 September 1870 the constitution creating the new super-rite was signed into effect by Pike and Mazzini.[102]

Occult Theocrasy states:

> The two founders divided their powers according to the following plan. To Pike was given dogmatic authority and the title of Sovereign Pontiff of Universal Freemasonry, while Mazzini held the executive authority with the title of Sovereign Chief of Political Action.[103]

Pike named the Order the New and Reformed Palladian Rite.[104] Historian Edith Starr Miller describes it as neo-gnosticism, "teaching that the divinity is dual and that Lucifer is the equal of Adonay."[105] It is in fact Lucifer who is worshipped within this Rite of Freemasonry. Miller goes on to state:

> The Holy See of the Dogma for the whole masonic world was set up at Charleston, the sacred city of the Palladium. Pike, the Sovereign Pontiff of Lucifer, was the president of the Supreme Dogmatic Directory, composed of ten brothers of the highest grades who formed his Supreme Grand College of Emeritus Masons. The Sovereign Executive Directory of High Masonry was established at Rome under Mazzini himself.[106]

In a letter to Albert Pike, dated 22 January 1870 (leading up to the founding of the new rite) Mazzini wrote:

> We must allow all the federations to continue just as they are, with their systems, their central authorities and their divers modes of correspondence between high grades of the same rite, organized as they are at present, but we must create a supreme rite, which will remain unknown, to which we will call those Masons of high degree whom we shall select. With regard to their brothers in masonry, these men must be pledged to the strictest secrecy. Through this supreme rite, we will govern all Freemasonry which will become the one international centre, the more powerful because its direction will be unknown.[107]

The main centers of operation for the Supreme or Palladian Rite were located in Charleston, Rome, and Berlin.[108] In addition to these headquarters, Pike and Mazzini established four Grand Central Directories for the purpose of gathering information vital to political and propaganda efforts. "These were, The Grand Central Directories for North America at Washington, for South America at Montevideo, for Europe at Naples, and for Asia and Oceania at Calcutta."[109] Later on, a Sub-Directory for Africa was founded at Port Louis on the Island of Mauritius.[110]

According to Edith Starr Miller, "To recruit adepts, they planned to use some members of the other rites, but in the beginning they meant to rely principally on those among the initiates of Ancient and Accepted Scottish Rites who were already addicted to occultism."[111] A thirty-third degree Mason, particularly, would be well received everywhere

> in any country, in any rite the existence of which is acknowledged. Thus it was particularly the initiates of the thirty-third degree Scottish Rites, who, owing to their extensive international ramifications, were privileged to recruit adepts for Palladism. That is why the supreme rite created its Triangles (the name given to Palladian Lodges) by degrees, but these were established on a firm base, the lowliest of its initiates being brothers long tested in ordinary masonry.[112]

On 14 July 1889 Albert Pike issued his instructions to the twenty-three Supreme Councils of the world, recorded by A.C. De La Rive in *La Femme et l'Enfant dans la Franc-Maconnerie Universelle* (page 588). The following is a brief excerpt from his speech.

> That which we must say to the crowd is—We worship a God, but it is the God that one adores without superstition.
>
> To you, Sovereign Grand Inspectors General, we say this, that you may repeat it to the Brethren of the 32nd, 31st and 30th degrees—The Masonic religion should be, by all of us initiates of the high degrees, maintained in the purity of the Luciferic doctrine.[113]

It is important to remember that at the time of this statement, Albert Pike simultaneously held the positions of Grand Master of the Central Directory of Washington, that of Grand Commander of the Supreme Council of Charleston, and that of Sovereign Pontiff of Universal Freemasonry.[114] Speaking as the leader of Freemasonry, he revealed the true character of his Order.

When Pike issued his instructions in 1889, Freemasons from the thirtieth degree up either already knew or were, for the first time, informed of the Luciferic nature of the Order. Today, however, the belief in Lucifer is not revealed until a higher level.

Pike intended the degrees leading up to the thirtieth degree to serve only as a training school to gradually condition and prepare the candidate for the ultimate acceptance of Luciferic initiation. Although perhaps not in a blatant fashion, Masonic rituals and ceremonies from the earliest stages are representative of occult rites. In Freemasonry everything has a double-meaning. Thus the candidate is practicing occultism throughout his degree work without knowing it. False interpretations are given to keep him from suspecting the institution to be anything less than noble and upright in purpose.

The success of a conspiracy depends on its ability to conceal from the masses the truth of what they are working for. The conspirators will, therefore, bring no more people into their inner circle than what is absolutely necessary for the success of their mission. With each new person initiated, the risk of defection or of leaks increases. This is one reason why those atop the hierarchy are so careful to screen out candidates along the way and reserve for themselves the right to hand pick those promoted to the thirty-third degree (and beyond). The logic is simple—why bring a hundred thousand into the know, if only ten thousand are needed to get the job done?

Therefore, the hierarchy uses millions of innocent people as dupes to serve as a shield between the public and themselves. These people who devote countless hours to establish hospitals, to help the crippled, and to do other good works unwittingly provide a cover under which the adepts operate—a perfect public relations ploy. Who would ever suspect a good works organization to be instead one massive conspiracy to usher in an occult New World Order? It is because the idea is so outrageous that few people believe it. But the intentions of the society's leaders are unmistakably clear. The following excerpt from *Morals and Dogma* explains the logic and intent of the Knights Templars, of which Freemasonry is the continuation.

> The tendencies and tenets of the Order were enveloped in profound mystery, and it externally professed the most perfect orthodoxy. The Chiefs alone knew the aim of the Order: the Subalterns followed them without distrust.

> To acquire influence and wealth, then to intrigue, and at need to fight, to establish the . . . Gnostic and Kabalistic dogma, were the object and means proposed to the initiated Brethren. The Papacy and the rival monarchies, they said to them, are sold and bought in these days, become corrupt, and tomorrow, perhaps, will

destroy each other. All that will become the heritage of the Temple: the World will soon come to us for its Sovereigns and Pontiffs. We shall constitute the equilibrium of the Universe, and be rulers over the Masters of the World.[115]

As a result of Pike's efforts, by the 1880s the United States was well on its way to becoming the dominant power in the drive to usher in the New World Order. The leadership role had shifted from Europe, specifically France, to the United States.

I discovered that some Masons and New Agers privately spoke of the United States as the power that will usher in the "New Atlantis." Occult tradition maintains that the world prior to the flood had become unified under a system of global government based upon ten regions. This global civilization was known as Atlantis and was the most advanced occult society ever. This is why God destroyed it.

Unfortunately, it appears as if history is about to repeat itself. Today we have come full cycle and are almost back to the way things were in Noah's day—the world is on the brink of taking a "quantum leap" into an occult based New World Order, which will consist of ten administrative regions. This knowledge gives new meaning to the words of Jesus spoken in Matthew. Concerning the time of the end and of His return Jesus said:

As it was in the days of Noah, so it will be at the coming of the Son of Man. (Matt. 24:37)

I now realized how literal Christ's words had been.

The Role of the Soviet Union

After learning about these things, there was one lingering question that I had. . . . What was the role of the Soviet Union in all of this, if anything? As I looked into this matter, I soon discovered that the same forces that have gained control of America have always had control of the Soviet Union, as they were responsible for the founding of the Soviet state in the first place. What follows is a brief overview of the events leading up to the creation of communism and the birth of the Soviet Union.

In 1847 an obscure intellectual by the name of Karl Heinrich Marx joined one of the branch organizations of the Illuminati called the League of the Just.[116] *Occult Theocrasy* states, "It is a fact that for a certain length of time Mazzini [the European leader of illuminized Freemasonry] and Marx were closely associated."[117] Mazzini and his International Masons would use Marx to penetrate and subvert the growing Socialist Labour movement.[118] So obvious was Marx's connection with Mazzini that, during the early days of the Russian Revolution, the revolutionaries called themselves Spartacusts (after Adam Weishaupt's Illuminati pseudonym) before becoming known as Bolsheviks and later as Communists.[119]

During the mid 1800s, the labor movement of France had begun to organize hoping to improve the conditions for their working class. Toward this end, they sent a deputation of French working-men to England in 1862 "to observe the utility of Trade Unions in protecting the interest of the workers."[120] Seeking to learn from their English counterparts they intended to bring about some peaceful changes in their own country. Illuminized Freemasonry, however, saw in the Working-men's Association "the very instrument they needed for carrying out their plans."[121]

Karl Marx, residing in London at the time, was frequently found in the clubs and cafes where the working-men gathered. Having successfully penetrated these circles, he was named to the sub-committee at the meeting in St. Martin's Hall on 28 September 1864 when the Internationale was founded.[122] The other members of the committee were Mazzini's personal secretary named Wolff; Le Lubez, a French Freemason; Cremer, the secretary of the English Masons' Union; and Weston, the Owenite.[123]

At the very first meeting of this committee "Wolff placed before it the statutes of Mazzini's working-men's associations, proposing them as the basis of the new association."[124] Although the statutes were presented by Wolff, Marx later stated, "My propositions were all accepted by the commission ... "[125] So close was Marx's affiliation with Mazzini that he viewed Mazzini's proposals as if they were his own. These "provisional statutes of the Internationale" were then sent from London to Paris in the following November where they were officially ratified and the French Internationale was founded.[126]

E.E. Fribourg, in his book *L'Association Internationale Des Travailleurs*, published in 1871, stated that "the Internationale everywhere found support in Freemasonry."[127] The support was particularly forthcoming from the lodges of the Grand Orient.[128] Historian Nesta Webster, in her book *World Revolution*, published in 1921, expressed her indignation:

> It is difficult to write of these things calmly. For to deceive the people, whose simple faith and lack of education prevents them seeing whither they are being led, is as cowardly as to guide a blind man into a ditch. Yet this is what the exploiters of the Internationale did for the working-men.[129]

This movement, which was completely dominated by the secret

societies, eventually worked its way into Russia where, with the help of existing Russian lodges, the assistance of Trotsky and Lenin, and the outside support of the international financiers, it forced itself upon the Russian people. Winston Churchill summarized these events in a statement appearing on 8 February 1920 in London's *Sunday Illustrated Herald*. It is worth repeating here.

> From the days of Spartacus-Weishaupt, to those of Karl Marx, to those of Trotsky . . . this worldwide conspiracy for the overthrow of civilization and for the reconstitution of society on the basis of arrested development and envious malevolence, and impossible equality has been steadily growing. It has been the mainspring of every subversive movement during the nineteenth century; and now at last this band of extraordinary personalities from the underworld of the great cities of Europe and America have gripped the Russian people by the hair of their heads and have become the undisputed masters of that enormous empire.[130]

Churchill must have known something about these matters as he had been a Mason himself.[131]

It is only logical to conclude that if Freemasonry founded the Soviet Union, it must still be the power in charge, pulling the strings from behind-the-scenes. But what could have been the reasoning behind Freemasonry's creation of such a ruthless dictatorial power? The answer—If the role of the United States was to lead us into the New World Order then Russia's role, being no less important, was to apply the pressure that would make it all possible.

In order for the occult hierarchy to succeed in establishing a world government, humanity first had to become convinced of the need for such a governing body. The conditions had to be created whereby people would accept this as an alternative. If the people of the world could somehow only be convinced that nations were responsible for war and that peace could only be achieved if nationalism were eliminated, then perhaps humanity would have finally arrived at a point of accepting a One World Authority as its only alternative. In order to lead mankind to this conclusion, however, wars had to be created, sparked, and fanned into existence by acts of terrorism and military aggression. No part of the world could be left unaffected by armed conflicts and violence. But such conflicts had to be incited and the weapons supplied by someone.

Enter the Soviet Union. Nearly every major conflict in the world over the past forty years has been the result of Soviet aggression or instigation. At one point during the early 1980s nearly one in every four nations was engaged in some kind of war.[132] Almost without exception the USSR was the main perpetrator.

This constant strife and fear that a conflict somewhere could escalate into a nuclear war, has played on peoples' minds psychologically, wearing them down. It has caused them to desire world peace more than anything else.

Now suppose that at some time in the future, a final conflict is precipitated, say in Europe or the Middle East, and the Super Powers are intentionally drawn into it. What if one of the powers was destroyed as a result, with additional destruction occurring elsewhere in the world?

Humanity would be awestruck and overwhelmed by such destruction, and would now be prepared to accept a proposed One World Government, which promises to prevent such a tragedy from ever occurring again. Effectively convinced that nations cause wars, and disillusioned by the needless loss of life resulting from such wars, the people of the world would finally be willing to surrender their national sovereignty to a higher authority claiming the ability to protect them from one another.

There is direct evidence to suggest that the hidden powers have been planning for the eventual merger of the United States and the Soviet Union all along, but not until after a prolonged period of Cold War had accomplished their objectives. This evidence surfaced during the Reece Committee investigations into tax-exempt foundations during the 1950s. Norman Dodd, the director of research for the committee, had at one point during the investigation been invited to the headquarters of the Ford Foundation by its president, H. Rowan Gaither, who was a member of the Council on Foreign Relations.

During this visit Gaither told Dodd:

> All of us here at the policymaking level have had experience, either in O.S.S. (Office of Strategic Services) or the European Economic Administration, with directives from the White House. We operate under those directives here. Would you like to know what those directives are? [133]

Dodd responded that he would, after which Gaither replied:

> The substance of them is that we shall use our grant-making power so to alter life in the United States that we can be comfortably merged with the Soviet Union.[134]

Dodd, who was jolted by the frankness of the remarks, asked if Gaither would be willing to repeat his statement before the Reece Committee; to which the Ford Foundation president responded: "That we would not think of doing."[135]

Chapter Six
Secret Teachings of the New World Order

It is not fair to assume that all Masons are aware of their organization's hidden agenda. My discussions with past and present members of Freemasonry have convinced me that an overwhelming majority of Masons haven't the faintest idea of what their organization is really all about. In defense of these people who are being used, I urge that the reader not be quick to judge.

All of us have been guilty, at one time or another, of jumping into decisions without first having a reasonable understanding of the facts. In the case of Freemasonry, it would take months of diligent study to gain a comprehensive view of the order, assuming that one could obtain copies of its secret books, which is difficult to do prior to joining. Once individuals belong to the organization and finally have the opportunity to examine its doctrinal materials, few have the interest or take the time to do so.

Most of the current members with whom I have spoken, while being well versed in the rituals and superficial workings of the order, showed few signs of possessing any knowledge of the organization's actual history or beliefs. Some members have belonged to the Lodge for more than thirty years without having spent so much as a single hour studying its reference works. For the benefit of these people and for those who are currently considering membership, I have prepared the following summary on Masonic beliefs.

Masonic Theology

In 1986, in order to determine which Masonic books best represent the beliefs of Freemasonry, talk show host John Ankerberg asked a couple who was studying Freemasonry to write a letter to each of the fifty Grand Lodges in America. Ankerberg relates:

> We asked that they address their letter to the Grand Master and ask him to respond to the following question: "As an official Masonic leader, which books and authors do you recommend as being authoritative on

the subject of Freemasonry?"[1]

Twenty-five (50 percent) of the Grand Lodges responded. According to the survey, the following books and authors were the most highly recommended by the Grand Masters: *Coil's Masonic Encyclopedia* by Henry Wilson Coil; *The Builders* by Joseph Fort Newton; *An Encyclopedia of Freemasonry* by Albert G. Mackey; *Introduction to Freemasonry* by Carl H. Claudy; *The Newly-Made Mason* by H.L. Haywood; *A Masonic Reader's Guide* by Alphonse Cerze; *History of Freemasonry* by Robert F. Gould; *The Craft and Its Symbols* by Allen E. Roberts; and *Morals and Dogma* by Albert Pike, in addition to a number of other highly respected Masonic authors including Manly P. Hall, G. Steinmetz, Thomas Smith Webb, and Louis L. Williams.[2]

Since these are the sources recommended by the leaders of Freemasonry themselves, it is only fair in examining Masonic theology that we quote directly from these books or from other sources written by the same authors. Therefore, unless otherwise specified, statements will be taken from the above sources. The key document that will be quoted is Albert Pike's *Morals and Dogma*. Because of the book's availability in Masonic libraries everywhere, Masons will easily be able to verify the following information for themselves. *Morals and Dogma* can also be found in some public libraries under catalogue number 366.1 although copies have become scarce.

Freemasonry *Is* a Religion!

> Every Masonic Lodge is a temple of religion; and its teachings are instruction in religion.[3] (*Morals and Dogma*, p. 213)

> I contend, without any sort of hesitation, that Masonry is, in every sense of the word, except one, and that its least philosophical, an eminently religious institution-that it is indebted solely to the religious element which it contains for its origin and for its continued existence, and that without this religious element it would scarcely be worthy of cultivation by the wise and good.[4] (*Mackey's Encyclopedia of Freemasonry*, p. 618)

> It [Masonry] is the universal, eternal, immutable religion, such as God planted it in the heart of universal humanity. No creed has ever been long-lived that was not built on this foundation. It is the base, and they are the superstructure. (*Morals and Dogma*, p. 219)

Pike goes on to describe Freemasonry as

> the custodian and depository of the great philosophical and religious truths, unknown to the world at large, and handed down from age to age by an unbroken current

of tradition, embodied in symbols, emblems and allego-
ries. (*Morals and Dogma,* p. 210)

Antichrist in Nature

It is typical of Freemasonry to omit the name of Jesus Christ
when quoting passages of Scripture. The following examples compare
Scriptures taken from The Holy Bible (KJV) with those used by Thomas Smith Webb in his book, *The Freemason's Monitor* (better known
as *Webb's Monitor*).[5]

Bible (1 Pet. 2:5)	Webb's Monitor (p.92)
Ye also, as lively stones, are built up a spiritual house, an holy priest-hood, to offer up spiritual sacrifices, acceptable to God by Jesus Christ.	Ye also, as living stones, be ye built up a spiritual house, an holy priesthood, to offer up sacrifices acceptable to God.

Bible (Matt. 21:42)	Webb's Monitor (p.94)
Jesus saith unto them, "Did ye never read in the scriptures, The stone which the builders rejected, the same is become the head of the cor-ner . . . ?	Did ye never read in the scrip-tures, The stone which the build-ers rejected, is become the head of the corner?

Bible (2 Thess. 3:12)	Webb's Monitor (p. 156)
Now them that are such we com-mand and exhort by our Lord Jesus Christ, that with quietness they work, and eat their own bread.	Now them that are such, we com-mand and exhort, that with quiet-ness they work, and eat their own bread.

These subtle omissions cause the initiate to think of God only
in a general sense, without the consideration of Christ.

The name of Jesus is also omitted from Masonic prayers.

> To offer prayer in the name of Christ, is contrary to the
> universality of Masonry. (Jud. Dec. Grand Lodge of Penn-
> sylvania)

Views on the Bible:

> The Teachers, even of Christianity, are, in general, the
> most ignorant of the true meaning of that which they
> teach. There is no book of which so little is known as
> the Bible. To most who read it, it is as incomprehensible
> as the Sohar. (*Morals and Dogma,* p. 105)

> The Bible, with all the allegories it contains, expresses,
> in an incomplete and veiled manner only, the religious
> science of the Hebrews. The doctrine of Moses and the

Prophets, identical at bottom with that of the ancient Egyptians, also had its outward meaning and its veils. (*Morals and Dogma*, p. 744)

The Hebrew books were written only to recall to memory the traditions; and they were written in Symbols unintelligible to the Profane. The Pentateuch and the prophetic poems were merely elementary books of doctrine, morals, or liturgy; and the true secret and traditional philosophy was only written afterward, under veils still less transparent. Thus was a second Bible born, unknown to, or rather uncomprehended by, the Christians; a collection *they* say, of monstrous absurdities; a monument, the adept says, wherein is everything that the genius of philosophy and that of religion have ever formed or imagined of the sublime; a treasure surrounded by thorns; a diamond concealed in a rough dark stone. (*Morals and Dogma*, pp. 744-745)

This "second Bible," which Albert Pike refers to, is the Kabalah— an ancient book of the occult.

Source of Knowledge

All truly dogmatic religions have issued from the Kabalah and return to it: everything scientific and grand in the religious dreams of all the illuminati, Jacob Boehme, Swedenborg, Saint-Martin, and others, is borrowed from the Kabalah; all the Masonic Associations owe to it their Secrets and their Symbols.

The Kabalah alone consecrates the alliance of the Universal Reason and the Divine Word; . . . it alone reconciles Reason with Faith, Power with Liberty, Science with Mystery; it has the keys of the Present, the Past, and the Future. (*Morals and Dogma*, p. 744)

One is filled with admiration, on penetrating into the Sanctuary of the Kabalah, at seeing a doctrine so logical, so simple, and at the same time so absolute. (*Morals and Dogma*, p. 745)

Source of Inspiration

LUCIFER, the *Light-bearer*! . . . Lucifer, the Son of the Morning! Is it *he* who bears the *Light*? . . . Doubt it not! (*Morals and Dogma*, p. 321)

Source of Power

When the Mason Learns that the Key to the warrior on the block is the proper application of the dynamo of living power, he has learned the Mystery of his Craft. The seething energies of Lucifer are in his hands and

before he may step onward and upward, he must prove
his ability to properly apply (this) energy.[6] (Manly P.
Hall, *The Lost Keys of Freemasonry*, p. 48)

Basic Doctrine

The theological dogma of Freemasonry was explained in the
"Instructions" issued by Albert Pike on 14 July 1889 to the twenty-
three Supreme Councils of the world. His words were recorded by
A.C. De La Rive in *La Femme et L'Enfant dans la Franc-Maconnerie
Universelle* (p. 588).

> If Lucifer were not God, would Adonay (The God of the
> Christians) whose deeds prove his cruelty, perfidy, and
> hatred of man, barbarism and repulsion for science,
> would Adonay and his priests, calumniate him?
>
> Yes, Lucifer is God, and unfortunately Adonay is also
> God. For the eternal law is that there is no light with-
> out shade, no beauty without ugliness, no white with-
> out black, for the absolute can only exist as two Gods:
> darkness being necessary to light to serve as its foil as
> the pedestal is necessary to the statue, and the brake
> to the locomotive.
>
> In analogical and universal dynamics one can only lean
> on that which will resist. Thus the universe is balanced
> by two forces which maintain its equilibrium: the force
> of attraction and that of repulsion. These two forces exist
> in physics, philosophy and religion. And the scientific
> reality of the divine dualism is demonstrated by the phe-
> nomena of polarity and by the universal law of sympa-
> thies and antipathies. That is why the intelligent disciples
> of Zoroaster, as well as, after them, the Gnostics, the
> Manicheans, and the Templars have admitted, as the
> only logical metaphysical conception, the system of the
> two divine principles fighting eternally, and one cannot
> believe the one inferior in power to the other.
>
> Thus, the doctrine of Satanism is a heresy; and the true
> and pure philosophic religion is the belief in Lucifer, the
> equal of Adonay; but Lucifer, God of Light and God of
> Good, is struggling for humanity against Adonay, the
> God of Darkness and Evil.[7]

Pike continues to pervert the truth in statements made on page
567 of *Morals and Dogma*.

> To prevent the light from escaping at once, the Demons
> forbade Adam to eat the fruit of "knowledge of good and
> evil," by which he would have known the Empire of
> Light and that of Darkness. He obeyed; an Angel of Light

induced him to transgress, and gave him the means of victory; but the Demons created Eve, who seduced him into an act of Sensualism, that enfeebled him, and bound him anew in the bonds of matter.

These doctrines are, in their entirety, heresy. Pike not only turns the truth upside down, but he adds material. In short, Masonic doctrine places Jesus Christ under the control and at the mercy of Lucifer, labelling the Holy God of Israel a demon.

Teaches Universality

As with the New Age movement, the central theme of Freemasonry is universality, an attempt to unite all of the world's religions under one umbrella. To do so, it conveniently demotes Jesus Christ from being the Son of God to being a mere spiritual master on the same footing with Buddha or any other religious leader.

Masonry . . . is Religion, a worship in which all good men may unite, that each may share the faith of all.[8] (Joseph Fort Newton, *The Builders,* p. 242)

Describing an experience he had in a London lodge with Masons of various faiths, Joseph Newton writes:

It was a scene no one could ever forget, a vision-hour deeply moving, at once a picture and a prophecy. . . . It was most impressive, as if one were listening-in on the future. It made me think of the words of a seer in a sacred book of China: "The broad-minded see the truth in different religions; the narrow-minded see only the differences." . . . Where else, except in a Masonic lodge, could men of many religions meet, each praying for all and all for each one? It taught me one lesson: If ever there is to be a Religion of Brotherhood on earth, it must begin with a Brotherhood of Religions. (*The Builders,* pp. 223-224)

If Masonry were simply a Christian institution, the Jew and the Moslem, the Brahman and the Buddhist, could not conscientiously partake of its illumination; but its universality is its boast. In its language, citizens of every nation may converse. At its altar men of all religions may kneel. To its creed, disciples of every faith may subscribe. (*Mackey's Encyclopedia of Freemasonry,* p. 439)

It [Masonry] reverences all the great reformers. It sees in Moses, the Lawgiver of the Jews, in Confucious and Zoroaster, in Jesus of Nazareth, and in the Arabian Iconoclast, Great Teachers of Morality, and Eminent Reformers, if no more: and allows every brother of the Order

> to assign to each such higher and even Divine Charac-
> ter as his Creed and Truth require. (*Morals and Dogma*,
> p. 525)

> Masonry, around whose altars the Christian, the Hebrew,
> the Moslem, the Brahmin, the followers of Confucius and
> Zoroaster, can assemble as brethren and unite in prayer
> to the one God who is above *all* the Baalim, must needs
> leave it to each of its Initiates to look for the founda-
> tion of his faith and hope to the written scriptures of
> his own religion. (*Morals and Dogma* p. 226)

> In a Lodge consisting entirely of Jews, the Old Testament
> alone may be placed upon the altar, and Turkish Free-
> masons may make use of the Koran. Whether it be the
> Gospels to the Christian, the Pentateuch to the Israel-
> ite, the Koran to the Mussulman, or the Vedas to the
> Brahman, it everywhere Masonically conveys the same
> idea—that of the symbolism of the Divine Will revealed
> to the man. (*Mackey's Encyclopedia of Freemasonry*,
> p. 133)

All of these beliefs are contrary to the teachings of Jesus who
said, "I am the way, the truth, and the life: no man cometh unto the
Father, but by me" (John 14:6, KJV).

Deification of Man

One of the many symbols of Masonry is a ladder, which is used
in the work of initiation. Mackey refers to this ladder as a

> symbol of progress . . . its three principal rounds, rep-
> resenting Faith, Hope and Charity, present us with the
> means of advancing from earth to heaven, from death
> to life, from the mortal to immortality. Hence, its foot
> is placed on the ground floor of the Lodge, which is
> typical of the world, and its top rests on the covering
> of the Lodge, which is symbolic of heaven. (*Mackey's
> Encyclopedia of Freemasonry*, p. 361)

Consistent throughout Masonic doctrine is the belief that man
reaches immortality not through the forgiveness of sin provided by
God when one believes in his son Jesus Christ, but rather through
good works. In the higher degrees this teaching is taken even one
step further when the initiate proclaims himself to be God.

> Man is a god in the making. And as in the mystic myths
> of Egypt, on the potter's wheel, he is being molded.
> When his light shines out to lift and preserve all things,
> he receives the triple crown of godhood. (*The Lost Keys
> of Freemasonry*, p. 92)

In the closing ceremonies of the ritual for the Royal Arch

degree, the candidate is asked, "Brother, Inspector, what
are you?" and he replies, "I AM THAT I AM."[9] (Ed Decker,
The Question of Freemasonry, p.9)

In the Bible, these are the words used in reference to God. When
Moses asked God to name himself, God said, "I AM THAT I AM" (Ex.
3:14, KJV).

Admitted Deception

Many honorable men have become Masons under the false
impression that Freemasonry is a Christian institution. Although certain ceremonies occasionally make use of Christ's name, this is usually in the form of a mockery (sometimes blatant, sometimes subtle),
unfortunately not often realized as such by one not grounded in the
Bible, thereby further confusing initiates' perceptions of the Order.

> The Blue Degrees are but the outer court or portico of
> the Temple. Part of the symbols are displayed there to
> the Initiate, but he is intentionally misled by false in-
> terpretations. It is not intended that he shall understand
> them, but it is intended that he shall imagine he under-
> stands them. Their true explication is reserved for the
> Adepts, the Princes of Masonry. (*Morals and Dogma*, p.
> 819)

> We teach the truth of none of the legends we recite.
> They are to us but parables and allegories, involving and
> enveloping Masonic instruction. (*Morals and Dogma*, p.
> 329)

> Masonry, like all the Religions, all the Mysteries, Hermeti-
> cism and Alchemy, *conceals* its secrets from all except
> the Adepts and Sages, or the Elect, and uses false expla-
> nations and misinterpretations of its symbols to mislead
> those who deserve only to be misled; to conceal the
> Truth, which it calls Light, from them, and to draw them
> away from it. Truth is not for those who are unworthy
> or unable to receive it, or would pervert it. (*Morals and
> Dogma*, pp. 104-105)

> Truth becomes deadly to those who are not strong
> enough to contemplate it in all its brilliance. . . . The
> truth must be kept secret, and the masses need a teach-
> ing proportioned to their imperfect reason. (*Morals and
> Dogma*, p. 103)

The immoral character of these words should not come as a
surprise when considering the philosophy of their author, Albert Pike.

> [A]ll truths are *"Truths of Period,"* and not truths for
> eternity. (*Morals and Dogma*, p. 37)

Mandate for Blind Obedience

The first duty of every Mason is to obey the mandate of the Master. . . . This spirit of instant obedience and submission to authority constitutes the great safeguard of the Institution. Freemasonry more resembles a military than a political organization. The order must at once be obeyed; its character and its consequences may be matters of subsequent inquiry. The Masonic rule of obedience is like the nautical, imperative: "Obey orders, even if you break owners." (*Mackey's Encyclopedia of Freemasonry,* p. 525)

Thus a Mason is sworn to blind obedience without having the slightest knowledge of what it is that he is really swearing to. The oaths taken by candidates in the first three degrees are as follows:

Entered Apprentice (1st degree)

To all of which I do most solemnly and sincerely promise and swear, without the least equivocation, mental reservation, or self evasion of mind in me whatever; binding myself under no less penalty than to have my throat cut across, my tongue torn out by the roots, and my body buried in the rough sands of the sea at low water-mark, where the tide ebbs and flows twice in twenty-four hours; so help me God, and keep me steadfast in the due performance of the same.[10] (Captain William Morgan, *Illustrations of Masonry,* pp. 21-22)

Fellow Craft (2nd degree)

. . . binding myself under no less penalty than to have my left breast torn open and my heart and vitals taken from thence and thrown over my left shoulder and carried into the valley of Jehosaphat, there to become a prey to the wild beasts of the field, and vulture of the air, if ever I should prove willfully guilty of violating any part of this my solemn oath or obligation of a Fellow Craft Mason; so help me God, and keep me steadfast in the due performance of the same. (*Illustrations of Masonry,* pp. 52-53.)

Master Mason (3rd degree)

. . . binding myself under no less penalty than to have my body severed in two in the midst, and divided to the north and south, my bowels burnt to ashes in the center, and the ashes scattered before the four winds of heaven, that there might not the least track or trace of remembrance remain among men, or Masons, of so vile and perjured a wretch as I should be, were I ever to prove willfully guilty of violating any part of this my solemn oath or obligation of a Master Mason. (*Illustra-tions of Masonry*, pp. 75-76)

The severity of these oaths continues to increase with each degree. Though these oaths have been taken from a book written in the 1820s, former Masons have told me that the oaths have changed very little over the past two centuries, and they are essentially still the same today.

Jesus warned in reference to oaths, "Do not swear at all. . . . Simply let your 'Yes' be 'Yes,' and your 'No,' 'No'; anything beyond this comes from the evil one" (Matt. 5:34, 37). Christ gave us this command for our own protection, yet many do not heed his words.

If a Mason finally discovers the underlying purpose of the Order and decides to get out, these oaths serve as a most effective intimidation to prevent him from disclosing any secret information. As a result, although a small percentage of Masons defect from the organization, only a few of them are willing to take the risk of speaking out against it.

However, Captain William Morgan of Batavia, New York (a Mason of thirty years) was one such courageous man, whose book, *Illustrations of Masonry*, revealed the secret rituals and oaths of the Masonic Order. This expose cost him his life.

When it was learned that Morgan had prepared the manuscripts and was planning to publish them, Masonic leaders acted to prevent the book's publication. Captain Morgan was kidnapped on 11 September 1826 and was drowned by several Masons in the Niagara River.[11] David Miller, the publisher, was also kidnapped; but the citizens of Batavia, finding it out, pursued the kidnappers, and finally rescued him. In spite of all the efforts by the Masons to prevent its publication, Morgan's book was published in 1827.[13]

Freemasonry did everything within its power to deny its role in the murder of William Morgan, but the incident threw the Eastern States into an all-out frenzy. Innocent Masons themselves believed that Morgan's execution was carried out by fellow Masons. During the decade that followed, forty-five thousand Masons withdrew from the Lodges over this incident. Masonic reference works such as *The Build-ers* (pp. 217-219), *Coil's Masonic Encyclopedia*, and others attest to this fact. Coil states:

> Masonic defections spread throughout New England, New York, New Jersey, Pennsylvania and Maryland. . . . In 1826, New York had 480 Lodges with a membership of 20,000 but from 1827 to 1839 only 40 or 50 Lodges were reporting to the Grand Lodge. . . . The Grand Lodge of Massachusetts surrendered its charter to the state and

became an unincorporated body.[13] (*Coil's Masonic Encyclopedia,* p. 58)

In the years that followed, Freemasonry continued to refute charges of the murder in spite of the fact that one of the three men appointed to carry out the assassination confessed the entire account on his death bed in 1848. The confession appears on pp. 11-16 of a book entitled *The Character, Claims and Practical Workings of Freemasonry,* written by Rev. Charles G. Finney, the great nineteenth century evangelist and longtime president of Oberlin College.

Early in his career as an attorney, Finney had himself been a Mason; but he left the Lodge following his conversion to Christ, becoming an evangelist instead. He spent much of his remaining life denouncing the evils of Freemasonry and had his life threatened repeatedly as a result.[14] His effort culminated in a 272 page book devoted entirely to exposing the Masonic Order. What Finney learned during his years as a Mason so alarmed him that it was largely responsible for his compelling drive and zeal in proclaiming the gospel of Christ throughout the world. Because Finney was a man of unquestionable integrity who is still widely respected today, I have chosen to quote him at length. The following excerpts are taken from his book, which was published in 1869.

> It is high time that the Church of Christ was awake to the character and tendency of Freemasonry. Forty years ago we supposed that it was dead, and had no idea that it could ever revive. But, strange to tell, while we were busy in getting rid of slavery, Freemasonry has revived, and extended its bounds most alarmingly. . . . I know something about it, for I have been a Freemason myself.[15] (p. 1)

> Upon reflection and examination, and after a severe struggle and earnest prayer, I found that I could not consistently remain with them. My new life instinctively and irresistibly recoiled from any fellowship with what I then regarded as "the unfruitful works of darkness." (p. 5)

> I came to the deliberate conclusion, and could not avoid doing so, that my oaths had been procured by fraud and misrepresentations, and that the institution was in no respect what I had been previously informed it was. And, as I have had the means of examining it more thoroughly, it has become more and more irresistibly plain to my convictions that the institution is highly dangerous to the State, and in every way injurious to the

Church of Christ. (p. 8)

Elderly men and women, especially in the Northern States, will almost universally remember the murder of William Morgan by Freemasons, and many facts connected with that terrible tragedy. But, as much pains have been taken by Freemasons to rid the world of the books and pamphlets, and every vestige of writing relating to that subject, by far the larger number of young people seem to be entirely ignorant that such fact ever occured. (p. 9)

Referring to Captain Morgan, Finney stated:

He . . . was aware, as Masons generally were at the time, that nearly all the civil offices in the country were in the hands of Freemasons; and that the press was completely under their control, and almost altogether in their hands. Masons at that time boasted that all the civil offices in the country were in their hands. I believe that all the civil offices in the county where I resided while I belonged to them, were in their hands. I do not recollect a magistrate, or a constable, or sheriff in that county that was not at that time a Freemason. (p. 10)

In his appeal to the Church, Finney proclaimed:

Believing, as I most assuredly do, that these works truly reveal Masonry, could I be an honest man, a faithful minister of Christ, and hold my peace in view of the alarming progress that this institution is making in these days. In your hearts you would condemn and despise me if, with my convictions, I suffered any earthly considerations to prevent my sounding the trumpet of alarm to both Church and State. . . . Would you have me cower before this enormously extended conspiracy? Or would you have me sear my conscience by shunning the cross, and keeping silence in the midst of the perils of both Church and State? (pp. 269-270)

Can a man who has taken and still adheres to the oath of the Royal Arch degree be trusted in office? He swears to espouse the cause of a companion of this degree when involved in any difficulty, so far as to extricate him from the same, whether he be right or wrong. He swears to conceal his crimes, murder and treason not excepted. Now, gentlemen, I appeal to you, is a man who is under a most solemn oath to kill or seek the death of any man who shall violate any part of the Masonic oaths a fit person to be at large amongst men? (pp. 270-271)

There are many seceding Masons throughout the land.

> Adhering Masons are under oath to seek to procure their death. . . . Ought a Freemason of this stamp to be fellowshipped by a Christian Church? Ought not such an one to be regarded as an unscrupulous and dangerous man? I appeal to your conscience in the sight of God, and I know that your moral sense must respond amen to the conclusions at which I have arrived. Be not offended with my telling you the truth in love. We must all soon meet at the solemn judgment. Let us not be angry, but honest. (p. 272)

Prominent ministers who joined Finney in exposing the Masonic institution included Rev. Torrey and Rev. Dwight L. Moody, both of whom went out of their ways to denounce Freemasonry. Torrey remarked, "I do not believe it is possible for a man to be an intelligent Christian and an intelligent Mason at the same time."[16] D.L. Moody likewise put himself on the line. At one of his conventions Moody invited Rev. Charles A. Blanchard D.D. to speak on the subject of Freemasonry. Great opposition resulted, and certain individuals threatened to stop supporting his schools if he continued to invite such men to expose the institution. Responding from the platform, Moody stated:

> Here is a man who knows what he is talking about and you say unless I silence him, you will not support the Schools. I say, if vital truth has to be sacrificed so that the Schools live on—then LET THE SCHOOLS DIE.[17]

Such was Moody's stance on Freemasonry.

John Marshall, the great chief justice of the United States Supreme Court, wrote:

> The institution of Masonry ought to be abandoned, as one capable of producing much evil, and incapable of producing any good which might not be affected by open means.[18]

Marshall was himself a famous Mason and had assisted in the establishment of two Lodges in Virginia.[19] His biography is one of only twenty-five appearing under the section "Statesmen, Founders, Officers" in the book *Famous Masons and Masonic Presidents*. He is included in the same section with Albert Pike and Adam Weishaupt. Marshall must have therefore known something about Masonry. His anti-Masonic statement came shortly before his death in 1835.

William H. Seward, secretary of state under Lincoln, wrote:

> Secret Societies, Sir? Before I would place my hands between the hands of other men in a secret lodge, order, class or council, or bending my knee before them, enter into combination with them for any object, I would

> pray to God that that hand and that knee might be para-
> lyzed, and that I might become an object of pity and
> mockery to my fellow men.[20]

Daniel Webster wrote:

> In my opinion, the imposition of such obligation as Free-
> masonry requires should be prohibited by law.[21]

Ulysses S. Grant stated:

> All secret oath-bound political parties are dangerous to
> any nation. . . [22]

Other U.S. presidents who condemned Freemasonry include John Adams, James Madison, John Quincy Adams (who campaigned openly against the Order), and Millard Fillmore. Madison and Fillmore had both been Masons and were therefore speaking from experience.[23]

Several generations have come and gone since these men warned the people of America and the world against Freemasonry; therefore, some might argue that the Order today is not the same as it was back in the 1800s. To see if this is true let us examine some more recent evidence.

Current Status

In the February 1987 issue of *The Northern Light*, the official publication of the Supreme Council for the Northern Masonic Jurisdiction, Louis L. Williams, a thirty-third degree Mason comments:

> Universality does not mean Christianity although some
> Masons think it should be so interpreted.
> . . . from Anderson* forward, efforts continued to re-
> move all Christian references from Masonry, and those
> efforts still continue to this day.[24]

As mentioned earlier, in certain Masonic degrees, as in the degrees of the earlier Knights Templars, various references to the life of Christ had been placed in the rituals, serving to make the Masonic organization appear open to Christians. These top dressings of Christianity have, from the beginning, been a deception. But more recently the leadership of Freemasonry has become more blatantly anti-Christ, admitting their efforts to remove any possible Christian commitment from the degrees.

For example, in specific reference to the rituals of the eighteenth degree, Louis Williams writes:

> . . . no candidate for the Scottish Rite degrees shall be
> required to assume any obligation to support any par-
> ticular religious belief, except as Dr. Anderson states, "to

*Dr. James Anderson was a renowned Masonic writer and a strong proponent of universality of religion.

oblige them to that Religion in which all Men agree."

The Southern Supreme Council adopted a universal 18°
under Pike in the 1860s. We eliminated any possible
Christian commitment in 1942 under Johnson. Any
matter of discord should be laid to rest, and the 18° of
the Northern Jurisdiction is "For All Men and All
Time. . . [25]

If the only religion of the Masons is "that Religion in which all
Men agree" which they admit is not Christianity, then what religion
is it? Clearly it is the religion of universality, which teaches that immortality is achieved through good works instead of faith in Christ.
This is actually a form of spiritualized humanism, which gives way
first to various principles of pantheism, and ultimately, to direct Lucifer worship in the highest levels.

Even more recently, on 14 July 1987 the anti-Christ character
of Freemasonry was again revealed when the Associated Press reported on the results of a study conducted by the Church of England.
The article, entitled "Church Calls Freemason Rituals Blasphemous,"
appeared in the *Indianapolis Star*. It states:

Church of England leaders overwhelmingly endorsed a
report Monday that called Freemason rituals blasphemous . . .

The report—"Freemasonry and Christianity: Are They
Compatible?"—said some Christians found Masonic rituals disturbing and "positively evil."[26]

The article continued:

Masons say their movement is not a religion and that
its aim is charitable works. However, the report said
much Masonic language has religious overtones, including chaplains, rituals, and a secret name for God—
"Jahbulon."*

*Although Masons publicly refer to their god as "The Grand Architect of the
Universe," a secret name for this god is revealed in the Royal Arch degree. This
name is "Jahbulon" (also Jaobulon). Ed Decker, a former Mormon who took up
the study of Freemasonry upon discovering the similarities between it and
Mormonism, defines the name as follows: "JAH" is the Greek word for Jehovah;
"BUL" is a rendering of the name, BAAL [the ancient demon-god]; and "ON" is the
term used in the Babylonian mysteries to call upon the [Ancient Egyptian] deity,
"OSIRIS"! The secret ritual book of the Craft prints the letters J.B.O.[29]
This name symbolically gives the god of the mysteries (Lucifer) authority over
Jehovah (the only true God and Creator). No one Mason may pronounce the entire
"sacred name" by himself, (apparently for fear that his soul would be eternally
damned). Therefore, it takes three Masons to repeat the name, each pronouncing
only one syllable.[30]

The report called the name blasphemous and said: "In Christian theology, the name of God must not be taken in vain, nor can it be replaced by an amalgam of the names of pagan deities."

It said Masonry smacked of heresy by promising salvation through good works alone.[27]

The report closed on an interesting note by revealing:

Many lodge members are civil servants, bankers, lawyers, military and police officers, judges, clergy, business executives and shopkeepers.

The nation's top Mason, with the title grand master, is the Duke of Kent, first cousin of Queen Elizabeth II.[28]

If more evidence is required concerning the diabolical character of the Masonic Order, consider the fact that Anton LaVey, the founder and leader of The Church of Satan, gives repeated reference to Freemasonry in his book, *The Satanic Rituals—Companion to the Satanic Bible*. On page 21 of this book he concedes that modern Satanism draws heavily on Masonic rituals and teachings.

Satanic Ritual is a blend of Gnostic, Cabbalistic, Hermetic, and Masonic elements, incorporating nomenclature and vibratory words of power from virtually every mythos.[31]

One of the rituals celebrated by the Church of Satan is *"The Ceremony of the Stifling Air,"* better known as *"L'Air Epais."* According to LaVey, this rite was originally performed *"when entering the sixth degree of the Order of the Knights Templar."*[32] (It should be remembered that the Knights Templars were the forerunners of Freemasonry.)

In describing the requirements for the performance of "L'Air Epais," LaVey comments:

The coffin may be of any type, although a traditional hexagonal style is recommended, as this is the type depicted in the actual sigil of the Sixth degree of the Templars and, combined with the skull and crossbones, is retained in Masonic symbology . . .[33]

LaVey continues:

The original Templars' rite of the Fifth degree symbolically guided the candidate through the Devil's Pass in the mountains separating the East from the West (the Yezidi domain). At the fork of the trail the candidate would make an important decision: either to retain his present identity, or strike out on the Left-Hand Path to Schamballah, where he might dwell in Satan's household, having rejected the foibles and hypocrisies of the everyday world.

A striking American parallel to this rite is enacted within the mosques of the *Ancient Arabic Order of the Nobles of the Mystic Shrine,* an order reserved for thirty-second degree Masons. *The Nobles* have gracefully removed themselves from any implication of heresy by referring to the place beyond the Devil's Pass as the domain where they might "worship at the shrine of Islam."[34]

The leader of the Church of Satan concludes:

L'Air Epais is impossible to perform without an indiscreet degree of blasphemy toward the Christian ethic. . . .

The numerous manifestations of Satanism in Masonic ritual, for instance, the goat, the coffin, the death's-head, etc., can easily be euphemized, but the rejection of certain values demanded by *L'Air Epais* cannot be cloaked in accepted theologies. Once the celebrant has taken this degree, he embarks upon the Left-Hand Path and chooses Hell in place of Heaven. Besides being both ritual and ceremony, *The Stifling Air* is a *momento mori* carried to its highest power.[35]

At this point one might say, "Alright, I can see your point that Freemasonry is not a good organization to belong to, but why be concerned about it if most of the people involved are not even aware of its secret agenda and can therefore be no threat to society?" The answer lies in the fact that Freemasonry encourages universalism of religion even at its lowest levels.

From its earliest degrees, Freemasonry subtly conditions its members to accept the false belief that all religions are pathways to the same God, rendering Christ's atonement on the cross insignificant and meaningless. A widespread acceptance of this view is a precondition for merging humanity into a system of world government. Without the existence of a synthetic global religion capable of uniting the religions of the world under a single umbrella, it would be impossible for the conspirators to succeed. Freemasonry provides this umbrella. It has already succeeded in preparing a significant portion of our world's population to embrace its universalist worldview. The Masonic religion is therefore not only a threat to the souls of its members, but to the sovereignty of nations and to the current world order as well; and for these reasons, I stand opposed to it.

Realizing that the words of a contemporary Mason carry more weight than my own, I have asked Reverend James Shaw, a former thirty-third degree Mason, to close this chapter by sharing his own experience with Freemasonry and his reasons for leaving the Order. The following is his personal account:

"Dear Friend,

"Membership in the Masonic Lodge has in many cases become a family tradition, with young men often joining because their fathers and grandfathers belonged. Because of their admiration for certain friends or relatives, these men join the Lodge without hesitation, certain that the Order is based on noble aspirations. This was the case with me. From the time I was a little boy, my mother encouraged me to become a Mason some day like my uncle whom she greatly admired. Her impression of Freemasonry was that of a club where good men met to plan on helping those in need.

"When I grew up, I married a fine woman who was a member of the Eastern Star and whose father was a Mason. Although her father would never talk to me about the Lodge, I was nevertheless proud of him. Surrounded by people I loved who were Masons, I finally decided to join the Lodge myself.

"Upon applying for membership in Indianapolis, I received a letter from the Lodge within two weeks telling me I had been accepted. I was instructed to be present at the Lodge at 6:30 p.m. on a particular day to receive my first degree. When the time came, I went to the Lodge and paid my dues for the first three degrees after which I was told to follow a man who they said was the Senior Steward. He took me to the Preparation Room where he told me to remove my clothes and to put on a pair of white pants (like pajama pants) and a white jacket. Before long, a man referred to as the Junior Deacon came in and told me to follow him. He took me to a door and put a blindfold on me. He also rolled up the left leg of my pants and turned back the collar of my shirt exposing my left breast. After some conversation between the Junior Deacon and the man inside the Lodge room, I was finally told to enter. Being hoodwinked, I could not see, but I could sure feel! Something hit my left breast (it hurt). A man's voice said, 'Jim Shaw, you are received into this Lodge on the sharp points of the compass, which (and he jabbed me again) is to teach you never to reveal any of the secrets of an Entered Apprentice Mason to anyone unless he be a Brother Mason.'

"I had come to the Lodge that evening expecting merely to be told what a Mason was supposed to do. However, by the end of the ceremony I had become disgusted. When it was over, my friend told me it was something that all Masons had to endure; so I put it out of my mind.

"After one year I was appointed Senior Deacon. This was a big jump for me as I had bypassed three chairs. I had told the Worshipful Master that I did not want to be a 'chairwarmer' but wanted to be of service to the Lodge and go through all the chairs. I also joined the Scottish Rite, and had become Prelate in the Lodge of Perfection, studying for Master of the 4th degree.

"About this time I received word from an old Army friend encouraging my wife and I to move to Florida where he was living. I didn't want to leave my job with the Post Office, but my friend told me he could get me a Civil Service job in Florida. My wife loved the idea of living there. So between the two of them begging me, I finally agreed to make the move. My Lodge membership was transferred from Indianapolis (which was in the Northern Jurisdiction) to my new Lodge in Florida (which belonged to the Southern Jurisdiction). Although the Ritual between the two jurisdictions varies somewhat, I found that the essence of the Lodges was still the same.

"The Lodge in Florida was in need of good officers; and I soon progressed to the position of Worshipful Master. I had to be elected to this particular office, but that was no problem. I worked with Lodge members in my Civil Service job, and there were numerous officers of the Scottish Rite who were also City Officials. In fact, I had a part in the initiation of the Mayor of the city. It was in the Skull lecture I gave in the 30th degree. He paid close attention.

"Soon I had served in many chairs and was given the Degree of K.C.C.H. (Knight Commander of the Court of Honor). I had this degree for four years when I, quite literally, entered the darkest period of my life. My sight began to deteriorate rapidly as I was developing a cataract on my left eye. A friend of my wife recommended I visit an ophthalmologist who she said was very good. I took her advice. After examining my eyes the ophthalmologist informed me that I had to have an operation on one eye and possibly on the other eye as well at a later time.

"He told me he had to see me every day for a week before he could operate because of an infection in my eyelid which had to be treated. During these visits he began to share with me about Jesus Christ and even read some verses to me out of the Bible. Although I knew of many ministers and preachers who were Masons, particularly those affiliated with the National Council of Churches, I had been trained by my family to stay away from churches. My stepfather said they were full of hypocrites and no one in his house was ever to go to a church. And here I was, with a doctor who was working on my eyes trying to read the Bible to me. On my job I began speaking with a few people who I knew to be Christians, and they also told me about Jesus. One went so far as telling me that no Christian should ever be a Mason. In the meantime, the doctor continued sharing with me while he was working on my eyes. I tried not to listen, but deep inside I knew he was right.

"Just one day after I had returned to work following my operation, I received a letter from The House of the Temple in Washington, D.C. I had been chosen to receive the 33rd degree and was to report to Washington in one week to accept the honor. Two men from the Scottish Rite who were 33rd degree Masons decided to go along with me to share in my time of joy. I remember being impressed by the size and the beauty of The House of the Temple. It was at least four times as large as our Scottish Rite Temple. After I had received the 33rd degree along with my white hat and ring, we all had a big feast and drank wine. It was all so much fun. Yet throughout this time I kept thinking of some of the passages the doctor had read to me from the Bible.

"Soon after returning home I received a call from the Secretary of the Scottish Rite telling me to prepare for the upcoming Maundy Thursday services prior to Easter. I can tell you that the Lodges always make a mockery of Christian Holy Days. Now I was Master of all degree work and had to conduct the service.

"In the meantime my wife and I had begun attending church with the ophthalmologist. He was still helping me understand the Bible and did not like the idea of me being a Mason. He told me he didn't think I understood just how evil the Lodge really was, and he urged me to read thoughtfully the books of John and Galatians. I studied these books and was on the verge of accepting Christ. But to become fully convinced I had yet to go through the Maundy Thursday ritual itself.

"We were all in our places for the Maundy Thursday Rose Croix service to begin, each of us dressed in black robes. I stood and clapped my hands three times, and everyone rose to their feet. I began to speak, 'My brothers, we meet this day to commemorate the death of our most wise and perfect Master—NOT as inspired or divine, but as at least the greatest of all humanity.'

"At this point I had to stop for a moment to think about what I had just said. I was denying the fact that Christ was inspired or divine, saying he was merely a human master no greater than Buddha, Mohammed, Confucious or other religious figures. I felt a tear run down my face, but I had to go on. I walked out to the menorah and lit a candle.

"The next speaker said his part and lit a candle on the menorah. All spoke and lit candles. I was feeling sad and bewildered, wondering how I could go on; but I did. We had the Black Mass, drinking wine from a skull and eating a piece of bread—passing it around the table—saying to each man, 'Take, drink, and give to the thirsty. Take, eat, and give to the hungry.' Then we all went back to our stations. As I got up, my knees were shaking. I knew what fear was, and I had never felt anything like this since being shot at in the Army.

"I stood and began to recite the closing words. 'We now close this commemoration of the death of our master. MOURN!! LAMENT!! CRY ALOUD!! HE IS GONE!! NEVER TO RETURN!! MOURN!! LAMENT!!' The candles were extinguished one at a time. I closed the ceremony by saying, 'It is over; we must depart.'

"I hurried to the disrobing room and got out of the black robe and into my street clothes. Some men came around and asked me if I was sick. I just said, 'Yes, I've got to go!'

"The very next day I wrote letters to the Blue Lodge, the Shrine, and the Scottish Rite saying that I had attended my last meeting. I was a Christian now and would not be back. That was 25 years ago. I have never regretted my decision.

"During my 19 years as a Mason, I witnessed and participated in numerous disturbing events, but the single most important reason causing me to leave was the fact that Jesus Christ was not the one being worshipped. Many gods in the Scottish Rite are revered and many religions taught, but never is the Blessed Name of Jesus Christ allowed. One is not even allowed to close a prayer in the name of Jesus, but instead must use a vague reference to God, which could mean anyone or anything. Teachings of the Kabbalah, Zend Avesta, and the Gnostics are used along with astrology and the doctrines of ancient false gods such as Osiris, Semiramis, Isis and Krishna. The Hindu gods Brahma, Vishnu, and Shiva are also given reference as deities. But whenever Christ was mentioned, it was only in the form of a mockery.

"For these reasons I left the Masonic Order. If you are currently a Mason, I urge you from the bottom of my heart to do likewise. It is the only right thing to do.

"In Christian Love,

Jim Shaw"
P.O. Box 884
Silver Springs, Florida 32688-0884

Chapter 7
The Coming World Crisis

Introduction

By the mid 1980s I had assembled enough convincing evidence that friends were forced to acknowledge the fact that there was indeed a plot to establish a New World Order. However, some of these same friends could not see how a world government could be brought about during our generation. They felt that too many people would resist such an effort and that it could therefore never happen.

Between the years of 1985 and 1987 I began to think about how something like this could happen during our lifetime. I believed that a world government was possible, even probable, within the next decade or two. But, how might it come about?

I felt that if I could develop a realistic example of how the New World Order "could" be achieved, perhaps people would take the threat more seriously and respond accordingly. So, in June 1987 I prepared the scenario presented in this chapter. It has undergone two revisions since that time to keep it up-to-date with current findings.

I wish to make clear that there is no way of knowing exactly how the final pieces will fall into place. Only God knows this. We only know from Scripture that at some point a one-world government will become a brief reality. I have prepared the following scenario to present an idea of how the enemy might be thinking. My hope is that we might be more discerning and less likely to fall into his traps.

There are many uncertainties. For one thing, we do not yet know the full consequences of the Persian Gulf War. It could be that the hidden powers believe this crisis was all that was necessary to take us the final step, and that we will see steps taken in the near future to install the New World Order. Most of the researchers in my immediate circle, however, believe that a much larger final crisis will be needed to accomplish this task, and that a little more groundwork remains to be laid before the world is prepared to take such a "quantum leap." I personally lean in this direction.

The recent war with Iraq might have been only a dress rehearsal for something much larger yet to come. The fact that Saddam Hussein is still in power and is believed to possess at least three or four nuclear bombs, seems to be an indicator of more trouble ahead. If there is another Middle East conflict, it could result from, or start out very similar to, the recent crisis; only this time, the chances of it escalating into a regional, or even a global conflict would be much greater.

One possibility is that the new order will be achieved in stages, with the United States first leading the nations into a loosely knit world federation under an empowered United Nations (something that appears to be happening presently). A major global conflict could then be precipitated at a future time to take humanity the rest of the way in to an all-out occult based world government.

Whatever happens, we may be certain of three things—a world government will be formed; the Antichrist will be revealed; and he and his world system will be destroyed by Jesus Christ at His second coming. The only thing we don't know is when this all will happen.

Before the nations of the world ultimately embrace a system of global government, they must first have a reason to do so. Humanity, convinced that permanent world peace cannot be attained without the creation of a powerful world authority capable of protecting countries from one another, will eventually sacrifice the current world order—seeing no alternative. Significant strides have already been made in this direction since the turn of the century, and if history repeats itself, further "progress" will be made soon.

Two world wars have already been fought in the twentieth century. In each case, an aggressive power was used to ignite a crisis that drew in the rest of the world; and both times the aggressor was defeated. After each war, a supranational organization was established for the alleged purpose of promoting world peace, first the League of Nations, then the United Nations. Each organization has brought us one step closer to the realization of a one-world government.

The United Nations today is the closest thing to world government that humanity has ever known. Unlike the incomplete League of Nations, which consisted of only 63 countries and did not include the United States, the United Nations consists of 159 nations, nearly every country in the world. Its infrastructure is all-encompassing and includes the World Court, the U.N. peace-keeping forces, and specialized organizations ranging from the International Monetary Fund (IMF) and the World Bank to the World Health Organization (WHO). It overseas dozens of additional agencies ranging from UNESCO to UNICEF, covering virtually every aspect of life. The U.N. lacks only the power to implement and enforce its strategies.

Could a third world war be used to finally lead mankind to

accept a New World Order? If so, how might such a war begin? Who would be its main players? And what would be the outcome? To answer these important questions, we must examine those areas where current events and the blueprints of the conspirators coincide with what the Bible teaches must yet take place.

A Possible Scenario

I believe that insiders will initiate a world crisis only if they feel it is necessary to get the public to accept their New World Order. The mere threat of a major world conflict could be enough to scare the public into accepting such a change—especially when coupled with the existing problems of world hunger and global debt, and the created panic over the environment. As their campaign slogan openly proclaims, "Global Problems Demand Global Solutions!"

Historically, however, wars have been effective in advancing the cause of world government; the fact is, major changes occur more easily during times of crisis.

Unlike the previous world wars in which Germany was the main instigator, the world's next major conflict will undoubtedly be sparked by the hotbed of tensions surrounding the Middle East. If not Iraq a second time, then perhaps Iran or Syria.

This writer believes that Syria might play a significant role in ushering in the New World Order, if not as an instigator of war, then as a middleman for negotiating peace. It is too critical a nation to remain on the sidelines for very long and, contrary to popular belief, Syria—not Iraq—is the most powerful Islamic military state in the Middle East. It therefore merits close watching.

During the past several years, Syria appears to have been laying the groundwork for its own attack against Israel. Syrian troops now hold long sought after positions in Lebanon and have been prepared for such an invasion since early 1987. According to the U.S. Department of Defense publication, *Soviet Military Power*, Syria has also become the site of the largest Soviet arms build-up in the Third World, having contracted for $19 billion in military hardware. It currently boasts the largest number of Soviet military advisors of any Third World country.[1]

The Syrian government, meanwhile, has effectively turned the tables by falsely warning its people of a coming Israeli attack on Syria, although Israel has repeatedly denied such allegations.[2] According to the *Jerusalem Post*, during one of Syria's propaganda campaigns several years ago, it took a personal statement from Israeli Prime Minister, Yitzhak Shamir, to maintain peace. Shamir voiced his "incomprehension" at Syrian "nervousness," "which, he said, had trig-

gered several strong Soviet warnings to Israel in recent days."[3] I believe the Syrian government was deliberately misleading its people
in order to justify its own "pre-emptive" strike against Israel down
the road. For these reasons, I have chosen to use Syria as our example
in this scenario (although a similar scenario could be constructed using
Iraq, Iran, or even Libya).

If the powers-that-be were to move Syria against Israel, it would
be Syria's fatal mistake, planned this way by the conspirators in order to precipitate a world crisis. Unlike previous invasions, the Jewish state this time would have almost no time to respond. Its back
would be to the wall quickly as Syrian MIGs would streak over Jerusalem within four minutes. Israel would be faced with a very difficult
decision—either allow itself to be conquered, or else launch its nuclear
arsenal against Syria and possibly Iraq. In late 1986, "London's *Sunday Times* printed an article stating that Israel may have a stockpile
of as many as 200 nuclear warheads."[4] So we know that a nuclear
exchange is a very real possibility.

There is an Old Testament prophecy concerning Damascus, the
capitol of Syria, which has yet to be fulfilled. Isaiah proclaimed: "See,
Damascas will no longer be a city but will become a heap of ruins"
(Is. 17:1). As it is, Damascus is the oldest standing city in the world,
never having experienced mass destruction. This prophecy must be
fulfilled sometime before the return of Christ.

Having lost several thousand of its military advisors in the exchange and with world opinion seemingly turned against Israel for
her use of nuclear force, the Soviet Union could seize this opportunity to do what it has long desired—move against Israel. Arab pressure on the Soviets to invade Israel would add to the temptation.

If the Soviet Union came to the rescue of Syria, it would suddenly find itself on opposite sides with the United States. What could
happen next is unthinkable. Mankind will have been brought to the
brink of destruction.

Wicked men in high places have been contemplating such a
crisis for years. In a letter to the Italian revolutionary leader Giuseppe
Mazzini dated 15 August 1871 Albert Pike, the leader of the Illuminati's
activities in the United States and the head of Scottish Rite Freemasonry at the time, described a distant final war, which he felt would
be necessary to usher in the New World Order.[5] According to Pike,
this conflict between two future superpowers would be sparked by
first igniting a crisis between Islam and Judaism. He went on to write:

> We shall unleash the nihilists and the atheists and we
> shall provoke a great social cataclysm which, in all its

horror, will show clearly to all nations the effect of absolute atheism, the origin of savagery and of most bloody turmoil. Then, everywhere, the people, forced to defend themselves against the world minority of revolutionaries, will exterminate those destroyers of civilization; and the multitudes, disillusioned with Christianity whose deistic spirits will be from that moment on without direction and leadership, anxious for an ideal but without knowledge where to send its adoration, will receive the true light through the universal manifestation of the pure doctrine of Lucifer, brought finally out into public view; a manifestation which will result from a general reactionary movement which will follow the destruction of Christianity and atheism, both conquered and exterminated at the same time.[6]*

Should such a crisis be permitted to occur, the amount of destruction would be staggering. Humanity would tremble with fear believing that man is about to destroy himself. For even if the Soviet Union or the United States were eliminated as military powers, over thirty countries would still have nuclear capacity. It would be a time of despair and mass confusion. Add to this the resulting chaos of global financial markets, which are already on the brink of disaster; the economic turmoil would only contribute to the world's state of panic.

Once such a war began, there would be no guarantee that the United States or Europe would remain entirely unscathed. But, it is important to remember that no matter how much the powers of darkness plot and scheme, in the end, they can only bring about what God

---

*Is it a pure coincidence that the most powerful figures of the Middle East are Freemasons? Have they been destined to trigger the conflict about which Albert Pike wrote? A prominent Arab-Christian leader recently informed me that according to his contacts in Lebanon, King Assad of Syria and King Hussein of Jordan are both Freemasons. If this is true, we could be closer to the New World Order than people realize. (He was uncertain about whether Saddam Hussein belonged to the same secret society.)

A few months ago the son of this same Arab-Christian gave me a Masonic document—a membership certificate—which he found in Lebanon, issued by a Phoenician lodge located in Lebanon. However, the document notes that the lodge is under the jurisdiction of The Grand Lodge of Jordan, which is under the authority of The Arab Supreme Council. For at least several centuries, Jordan has been a bastion for the secret societies in the Middle East and has much more influence in the region's behind-the-scenes politics than most people realize. The same Masonic symbol appearing on our dollar bill and found at ancient occult worship sites throughout the world, the all-seeing eye, is prominently displayed on the certificate.

allows. Only He knows with certainty what the future holds. Thus far, God has prevented the hidden forces from making their move. But the time could soon come when the world will have become so wicked and abominable in the eyes of God that He will say "enough is enough," and He will permit the powers of darkness to succeed for a time (Dan. 11:24).

As a result, man would be disillusioned and searching for answers. Many would blame God for the devastation, not even considering the fact that it was man's own wickedness and willingness to be deceived that brought it about. For one professing to provide the solutions, the time would be ripe. The real crisis is about to begin.

If You Build It, I Will Come!

The moment for which Satan has so long awaited and for which his disciples have diligently labored, will have finally come. The conspirators will submit their power to one who will rise to the occasion and whom they will recognize as their undisputed leader. Their complete allegiance and devotion will be given to him—truly a first since the Tower of Babel. He will be Satan personified and will have all the powers of darkness at his disposal—capable of performing every sort of sign and wonder imaginable. He is the one spoken of in the Bible as the lawless one or the beast; he is also referred to in the first letter of John as the Antichrist.

For a while, he will remain in the background; his servants overseeing the final phase. Tens of thousands of New Agers will appear on the world scene, fully organized, demanding that a one-world government be established. This restructuring of the old order, they will claim, is necessary to deal with existing global problems and to prevent any future catastrophes from taking place. The international media will give full coverage to this unfolding drama. Most of the public will be unaware that this network had been organized specifically for this purpose years in advance; it will simply appear to be a spontaneous democratic grassroots movement, held together by people with a common pursuit—the desire for world peace and unity.

Every problem, no matter how small (or how fabricated), will suddenly become a reason for why we need a world government. The most convincing arguments will have to do with the environment, global debt, world poverty, and the prevention of war. A New World Order, they will say, is needed because individual nations are no longer capable of dealing with these complex problems on their own.

The New World Order will appear to come from the bottom up, as something that the people of the world want. It will come in the name of democracy, non-threatening—not as a system being forced upon us by our politicians. Too many people would become suspicious, otherwise, sensing that they are being manipulated. Instead, the inhabitants of "Mother Earth" will believe that they are in control of their own destiny, unaware of the hidden agenda of those really in charge behind-the-scenes.

Most of those initially involved at the core of this movement will in some way be connected with the secret societies, having in common an obsession with mysticism and the occult—a fact not readily apparent to the public. One popular battle cry among New Agers is, "If you build it, I will come." More clearly put, if you build the New World Order and put all the pieces into place, then I (the Antichrist) will come and take my seat of power.

Once this movement goes public, it will gain momentum rapidly; many unsuspecting citizens who are not involved in the occult will join the effort, simply because it seems like the most logical thing to do. The call for democratic world government will sound most appealing.

At some point, the beast, or one of his representatives, will step forth with what will appear to be a brilliant plan for Mideast peace. The initiative will include some type of settlement between the Jews and the Palestinians, claiming to ensure permanent peace in the war torn region. The agreement would probably guarantee Israel's security and would allow the Jews to rebuild their long-anticipated temple, in exchange for allowing the Palestinians to have their own homeland with autonomous rule. The beast will succeed where others before him have failed.

His appearance will most likely be as a democratic leader, riding into power on the back of the democracy movement, appearing as a genuine man of peace. Whether he first emerges as a world diplomat or as a religious leader (such as the pope or the Dalai Lama) remains to be seen; remember, he could be someone who is still unknown to the world. However, once he and his main accomplice, the false prophet take their positions, discerning Christians will recognize them for who they are.

The Antichrist will come to reside over an empowered United Nations or, perhaps, over a newly created global authority, such as the Federation of Earth, at first a loosely knit federation of nations. However, it would most likely emerge rapidly into a powerful structure administrated on the basis of [probably] ten world regions.

A World Constitution will be proposed, and a "democratic" World Parliament will be created. World citizens will believe they have a say in matters, not realizing that occult-based secret societies are really the ones in control. If the New World Order, for example, were to be based on a two or three party system, all that New Age occultists would have to do is control each of these parties—something easily accomplished since they were the ones responsible for proposing the world government in the first place. These insiders would determine the tempo of change and the rest of the world would follow their lead.

The public would be content because it would retain its right to vote and choose candidates, seeing itself as part of a representative government. But in reality, it wouldn't matter who was elected; the result would always be the same: supporters of the Antichrist would be running the system unchecked. As a worldwide system, there would be no place to run.

Sovereign nations would cease to exist. A single global economic system would be established and anything left from the old order of things would be purely superficial, such as languages, cultures, names of countries, etc. Any real authority would now rest with an international body controlled by Satan himself.

The disputing world religions will become unified, and as he will be a master of spiritual intrigue, it is not inconceivable that, at some point during his ascent to power, he declares himself to be "the Christ."* If this were to be the case, he might also claim to be the long awaited Messiah to the Jews. To the Buddhists he would be the fifth Buddha; to Moslems, the Imam Mahdi; to Hindus, Krishna. Those Christians accepting this lie would unfortunately see in him the fulfillment of the second coming of Christ.

But regardless, Scripture tells us that a majority of the world's inhabitants will be deceived (Rev. 13 and 2 Thess. 2); thus, the rise of the Antichrist will be extremely convincing to those who are unprepared and who are not firmly grounded in God's Word.

New Age principles, which have subtly worked their way into many churches disguised as sound biblical teachings, will prevent unsuspecting Christians from recognizing the Antichrist. If he would come proclaiming to be a servant of Satan, few would be foolish enough to follow him. Instead, he will come in the name of Christ, posing as an angel of light. Discerning Christians will be astonished at who steps forth to head the New World Order—possibly the last person ever suspected.

Jesus Warned of This Time

For false Christs and false prophets will appear and
perform great signs and miracles to deceive even the

*Unbeknownst to many, the term "Antichrist," in 1 John 2:18, may also be interpreted as "in place of Christ."

elect—if that were possible. See, I have told you ahead
of time. (Matt. 24:24-25)

The Christianity represented by the Antichrist will be a complete counterfeit, saturated with all the pantheistic teachings of eastern mysticism and the ancient mystery religions—the same beliefs held
by New Agers and promoted by the secret societies. The topdressing
of Christianity will be necessary to make it acceptable to the public.

The focus will be on elevating self rather than God. It will be a
popular religion to a me-oriented generation seeking fulfillment in
the empty teachings of self-esteem. The false teachings of me-ism have
already permeated churches to an alarming degree. Most people do
not realize that self-worship and occultism go hand in hand. The naive will actually be practicing occultism in the name of Christ, while
worshipping the father of lies. It will be the ultimate deception.

In 2 Thessalonians 2:9-12, the Apostle Paul warned:

> The coming of the lawless one will be in accordance with
> the work of Satan displayed in all kinds of counterfeit
> miracles, signs and wonders, and in every sort of evil
> that deceives those who are perishing. They perish be-
> cause they refused to love the truth and so be saved.
> For this reason God sends them a powerful delusion so
> that they will believe the lie and so that all will be con-
> demned who have not believed the truth but have de-
> lighted in wickedness.

At first, the Antichrist will be remarkably successful in keeping
peace on the planet. This is because most of the world's conflicts were
incited by his followers. With the prince of darkness now in power,
his followers will cease fomenting wars, giving him credibility among
the people as a genuine peacemaker.

According to Scripture, the length of his reign will be seven
years (Dan. 9:27). The first 3 1/2 years will most likely be used to
consolidate his power and to put in place any final mechanisms
needed to ensure absolute control of the world.

During the second 3 1/2 year period, his nature will be fully
revealed as he will demand the loyalty and worship of the earth's
inhabitants (Rev. 13). This moment will mark the beginning of the
great tribulation spoken of in Revelation 7:14. Regarding the reign
of the Antichrist, the Bible says:

> And he was given authority over every tribe, people,
> language and nation. All inhabitants of the earth will
> worship the beast—all whose names have not been writ-
> ten in the book of life belonging to the Lamb that was
> slain from the creation of the world. (Rev. 13:7b-8)

The tragedy is that most people will voluntarily serve this man of lawlessness and his system, seeing him as their savior. He will have a way of making people feel good about themselves, teaching them how to get in touch with their "higher selves," and showing them how to receive supernatural power. During this time, man will indulge in every sort of perverted demonic activity that God has ever warned against. Evil will go forth in the name of goodness.

Of this time, it may be said that the principalities and powers of darkness will be unleashed upon the world. The Bible warns: ". . . woe to the earth and the sea, because the devil has gone down to you! He is filled with fury, because he knows that his time is short" (Rev. 12:12b). It will be Satan's moment. He will receive that which only God deserves—the worship of man, the worship that Satan most desires and which he wants to deny to God.

In order to ensure that he will receive the world's allegiance and worship, the Antichrist will force everyone

> small and great, rich and poor, free and slave, to receive a mark on his right hand or on his forehead, so that no one could buy or sell unless he had the mark, which is the name of the beast or the number of his name. (Rev. 13:16-17)

The mark will probably be similar to the bar code system of the Universal Product Code, each person tagged with their own permanent identification number easily read by scanners. The mark, however, will most likely come in the form of an invisible laser tattoo.

Those accepting the mark will be seen by God as submitting to the worship of Satan and his system, a terrible offense in the eyes of God—like spitting in his face. In Revelation 14:9-11 God warns us:

> If anyone worships the beast and his image and receives his mark on the forehead or on the hand, he, too, will drink of the wine of God's fury, which has been poured full strength into the cup of his wrath. He will be tormented with burning sulfur in the presence of the holy angels and of the lamb. And the smoke of their torment rises for ever and ever. There is no rest day or night for those who worship the beast and his image, or for anyone who receives the mark of his name.

The passage goes on to acknowledge that "this calls for patient endurance on the part of the saints who obey God's commandments and remain faithful to Jesus."

Yet those remaining obedient to God, refusing the mark, will be pursued like animals. Many will be put to death. In Matthew 24:9-10, Jesus warned:

> Then you will be handed over to be persecuted and put
> to death, and you will be hated by all nations because
> of me. At that time many will turn away from the faith
> and will betray and hate each other.

Christians who are alive during this period and who refuse to participate in this system will be seen as obstacles to world peace. They will be labelled as uncooperative troublemakers and warmongers. That remnant of believers determined to remain faithful to God during the tribulation are repeatedly warned in Revelation 13 and 14 to take heart and to prepare for this time of persecution.

> He who has an ear, let him hear. If anyone is to go into
> captivity, into captivity he will go. If anyone is to be
> killed with the sword, with the sword he will be killed.
> This calls for patient endurance and faithfulness on the
> part of the saints. (Rev. 13:9-10)

Those families who are free of debt, who own some land on which to grow food, and who own precious metal coins, which could be used as barter for needed goods, will initially fare better than others. However, eventually even they will find life difficult if they refuse the mark. They might be unable to pay taxes, for example, since all transactions with the new government will probably be conducted via the mark. Those unable to pay taxes will have their possessions taken and will be pursued. One might wonder, how will anyone be able to stand under such intense persecution? But the same God who warns of tribulation offers comfort and hope.

First of all, we know that the severest persecution will last for a time only, namely 3 1/2 years (Dan. 7:25, 12:7; Rev. 13:5). Secondly, those who are pursued will find pockets of refuge where they will receive help. Apparently some of those having accepted the mark will finally realize their mistake when they see the ruthlessness of the new order against uncompromising Christians. They will recognize that such a system cannot possibly be of God and will try to help those being persecuted. Daniel 11:34 states, "When they fall, they will receive a little help, and many who are not sincere will join them."

Finally, those who keep their eyes fixed on the eternal and strive to please God during this period, whether they die or remain alive until the end, are promised a tremendous reward in eternity with God.

> And he said, "These are they who have come out of the
> great tribulation; they have washed their robes and
> made them white in the blood of the Lamb. Therefore,
> they are before the throne of God and serve him day
> and night in his temple; and he who sits on the throne
> will spread his tent over them. Never again will they

hunger; never again will they thirst. The sun will not beat upon them, nor any scorching heat. For the Lamb at the center of the throne will be their shepherd; he will lead them to springs of living water. And God will wipe away every tear from their eyes." (Rev. 7:14-17)

In the same spirit, Revelation 14:13 continues, " . . . Blessed are the dead who die in the Lord from now on."

"Yes," says the Spirit, "they will rest from their labor, for their deeds will follow them."

Scripture indicates that there would even be a spiritual revival of sorts in the midst of this persecution. Daniel 11:32-33 states:

And such as do wickedly against the covenant shall he corrupt by flatteries: but the people that do know their God shall be strong, and do exploits.

And they that understand among the people shall instruct many. . .

Daniel 12 goes on to say:

Those who are wise will shine like the brightness of the heavens, and those who lead many to righteousness, like the stars for ever and ever. But you, Daniel, close up and seal the words of the scroll until the time of the end. Many will go here and there to increase knowledge.

Many will be purified, made spotless and refined, but the wicked will continue to be wicked. None of the wicked will understand, but those who are wise will understand. (Dan. 12:3-4,10)

The Bible makes it very clear that the time of the Antichrist must come, but it also assures us that Jesus Christ will put an end to the tribulation when He returns. Paul wrote:

Concerning the coming of our Lord Jesus Christ and our being gathered to him . . .

Don't let anyone deceive you in any way, for that day will not come until the rebellion occurs and the man of lawlessness is revealed, the man doomed to destruction . . . whom the Lord Jesus will overthrow with the breath of his mouth and destroy by the splendor of his coming. (2 Thess. 2:1,3,8b)

Jesus described His coming in detail to His disciples:

Immediately after the distress of those days "the sun will be darkened, and the moon will not give its light; the stars will fall from the sky, and the heavenly bodies will be shaken."

At that time the sign of the Son of Man will appear in the sky, and all the nations of the earth will mourn. They

> will see the Son of Man coming on the clouds of the sky
> with power and great glory. And he will send his angels
> with a loud trumpet call, and they will gather his elect
> from the four winds, from one end of the heavens to
> the other. (Matt. 24:29-31)

Those who remain faithful to Jesus will be avenged. They will
receive their just reward, reigning with the Lord forever.

I believe that God wants us to heed His warnings and to take
His prophecies seriously, otherwise He would not have given them
to us. By His prophecies we are warned, prepared, and encouraged.
Unlike the thousands of psychics and spiritualists whose predictions
are mostly inaccurate and originate in the occult, the prophetic statements of the Bible are proven and true. They are God's revelations
directly to His prophets through the Holy Spirit.

> You must understand that no prophecy of Scripture
> came about by the prophet's own interpretation. For
> prophecy never had its origin in the will of man, but
> men spoke from God as they were carried along by the
> Holy Spirit. (2 Pet. 1:20-21)

The Apostle Paul warned, "Do not treat prophecies with con-
tempt" (1 Thess. 5:20). And Jesus, speaking through His angel to John,
promised, "Blessed is he who keeps the words of the prophecy in this
book" (Rev. 22:7b).

Some may consider the scenario presented in this chapter too
overwhelming. Yet the Lord has impressed it upon my heart to warn
people, particularly Christians, of coming hard times so that they
might be spiritually prepared. I must remain true to this regardless
of what the world might say or think.

The Rapture

Jesus said that no one would know the exact day of His return,
"not even the angels in heaven, nor the Son, but only the Father"
(Matt. 24:36). However, from the multitude of prophecies given concerning Christ's second coming, God clearly wants us to know when
this time draws near so that we might be prepared. The same may
be said concerning the rapture.

Over the years, two primary views have arisen within the
Church regarding the general time when God would rescue His remnant from the earth. One view first became popular in the 1800s and
contends that God will take Christians from the world before the
beginning of the great tribulation. This is commonly referred to as
the pre-tribulation rapture theory. According to this view, those Christians alive during the tribulation are new Christians who will accept
Christ following the rapture.

The other view contends that Christians will go through the entire tribulation period, not being rescued until the actual second coming of Christ. This interpretation is known as the post-tribulation rapture theory and has been the more traditional view.

Other less accepted views also exist, placing the rapture at some point during the seven year period.

The question of the rapture remains a source of debate within the Church, as it is truly difficult to determine from the Bible the precise moment when the rapture will occur. But regardless of when the Lord takes His people home, too many Christians believe as they do for the wrong reasons.

I have heard it said repeatedly that God will spare the Church from going through the tribulation because He would never allow Christians to endure such hardship or persecution. But people forget that many in the early church were martyred for the sake of Christ. Nearly everyone of Jesus' disciples died in the face of persecution. And these were the very ones who were closest to God. Are we to believe that He had forgotten them?

And what about the millions of faithful Christians of our own generation who have suffered death and persecution at the hands of communism. Are they not as important to God since they have suffered and we have not?

Some believers tend to confuse Satan's persecution of Christians with God's judgment of a sinful, unrepentant world. They do not believe that Christians will be persecuted, because God would never judge His own. The fact is, the earthly persecution of Christians has nothing to do with God's judgment. To the contrary, it is Satan, the prince of this world, who persecutes us.

God's judgment falls only upon those who have denied Him or rebelled against Him; whereas the persecution of God's people is the result of Satan lashing out in anger against those whom he is unable to deceive or overcome.

During the time of the great tribulation, as described in Revelation, God's wrath will be poured out upon those who take the mark. This wrath will be in the form of plagues (Rev. 16:2). It will later be followed by His judgment—eternal damnation (Rev. 14:9-12). Satan's fury, on the other hand, will be experienced by those who do not take the mark or bow to worship him. This persecution will be in the form of imprisonment, torture, or death. Christians, however, should draw comfort from the fact that Satan's persecution is limited to this world; God's principle judgment against the wicked will last for eternity.

This ongoing battle is part of the spiritual warfare being waged between God and Satan over our souls. It explains why those who are doing the most for God are often the ones who suffer most.

The life of the apostle Paul best illustrates this point. He was probably the most resilient and dedicated follower of Christ in the early church. Yet, he suffered more tragedy, pain, and suffering than anyone else of his time. He was pursued everywhere he went and was eventually put to death.

Paul summarized his persecution in 2 Corinthians.

> I have worked much harder, been in prison more fre-
> quently, been flogged more severely, and been exposed
> to death again and again. Five times I received from the
> Jews forty lashes minus one. Three times I was beaten
> with rods, once I was stoned, three times I was ship-
> wrecked, I spent a night and a day in the open sea, I
> have been constantly on the move. I have been in dan-
> ger from rivers, in danger from bandits, in danger from
> my own countrymen, in danger from Gentiles; in dan-
> ger in the city, in danger in the country, in danger at
> sea; and in danger from false brothers. I have labored
> and toiled and have often gone without sleep; I have
> known hunger and thirst and have often gone without
> food; I have been cold and naked. (2 Cor. 11:23b-27)

Was this God's judgment against Paul?—obviously not. It was Satan's persecution against an unswerving man of God. Paul under-stood the nature of this warfare and even took comfort in the fact that he was being afflicted. He knew that his problems were a direct result of his faithful service to Christ. This enabled him to keep things in perspective.

> That is why, for Christ's sake, I delight in weaknesses,
> in insults, in hardships, in persecutions, in difficulties.
> For when I am weak, then I am strong. (2 Cor. 12:10)

Paul adds that all Christians must be prepared.

> For it has been granted to you on behalf of Christ not
> only to believe on him, but also to suffer for him, since
> you are going through the same struggle you saw I had.
> . . . (Phil. 1:29-30a)

Beginning with the first century church and continuing to the present day, those who have suffered the greatest persecution have commonly been those who were closest to God. Yet today the mes-sage of self-sacrifice and suffering for the cause of Christ has all but disappeared from our churches. It is no longer taught that crosses in life must precede the crown. Yet Jesus said to His disciples, "If anyone would come after me, he must deny himself and take up his cross and follow me" (Matt. 16:24). And John recorded Jesus as saying, "No servant is greater than his master. If they persecuted Me, they will persecute you also" (John 15:20). This theme remained constant throughout Jesus' teachings.

Suffering is therefore obviously not just limited to the great tribulation, but may be experienced in Western society and in the world as a whole, prior to the rapture, whenever it occurs.

Conclusion

If we might soon face this type of persecution and deception, what, if anything, can we do to prepare for it? Getting out of debt and positioning ourselves so that we are less dependent on worldly institutions is all good and well, and Christians are encouraged to do so. However, physical preparation should not be our principle concern. Instead, we should see to it that we are spiritually prepared.

Assuming that you are already a believer, here are some things you can do to get ready for difficult times.

1. Be an informed and educated Christian.

Equip yourself to discern good from evil—truth from deception. This involves striving to know the truth about what is going on in the world around you and becoming aware of Satan's schemes and tactics. However, while an awareness of current events and critical issues is strongly encouraged, the most important step you can take in gaining spiritual discernment is to know the Bible inside out. Don't take a preacher's word for what it says; find out for yourself! Know what you believe and why you believe it. How can you avoid being deceived if you don't know what the Bible teaches? Someone may be misleading you, but unless you are fluent in Scripture, you will never know it. The time for lukewarm Christianity and Bible illiteracy is over.

Be prepared to defend your faith at all cost; always stand ready to give the reason for the hope that you have in Christ (1 Pet. 3:15). How can we expect others to come to love and to serve Jesus if we can't tell them who He is or what He has done for us? Only if we know and understand God's Word can we truly be effective witnesses. Knowledge of Scripture must be accompanied by a life of example; we must know (God's Word) how to live according to God's will.

An understanding of the Bible is part of the armor of God, which Paul exhorts us to put on. Writing to the church in Ephesus, he states:

> Be strong in the Lord and in his mighty power. Put on
> the full armor of God so that you can take your stand
> against the devil's schemes. For our struggle is not
> against flesh and blood, but against the rulers, against

the authorities, against the powers of this dark world and against the spiritual forces of evil in the heavenly realms. Therefore, put on the full armor of God, so that when the day of evil comes, you may be able to stand your ground, and after you have done everything, to stand. (Eph. 6:10-13)

2. Draw near to Christ.

The first step in developing a closer walk with God is to obey His commands. Jesus said, "If you love me, you will obey what I command" (John 14:15). Either we love Him or we don't! Are you holding on to something, or have you truly surrendered every aspect of your life to Jesus Christ? It is important to root out any remaining sins and destructive habits by committing them to the Lord.

> Those who belong to Christ Jesus have crucified the sinful nature with its passions and desires. (Gal. 5:24)

> Since you died with Christ to the basic principles of this world, why, as though you still belonged to it, do you submit to its rules. (Col. 2:20)

> Dear friends, I urge you, as aliens and strangers in this world, to abstain from sinful desires, which war against your soul. (1 Pet. 2:11)

> Put to death, therefore, whatever belongs to your earthly nature: sexual immorality, impurity, lust, evil desires and greed, which is idolatry. Because of these, the wrath of God is coming. You used to walk in these ways, in the life you once lived. But now you must rid yourselves of all such things. (Col. 3:5-8a)

> So I say, live by the Spirit, and you will not gratify the desires of the sinful nature. (Gal. 5:16)

> Set your minds on things above, not on earthly things. For you died, and your life is now hidden with Christ in God. (Col. 3:1b-3)

The more we die to self, the more Christ can live through us; we must become less so that He can become more. The apostle Paul applied this principle to his own life with amazing results. The impact of his all-out commitment is still being felt today. Paul's devotion is reflected in his testimony.

> I have been crucified with Christ and I no longer live, but Christ lives in me. The life I live in the body, I live by faith in the Son of God, who loved me and gave himself for me. (Gal. 2:20)

> Whatever was to my profit I now consider loss for the sake of Christ. What is more, I consider everything a loss compared to the surpassing greatness of knowing Christ

> Jesus my Lord, for whose sake I have lost all things. I
> consider them rubbish, that I may gain Christ. (Phil. 3:7-
> 8)

Are you willing to pay the price to have this type of relationship with God? If so, it will require making some personal sacrifices and commitments . . . the type of a permanent nature. You must be willing to give up absolutely everything! If anything is more important to you than God, it must be surrendered to Him!

Purpose right now, to live in "daily" communion with Him, by reading His Word and by talking to Him regularly. God wants our fellowship and praise more than anything. This is part of living an obedient life. If we reject the prompting of His Spirit to draw near, our hearts will soon grow hardened, and we will no longer want to be in His presence. Instead, we will want to hide from God. Don't allow this to happen. You will have to know God intimately to make it through the difficult times ahead!

3. Keep life in its proper perspective.

This involves continually reminding ourselves of the real reason for being here . . . which is to love, serve, and please God. This, we must remember, is the heartbeat of our mission.

Only that which is done for the Lord will last. Everything else—our earthly belongings, our physical bodies, our sense of prestige and career accomplishment—will pass away. None of these things can be taken with us. So why do we insist on placing so much importance on things with no eternal value? Why do so many people love "things" more than they love God?

> Do not love the world or anything in the world. If any-
> one loves the world, the love of the Father is not in him.
> For everything in the world—the cravings of sinful man,
> the lust of his eyes and the boasting of what he has and
> does—comes not from the Father but from the world.
> The world and its desires pass away, but the man who
> does the will of God lives forever. (1 John 2:15-17)

As Christians we must see our earthly lives for what they really are. James reminds us:

> Why, you do not even know what will happen tomor-
> row. What is your life? You are a mist that appears for
> a little while and then vanishes. (James 4:14b)

The fact is, our body is only the temporary dwelling place of our soul. Only our soul (our spiritual being) will live forever. So wouldn't it be wise to place our main emphasis on the spiritual?

> For you have been born again, not of perishable seed
> but of imperishable, through the living and enduring

word of God. For all men are like grass, and all their glory is like the flowers of the field; the grass withers and the flowers fall, but the word of the Lord stands forever. (1 Pet. 1:23-25)

What God has prepared for us in eternity is far better than what we leave behind (John 14:1-6). We must, therefore, train ourselves to see the overall picture of our existence, remembering that we are only temporary dwellers on this earth. Since our time here is so short, let us live to please our eternal Father—not to satisfy the sinful longings of our flesh.

Paul summarizes this issue of the temporal versus the eternal:

Many live as enemies of the cross of Christ. . . . Their mind is on earthly things. But our citizenship is in heaven. And we eagerly await a Savior from there, the Lord Jesus Christ, who, by the power that enables him to bring everything under his control, will transform our lowly bodies so that they will be like his glorious body. (Phil. 3:18b-21)

Whatever happens, conduct yourselves in a manner worthy of the gospel of Christ . . . without being frightened in any way by those who oppose you. This is a sign to them that they will be destroyed, but that you will be saved—and that by God. (Phil. 1:27a-28)

This hope we have comes only through the Lamb of God, whose blood was shed for our sins. Jesus said:

My sheep listen to my voice; I know them, and they follow me. I give them eternal life, and they shall never perish; no one can snatch them out of my hand. (John 10:28)

Since we have so great a hope, let us not fret over what may happen to our possessions or to our bodies. Rather, let us seek God wholeheartedly and submit our lives to Him on a daily basis. As we do so, we will grow closer and closer to Him; and His Holy Spirit will empower us with a boldness to do things, even in the midst of persecution, which we never thought were possible before. By keeping our lives focused on Jesus Christ and the eternity that He has planned for us, we will be able to persevere under pressure, while maintaining His peace and joy.

Rejoice in the Lord always. I will say it again: Rejoice!. . . Do not be anxious about anything, but in everything, by prayers and petition, with thanksgiving present your requests to God. And the peace of God, which transcends all understanding, will guard your hearts and your minds in Christ Jesus. (Phil. 4:4, 6-7)

IF YOU WOULD LIKE TO EXPERIENCE THIS KIND OF PEACE AND
JOY, BUT HAVE NEVER ACCEPTED JESUS CHRIST AS YOUR SAVIOR,
HERE IS WHAT YOU MUST DO:

First of all, you must understand what it is that God has done
for you through Jesus Christ. John 3:16 explains:

> For God so loved the world that he gave his one and
> only Son, that whoever believes in him shall not per-
> ish but have eternal life.

God sent his son to die in our place, so that we might be saved
from the penalty of our sins. Had we been perfect, this would not
have been necessary; we could have entered Heaven on our own
merits.

God created man perfect without sin. However, He gave man
the freedom to make decisions; this included the right to choose between obeying God or following the empty lies and temptations of
Lucifer (Satan)—the master deceiver.

Lucifer was once a powerful angel, but rebelled against God,
wanting to be as God himself. Filled with self-pride and arrogance,
he wanted to be worshiped like his Maker. Rather than submitting
to the one Creator, he wanted to be exalted himself. (He apparently
suffered from too high a self-esteem!)

Having failed at his attempt, Lucifer was removed from God's
presence, and became known as Satan. With the creation of man, his
goal became to upset God's plan by luring man to make the same
mistake he made—desiring to be elevated to the position of God. So
he held out the forbidden fruit.

> "You will not surely die," the serpent said to the woman.
> "For God knows that when you eat of it your eyes will
> be opened, AND YOU WILL BE LIKE GOD. . . ."
>
> When the woman saw that the fruit of the tree was good
> for food and pleasing to the eye, and also desirable for
> gaining wisdom, she took some and ate it. She also gave
> some to her husband, who was with her, and he ate it.
> (Gen. 3:4-5a, 6)

The moment that Adam sinned, his seed became corrupted. As
a result, every future human being would be born into sin and would
wage a life-long struggle between doing what he knows is right (obeying his spiritual conscience) and doing what is wrong (yielding to the
sinful nature of his flesh). Contrary to popular belief, sin is not only
learned, it is also inherited. Romans 5:12 states that ". . . sin entered
the world through one man, and death through sin, and in this way
death came to all men, because all sinned" (also see Rom. 3:23).

When Satan succeeded in getting man to disobey God, it gave

him the right to condemn our souls; this fallen angel became our accuser. According to Scripture, he stands accusing us before God day and night (Rev. 12:10).

By yielding to Satan's temptation and choosing to live a life independent of God's will, man inflicted upon himself the penalty for sin, which is death (Rom. 6:23). Death, according to Scripture, includes permanent separation from God and eternal damnation in hell.

Man's sin, therefore, presented what appeared to be an insurmountable problem, since only that which is perfect may enter heaven and live forever with God. This standard of perfection had to be maintained, or else heaven itself would have become corrupt. (This is why Lucifer and his conspiring angels were dealt with accordingly.)

God could have allowed all of us to go to hell, a punishment we justly deserve. But because of His great love, He chose instead to intervene by paying the penalty for our sins Himself. God came to earth in the flesh, in the form of Jesus Christ, to suffer and die in our place on the cross. "But God demonstrates His own love for us in this: While we were still sinners, Christ died for us" (Rom. 5:8).

In this one act of love and mercy God took upon Himself the punishment for all our sins. He paid the price so that we might be set free from the hold of death and have eternal life. This, completely undeserving though we are, is God's gift to us. He did not have to do this but chose to do it anyway.

Such an act of mercy runs completely contrary to the thinking of the secular mind. We are not used to receiving something for nothing. It seems unfathomable that God would do something like this for us simply out of mercy or love. That the very Creator of the universe would humble Himself by coming as a man, to be mocked and scorned, and to die a grueling death at the hands of His own creation in order to save them, is incomprehensible. It defies all human logic. It can only be understood as an act of extraordinary, unjustifiable love!

> For he has rescued us from the dominion of darkness
> and brought us into the kingdom of the Son he loves,
> in whom we have redemption, the forgiveness of sins.
> (Col. 1:13-14)
> Once you were alienated from God and were enemies
> in your minds because of your evil behavior. But now
> he has reconciled you by Christ's physical body through
> death to present you holy in his sight, without blemish
> and free from accusation. (Col. 1:21-22)

This is the good news of the gospel! There is nothing we can do to earn this eternal life, for it cannot be obtained through works or human effort. It is purely a gift from God to us.

> The gift of God is eternal life in Christ Jesus our Lord.
> (Rom. 6:23b)

> For it is by grace you have been saved, through faith-
> and this not from yourselves, it is the gift of God-not
> by works, so that no one can boast. (Eph. 2:8-9)

The gift of salvation is available only through Jesus Christ, because He is the only one who, as a perfect being—God in the flesh—
was able to pay the necessary price for our sins. It took a perfect
sacrifice to overcome Satan's claim to our souls.

> Jesus answered, "I am the way and the truth and the life.
> No one comes to the Father except through me." (John
> 14:6)

> For there is one God and one mediator between God
> and men, the man Christ Jesus, who gave himself as a
> ransom for all men—the testimony given in its proper
> time. (1 Tim. 2:5-6 also read John 3:36 and Acts 4:12)

If Jesus is man's only hope for eternal life, and if we are unable to earn this gift, then what must we do to receive it? We must
accept the fact that Jesus paid the penalty for our sins and believe
that we have eternal life as a result of what he did. It's that simple!

> Yet to all who received him, to those who believed in
> his name, he gave the right to become children of God.
> (John 1:12)

> Whoever believes in him is not condemned, but who-
> ever does not believe stands condemned already be-
> cause he has not believed in the name of God's one and
> only Son. (John 3:18)

If you sincerely wish to accept the gift of eternal life through
Jesus Christ, simply pray to God in your own words. Do it right now.
Confess to him that you are a sinner and would like to be forgiven.
Tell Him that you accept His Son, Jesus Christ, and that you believe
His sacrifice on the cross was sufficient to cover your sins. Thank God
for what He has done, and ask Him to help you live the kind of life
that would be pleasing to Him. GOD WILL HEAR YOUR PRAYER IF IT
COMES FROM A SINCERE HEART!

If you have just accepted Christ as Lord, you now have eternal
life. Satan no longer has a claim to your soul. You are at peace with
God and have entered into a permanent relationship with Him. The
quality of this relationship, however, is up to you. Please allow God
to take "complete" control of your life!

As you grow in your Christian walk, you will gain wisdom and
understanding. God's Holy Spirit will convict you of what changes
need to be made in your life in order to serve Christ most effectively.

Repentance (turning your back on sin) is an ongoing process. God will give you the strength and resolve to be obedient to Him if this is truly your heart's desire.

It is important that you find a sound, Bible-teaching fellowship and become involved. Worshipping Christ with other believers is a very special privilege from which you will draw strength. There is nothing more valuable than true Christians friends. They are dependable and loving.

Remember, however, that every church, no matter how sound, has its share of hypocrites—people who hear with their ears but not with their hearts. But we are all accountable to God and must not compare ourselves to others. Rather, we must strive to follow the example of Jesus, which has been revealed to us through Scripture.

Make a special effort to read the Bible every day, beginning with the books of John and Philippians. Talk to God regularly, making your requests known. He is always ready to listen. Thank Him for all that He has done and delight in praising His name. Ask Him for opportunities to share the good news of Jesus with your family and friends. He will give you the words to speak along with the courage to do so. Above all, "Love the Lord your God with all your heart and with all your soul and with all your mind" (Matt. 22:37).

As you grow in your walk, there will be moments of difficulty and distress when your faith is tested. When such times arrive, remember, "Greater is he that is in you, than he that is in the world" (1 John 4:4b KJV). Take comfort in the fact that you are not alone in your struggle. Millions of other Christians are facing the same obstacles as you; so don't lose heart! Give it your all! Run to win!

> Do you not know that in a race all the runners run, but only one gets the prize. Everyone who competes in the games goes into strict training. They do it to get a crown that will not last; but we do it to get a crown that will last forever. (1 Cor. 9:24-25)

The eternal victory is already ours through Jesus Christ. Through Him we are destined to win!!

Holy , holy , holy
is the Lord God Almighty,
who was, and is, and is to come.

Revelation 4:8b

Part 2
The World Constitution and Parliament Association

Hear me, O God, as I voice my complaint;
protect my life from the threat of the enemy. Hide me from the
conspiracy of the wicked . . . . They encourage each other in evil
plans, they talk about hiding their snares; they say, "Who will see
them?" They plot injustice and say, "We have devised a perfect
plan!" Surely the mind and heart of man are cunning.
Psalm 64:1-2a, 5-6

Overview

Although the World Constitution and Parliament Association (WCPA) was not founded until 1959, the events leading up to its formation can be traced to the World War II Era, through the activities of its eventual founder, Philip Isely. Isely first surfaced as a leader in the one-world movement during the 1940s, serving as the Organizer of "Action for World Federation" from 1946-50. He would later become the Organizer of the "North American Council for the Peoples World Convention," (1954-58). Soon thereafter, in 1958 and 59, he went on to head the Committee for the World Constitutional Convention, eventually becoming its secretary general. These efforts, and others, finally culminated in the official forming of the World Constitution and Parliament Association of which Isely became the Secretary general in 1966.*

The original "Agreement to Call a World Constitutional Convention" was first circulated by Isely and his accomplices from 1958 to 1961. Several thousand dignitaries from around the world responded by signing this agreement. The signers included former prime minis-

*Who's Who in the World, 8th ed. (Chicago: Marquis Who's Who, 1987-1988 ed.), 499.

ters and cabinet ministers, many nobel laureates, and other prominent "world citizens."

As a result of this favorable response, work soon got underway on the preparation of a world constitution. This process began in 1965, in Milan, Italy, and it was continued in the City Hall of Wolfach, West Germany, in June of 1968. The Wolfach meeting was followed with a call to hold a second session, which would be referred to as the World Constituent Assembly—the new name given to the convening of the World Constitutional Convention. (Perhaps it was felt that the old name too accurately described the real intent of the WCPA—to replace the constitution of the United States with a world constitution). During this second session, held in June of 1977, at Innsbruck, Austria, the world constitution went under a further review, was amended, and then adopted by participants from twenty-five countries. The resulting document came to be known as the Constitution for the Federation of Earth.

The third Session of the World Constituent Assembly took place in January, 1979, in Colombo, Sri Lanka. Here, a strategy was devised on how to get the world constitution ratified by national parliaments and governments. Since Colombo, there have been three additional meetings of what is being called the Provisional World Parliament: 1982 in Brighton, England; 1985 in New Delhi, India; and 1987 in Miami Beach, Florida.

A total of eleven World Legislative Acts were adopted during these sessions. They appear in Exhibit O1.

At the "productive" third session, in Miami Beach, a Provisional World Presidium and World Cabinet were appointed to serve along with the already established Provisional World Parliament. These entities are to serve as the Provisional World Government until twenty-five countries have ratified the world constitution, at which time we would witness the emergence of a full-blown world government.

A fourth session of the World Constituent Assembly (or World Constitutional Convention) was held from April 29-May 9, 1991, in Lisbon, Portugal and the final ratification campaign for the world constitution was launched.[*] A more detailed history of the WCPA's attempt to establish a New World Order is provided in the Plan for Collaboration (Exhibit M); where you can read an account of this

---

[*] *Plan for Collaboration in Organizing a World Constituent Assembly for 1990*, (Lakewood, CO: World Constitution and Parliament Association, 1987), 1-5. NOTE: Most of the information presented in this overview has been taken from the Plan for Collaboration.

misguided undertaking in the words of the schemers themselves.

The following pages contain salient parts of some of the more important documents I received from the WCPA, including various letters on WCPA letterheads, lists of sponsors and collaborating organizations, copies of legislative acts already passed by the Provisional World Parliament and excerpts from the world constitution.

Please examine these documents carefully and become familiar with the terminology and tactics of the WCPA. Make a special effort to recognize the names of those involved, so that you will be able to identify them in the coming months and years. By knowing who they are and where they are coming from, you will not fall prey to their cleverly disguised proposals.

Finally, if you are wondering what, if anything, you can do to help stop, or, at least, to slow down the rapid progress of this movement, please take note of the sample letter at the back of this section, which you are encouraged to send to your elected officials. In addition, consider the survey on the last page requesting individuals interested in a newsletter to notify the author.

Letters from the World Constitution and Parliament Association

Over the past few years I have received numerous letters from the WCPA (note letters in Exhibits B through F), some of which have been written to me personally by Phil Isely. I have chosen to present a sampling of these letters spanning a four year period, representative of the correspondence sent out to "members and friends" of the WCPA. Although not fully reproduced here, there are at least two pages to each letter since the WCPA letterhead commonly lists the names of prominent members on both the front and back sides.

In examining the letterheads you will notice that WCPA membership is composed of prestigious leaders from around the world, including current and former mayors, members of parliaments, prime ministers, ambassadors, foreign ministers, key members of the United Nations, Nobel Prize winners, prominent World Court judges, influential financiers and attorneys, as well as leading educators and religious leaders.

A high percentage of members are from Asia and the Far East—in particular from India. This, of course, is where the religions of pantheism are rooted, and, therefore, where occult influence is strongest. Although every major world religion, including Judaism and Christianity, is represented in the WCPA, participating members typically have a strong disposition toward pantheistic beliefs, regardless of their outward religious affiliation. You will also notice that a disproportionate number of members are in some way connected with the United Nations, especially through UNESCO (United Nations Educational, Scientific, and Cultural Organization). Here is a statistical breakdown.

Out of 150 Honorary Sponsors listed on one of the letterheads, a total of thirty-four were identified with the United Nations; fourteen came from the area of commerce, banking or finance; and eight were Nobel Laureates. As far as countries are concerned, twenty-six came from India; ten from Nigeria; nine each from the U.S.A. and the United Kingdom; eight from Canada; and six from Pakistan. A total of forty-five sponsors came from the East Asian countries.

Many distinguished names appear on these letterheads (as noted in Exhibit A), and it is important to remember that while these individuals are certainly instrumental in the forming of the world government, they are not the most powerful figures of the one-world movement. They are only the figureheads. The real movers and shakers remain behind-the-scenes. There is a deeper center of direction, of

EXECUTIVE CABINET

CO-PRESIDENTS
Ing. Reinhart Ruge, *Mexico*
  Civil Engineer
Prof. Dr. Dennis Brutus, *Africa and USA*
  Poet; University Prof., USA and UK;
  Organizer of Africa Network
Dr. Terence P. Amerasinghe, *Sri Lanka*
  Attorney; Editor; Civic Leader

VICE PRESIDENTS
Rt. Hon. Tony Benn, *U.K.*
  M.P.; fmr. Cabinet Minister
  and Chairman of Labor Party
Hon. Gordon M. Bryant, *Australia*
  Civic Leader; x-M.P.; Cabinet Minister
Hon. Ramsey Clark, *U.S.A.*
  Lawyer, former Attorney General
Dr. Douji Gupta, *India*
  Mayor of Lucknow, three terms;
  Former Magazine Editor; Professor
Gerhard Havel, *Germany*
  President, Weltfoderalisten e. V.
Dr. Inamullah Khan, *Pakistan*
  Sec. Gen., World Muslim Congress
Dr. Jur. Adam Lopatka, *Poland*
  President of the Supreme Court
Rev. Toshio Miyake, *Japan*
  Minister and Peace Leader
Chief Adeniran Ogunsanya, *Nigeria*
  Lawyer; Political Leader; x-Mayor Lagos
Hon. Madan B. Pradhan, *Nepal*
  Fmr. Cabinet Minister and M.P.
Hon. Alex Quaison-Sackey, *Ghana*
  Fmr. Foreign Minister, and Pres.
  United Nations General Assembly
Prof. Josel Simuth, *Czechoslovakia*
  Prof. Molecular Biology; Fmr. M.P.
  and V. Chair., Federal Assembly
Mrs. Helen Tucker, *Canada*
  Elected Deputy to Peoples' Congress

SECRETARY GENERAL
Philip Isely, *U.S.A.*
  Integrative Engineer; Writer

TREASURER
Mrs. Margaret Isely, *U.S.A.*
  Businesswoman and Nutritionist

COMMISSION CHAIRPERSONS
(Members of the Executive Cabinet)
COMMUNICATIONS
Prof. Ram K. Jiwanmitra, *Nepal*
  Pres. Universal Correspondence Org.
Scott Jefferson Starquester, *U.S.A.*
  Writer; Political Scientist
ENERGY ALTERNATIVES
Dr. T. Nejat Veziroglu, *U.S.A.*
  President, International Association
  for Hydrogen Energy; Professor
ENVIRONMENT
Dr. Rashmi Mayur, *India*
  Director Urban Environment Institute
Emil Peter, *Germany*
  Greens Party Activist; x-Town Councilman; Secretary German Br. WCPA

Exhibit A

which this group is only the outward manifestation.

As mentioned in chapter 4, I received an additional letter from the WCPA in late February, announcing that the location of its World Constituent Assembly had been moved from Alexandria, Egypt, to Lisbon, Portugal, due to the Gulf War. This letter, received on 28 February 1991 would be my last correspondence from the Association before this book would go to press.

In reviewing this letter (Exhibit F) you will notice the frequent mention of the New World Order. You will also discover some disagreement over the precise meaning of the term. Some insiders envision a New World Order built around an empowered United Nations; while the WCPA advocates a more radical, all-encompassing form of global government. Either version however, would move us into a one-world system. It is possible that an empowered U.N. will serve as a stepping stool toward the more comprehensive version of world government proposed by the WCPA.

World Constitution and Parliament Association

1480 Hoyt St., Suite 31 / Lakewood, Colo. 80215, USA / Ph. 303-233-3548

TELEX: 3712957 EARTH RESCUE

27th March, 1987

To Participants in the Provisional World Parliament,
Officers and Trustees of the W.C.P.A., and Other Friends:

Plans are moving ahead for the 1987 session of the Provisional World Parliament, to be held from 18th to 28th June, 1987, at the Fontainebleau Hilton, Miami Beach, Florida. More than 200 delegates are now registered or expected from 30 countries. With travel assistance, the number of qualified delegates could easily be multiplied several times, from more than 50 countries. But this session of the Parliament will certainly go ahead, and make history, in any event.

Recently added to the plans for the Provisional World Parliament and concurrent International Arts and Crafts Fair, is a "Children's Peace Circle." The Childrens Peace Circle with various performances and events, is being organized by Ms. Yolanda Ariyana and Yogi Shanti Swaroop. Yolanda, who is from San Diego, California, brings to this project professional experience with similar events, music festivals, and Arts & Crafts shows. Delegates are invited to bring their children, who may have abilities to perform in the Childrens Circle. Also, children who want to participate are encouraged to bring drawings, poems and art work on the theme of world peace and human unity. Children under 12 years old may be accommodated at no extra cost at the Fontainebleau when sharing room with parents. You may write to Yolanda Ariyana at 4832 Auburn Drive, San Die   . CA 92105 (p⊦   619/ 563-9934.)
After M   she will '   ⌐n address·   Beach

F·

Exhibit B

PARTIAL LIST OF SPEAKERS AT THE PROVISIONAL WORLD PARLIAMENT
AND WORLD PROBLEMS DISCUSSION SERIES
(more speakers being added; some not confirmed)

AUSTRALIA
Hon. Gordon M. Bryant
Former M. P., Cabinet
Minister and UN Delegate
BANGLADESH
Mohammad Fazlul Haque
Pres., National Youth Org.
H. E. Awar Sahid
Minister of Information
BRAZIL
Hon. Jose Sette-Camara
V. Pres. of World Court,
Former Mayor of Brazilia
CANADA
Mrs. Helen Tucker
Dir., World Citizens Center
COLOMBIA
Prof. Dr. Jose Consuegra
Chancellor, Simon Bolivar
Univ.; Editor of Desarrollo
COSTA RICA
Hon. Rodrigo Carazo
Pres., University of Peace
CZECHOSLOVAKIA
Dr. Ivan Malek
V.Pres., Czech Academy Sc.,
and Int. Union Biological Ses.
GERMANY (West)
Emil Peter
Member Wolfach Town Council
Gerhard Havel
Pres., Weltfoderalisten e. V.
GHANA
Perry Matson
Gen. Secy, Ghana WCPA
HONGKONG
Kowie S. M. Yun
Pres., Enertec Engineering
INDIA
W. James Arputharaj
Chmn., Asian Youth Center
Hon. Bal Ram Jakhar, M.P.
Specker of the Lok Sabha
Dr. Rashmi Mayur
Dir., Urban Development Inst.;
Pres., Global Futures Network
Sudhir Kumar Ranga
Gen. Sec. All-India Youth Fed.
Hon. Mohinder Singh Saathi
Mayor of Delhi
Nirmal N. Salgal
Pres., Inst. Ecological Studies,
and Human Rights Foundation
Ratansinh Rajda
Member Parliament 1977-84;
Pres., All-India W.C.P.A.
Digvijay Sinh, M.P.
Member Lok Sabha; Pres., Par-
liamentarians Global Action
Ram Awadhesh Singh, M.P.
Pres., Federation of Minorities
S. Vizvesworiah
Journalist; Editor "World State"

IRAQ
Shebib Al-Maliki
Gen. Sec. Union Arab Jurists
IVORY COAST
Dr. Philip Glover-Hemans
Educator; Organizer of WCPA
in Ghana and Ivory Coast
JAMAICA
Dr. Roy E. Johnstone
Pres. Caribbean Action Group
JAPAN
Prof. Dr. Takeshi Haruki
Prof. of Political Science
Rev. Toshio Miyake
Minister, Konko Kyo Church
of Izuo; World Peace Leader
KENYA
Ms. Ravi Sharma
Editor of "Ecoforum"
LIBYA
Dr. Mohammed M. Eliofi
Law Prof., Nasar University
MALAYSIA
David Heah
Organizer, Asia-Pacific Peo-
ples Environment Network
MALTA
Prof. Arvid Pardo
Original proponent at U.N. of
Oceans & Seabeds as Common
Heritage of Humanity
MEXICO
Ing. Reinhart Ruge
Civil Engineer; Pres. WCPA
Dr. Modesto Seara-Vazquez
Prof. Political Sc., Univ. Mex-
ico; Author "La Hora Decisiva"
NEPAL
Hon. Madan Bahadur Pradhan
x-M.P. and Cabinet Minister
Mrs. Indira Shrestha
Civic Leader, Former M.P.
Rabi Charan Shrestha
Candidate for Mayor of Kath-
mandu; Secy Nepal WCPA
NIGERIA
Justice Taslim O. Elias
Recent President of World Court
Gerry Kraus
Organizer of first Peoples World
Constitutional Convention 1950
Hon. Shettima Ali Monguno
x-Cabinet Minister, UN Deleg;
Univ. Chancellor, Pres. OPEC
Chief Adenijian Ogunsanya
Lawyer, Former Mayor of Lagos
NICARAGUA
(To Be Announced)
PAKISTAN
Hon. Shahzada Kabir Ahmad
Judge, Punjab Labour Court
Ahmed E. H. Jaffer
Former M.P.; Businessman

PERU
(To Be Announced)
PHILIPPINES
Dr. Benjamin Salvosa
College President; Journalist
SINGAPORE
Dr. Tommy Kwik
Pres., Council of World Citizens
SOMOLIA
Abdulrahim Abby Farah
Under Sec. Gen. of U.N. for
Special Political Questions
SRI LANKA
Dr. Terence P. Ameralsinghe
Attorney, Civic Leader,
Exec. V. Pres. of WCPA
Hon. Dr. Nissanka Wijeraine
Minister of Justice
SUDAN
(To be announced)
THAILAND
Hon. Suchart Kosolkitlwong
President, International Feder-
ation of Religions
Hon. Chalermchai Jarupaibul
Judge; Pres. Thailand WCPA
TANZANIA
Hon. Joseph J. Mungal, M.P.
x-Minister of Agriculture
UNITED STATES OF AMERICA
Carl Casebolt
Coordinator, Peace and Environ-
ment Platform Project
Hon. Ramsey Clark
Lawyer; x-U.S. Attorney General
Philip Isely
Integrative Engineer
Dr. Lucile Green
x-Pres., World Citizens Assembly
Rev. Jesse Jackson
Leader, Rainbow Coalition;
Presidential Candidate
Dr. Roger Kotila
Psychologist; Field Organizer
for WCPA; Radio Publicist
Dr. Charles Mercieca
Exec. V. Pres., International Assn
Educators for World Peace
Dr. T. Nejat Vezsrioglu
Pres., Intern'l Assn. for Hydro-
gen Energy; Prof. Engineering
Dr. Fred Wood
Environment & Climate Consultant
VANUATU
Rev. Allen Nafuki
Leader, Pacific Community Center
YEMAN ARAB REPUBLIC
Hon. Mohsin Alaini
Ambassador to various countries
YUGOSLAVIA
Prof. Dr. Ivan Supek
Dir. Inst. History and Philosophy
Pres., Yugoslav Pugwash Group
ZAMBIA
Dr. A. Namakube Chimuka
Asst. Sec. Gen., Organization
of African Unity

WORLD SPIRITUAL LEADERS
Mahayogi Pilot Baba   Ma Yoga Shakti   Santa Kesha Va Das
Swami Bua Ji   Yogi Shanti Swaroop

Exhibit C

170

EXECUTIVE CABINET

HONORARY PRESIDENT FOR LIFE
SRI. A. B. PATEL, India
  General Secretary World Union
CO-PRESIDENTS
ING REINHART RUGE, Mexico
  Civil Engineer
N S RAO, India
  Businessman, Chmn World Union
VICE PRESIDENTS
HON. GORDON M. BRYANT, Australia
  Former Cabinet Minister and M P
RAMSEY CLARK, USA
  Trial Law, former Attorney General
GERHARD HAVEL, W Germany
  President, Weltföderalisten e V
HON SYED M. HUSSAIN, Bangladesh
  Advocate, ex Supreme Court Judge
AHMED E. H. JAFFER, Pakistan
  Businessman, former M P
HON. RAM NIWAS MIRDHA, India
  Cabinet Minister and M P
REV. TOSHIO MIYAKE, Japan
  Minister, Peace Leader
CHIEF ADENIRAN OGUNSANYA, Nigeria
  Lawyer, Political Leader
MRS INDIRA SHRESTHA, Nepal
  Civic Leader, former M P
MRS. HELEN TUCKER, Canada
  Director, World Citizens Center
SECRETARY GENERAL
PHILIP ISELY, USA
  Integrative Engineer, Writer
EXECUTIVE VICE PRESIDENT
DR TERENCE P. AMERASINGHE, Sri Lanka
  Attorney, Editor Avon World
  Pres. Sri Lanka Branch W C P A
TREASURER
MRS. MARGARET ISELY, USA
  Businesswoman, Pres. National
  Foundation Nutritional Research

HONORARY SPONSORS OF THE PROVISIONAL WORLD PARLIAMENT

EGIL AARVIK, Norway, Chmn Norwegian Nobel Cttee, M P since 1961, Pres. Laging (upper house par) Min Social Affairs 1965-70
DR. NORMAN Z. ALCOCK, Canada, Nuclear Physicist, Pres Canad Peace Research Inst
* SHEIKH MOHAMMAD ABDULLAH, India, Chief Minister of Jammu & Kashmir, was Pres. All-India States People's Conf Delegate to U N
ALEXEY A. ABRIKOSOV, U.S.S.R., Physicist, Lenin Prize 1966, Corr Mem USSR Academy Sci, Prof. Leningrad, Theoretical Physics.
NICHOLAS Y B. ADADE, Ghana, Lawyer, was Minister Justice Dir Ghana News Agency Dir Ghana Commercial Bank
DR. ADEBAYO ADEDEJI, Nigeria, U N Under-Sec Gen & Exec Sec Economic Comm for Africa Plus African Assn Public Admins.
CHIEF J. O. AGBOYE, Nigeria, Pres Nigerian Inst Administrative Mgmt., Nigerian Society Commerce and Inst Internal Auditors
AZIZ AHMED, Pakistan, Min. Foreign Affairs 1971-77, Ambas USA 1959-63, Chmn Press Trust Pakistan, many other diplomatic posts.
MOHSIN AHMED ALAIMI, Yemen Arab Republic, twice Prime Minister, three times Foreign Min Ambas UK, France, USA, USSR, UN, W Ger
JUSTICE ZVI BAR-NIV, Israel, Judge and Pres Natl Labor Court, ex-Solicitor General
* DR. RICHARD REDGOOD, New Zealand, Prof. Education, V Pres Int'l Community Educ Assn
PROF. SURI BHAGAVANTAM, India, Prof. Physics, Hon. V Chancellor, Pres Cttee on Science & Technology in Developing Countries.
PROF. S. O. BIOBAKU, Nigeria, Dir. Inst. African Studies, Univ Ibadan, V Chancellor Univs Ife and Lagos, Pres Historical Society Nigeria
PROF. GORAN VON BONSDORFF, Finland, Prof. Politics Sci Univ Helsinki, Author, "World Politics in Age of Technology
FR PHIL BOSMANS, Belgium, Priest, Radio Caller Couns Author, Give Happiness A Chance
DENNIS BRUTUS, South Africa, Poet, Dir World Campaign to Release S African Pol Prisoners, V Pres Union of Writers of African People
HON GORDON M. BRYANT, Australia, M P 1955-80, Cabinet Min 1972-75, UN Delegate
CHIEF MANGOSUTHU GATSHA BUTHELEZI, Kwazulu S Africa, Chief Minister, Leader S Africa Black Alliance, Leader 5,000,000 Zulus.
PROF. ADRIANO BUZZATI-TRAVERSO, Italy, Ltd Ind Genetics Univ Pavia 1946-62, Sr. Sc. Advisor UN Environment Prgm, WHO Advisor
PROF. HENRI CARTAN, France, Prof. Math. Univ Paris 1940-76, Pres European Assn Teachers (f r) 1957-75 Pres Ment Federatiale European
VEDAT CELIK, Cyprus, was Deputy Prime Min. and Min. Foreign Affairs, Turkish Fed State Cyprus, UNSC Rep to UN, was Legislature
KIRIB CHAND, India, Ambas and High Commr to Many Countries of Europe, Africa and Mid-East, Consultant for International Development
HON. Y. V. CHANDRACHUD, India, Chief Justice Supreme Court, Pres Ind Law Association
DR JOSEF CHARVAT, Czechoslovakia, Prof. Medicine on Science Council, Ministry of Health
DR A. NAMAKURE CHIMUKA, Zambia, Asst Secretary Gen Organization of African Unity, many posts with Ministry Foreign Affairs.
RAMSEY CLARK, USA, Lawyer, US Attorney Gen 1967-69, Prof. Law Brooklyn Law School

(continued on back)

World Constitution and Parliament Association

1480 Hoyt St., Suite 31 / Lakewood, CO 80215, USA / Ph. 303-233-3548, Telex: 3712957 EARTH

February -- April, 1987

Dear Friend of Peace and Humanity:

At this time of extreme global crises, we should like to invite you to participate in the Third Session of the Provisional World Parliament, as a way to help obtain control over world events for the good of all people on Earth.

The Third Session of the Parliament will convene from 18 to 28 of June, 1987, at the Fontainebleau Hilton, Miami Beach, Florida. This location is particularly convenient for delegates from Central and South America and the Caribbean area. An agenda for the Third Session is enclosed, together with a registration page and further information.

The Provisional World Parliament offers a constructive way for people who want peace and human welfare (including both private citizens and government leaders) to begin taking charge of world affairs -- all in the context of an emerging World Federation and Democratic Non-Military World Government. The Parliament is organized under Article 19 of the Constitution for the Federation of Earth, and convenes each year until replaced by a formally elected World Parliament under a ratified World Constitution.

Major objectives of the Third Session of the Provisional World Parliament are to work on implementation of World Legislation adopted at previous sessions of the Parliament, to promote the campaign for ratification of the Constitution for the Federation of Earth, to take action on other world problems (such as world food supply, the Third World debt situation, world energy supply, and human rights) and to establish a Provisional World Cabinet.

At previous sessions of the Parliament, held in England and in India, eight World Legislative Measures have been adopted. These include:

Bill #1, to outlaw nuclear weapons and other weapons of mass destruction, and to establish a World Disarmament Agency;
Bill #2, for a World Economic Development Organization, which will establish a new global system of finance and credit;
Bill #3, for ownership by the people of Earth all oceans and seabeds from 20 km offshore, no exclusive economic zones beyond territorial waters;
Bill #4, for a Graduate School of World Problems;
Bill #5, for Provisional District World Courts;
Bill #6, for an Emergency Earth Rescue Administration, to bring carbon dioxide levels under control, save the environment, and prevent universal starvation as a result of global climatic catastrophe;
Bill #7, for a World Government Funding Corporation;
Bill #8, for a World Commission on Terrorism.

Ways for you to qualify as a fully accredited delegate to the Provisional World Parliament are listed on the registration page. Upon receipt of your registration, we will send you the appropriate forms to fulfill the requirements for an accredited delegate, including alternatives of (a) an announcement which you can publish in periodicals and papers; (b) on election petition form; (c) a model resolution for adoption by an organization, community, university or Parliamentary body, which thereby designates its delegates.

If you are unable to attend the Provisional World Parliament, then we invite you to take part in the on-going action program of the World Constitution and Parliament Association.

Please let us hear from you soon, by return of the enclosed reply form and registration page, also by personal letter.

for Peace and Humanity,

Philip Isely, Secretary General

Reinhart Ruge, President

"Let Us Raise A Standard To Which The Wise And The Honest Can Repair!"

Exhibit D

World Constitution and Parliament Association

ORGANIZING AGENT FOR THE PROVISIONAL WORLD PARLIAMENT
and PREPARATORY COMMITTEE 1990 WORLD CONSTITUENT ASSEMBLY
1480 Hoyt St., Suite 31/Lakewood, Colo 80215, USA/Ph. 303-233-3548
Telefax: 303-526-2185, and 303-233-4800, Attn: WCPA

14 March 1990

Gary Kah

Dear Gary:

I was glad to hear from you by telephone today, and hope you will be able to participate actively.

I reviewed your previous file, and believe that you could be a positively contributing participant in achieving the objectives.

for adequate action in time for the survival of humanity on Earth,

Philip Isely

"We are as small as our fear and despair, as great as our courage and hope!"

Exhibit E

World Constitution and Parliament Association

ORGANIZING AGENT for the PROVISIONAL WORLD PARLIAMENT and
PREPARATORY COMMITTEE 1991 WORLD CONSTITUENT ASSEMBLY
1480 Hoyt St., Suite 31/Lakewood CO 80215, USA/Ph. 303-233-3548 or 526-0463
Telefax, 303-526 2185 or 233-4800

Dear *Gary Kah*:   February, 1991

We are happy to have your recent support for, or inquiry about, the World Constituent Assembly and the work of the World Constitution and Parliament Association. Enclosed is the latest information. Originally the World Constituent Assembly was planned for Alexandria, Egypt. But due to war related dangers, the location has been changed to Portugal -- at the Troia Convention Center, 40 km. south of Lisbon on the sea-coast, as described by the enclosures.

On the days of writing this letter, no one knows whether the war in the Persian Gulf will last another week or several months. It is certain, however, that a comprehensive peace conference must follow the war, and there is talk of a "new world order."

We are ready for the peace conference. In fact, **WE HAVE ALREADY CALLED THE COMPREHENSIVE PEACE CONFERENCE: IT IS THE WORLD CONSTITUENT ASSEMBLY.** The purposes are summarized, again, in the enclosed reprint of an ad appearing in SOUTH Magazine. To the agenda, we have added two specific items: Mid-East Peace; and Global Energy Network, to replace oil and fossil fuels.

For the New World Order, almost all talk is in the familiar terms of re-arrangements of the balance of power among sovereign nations, enforced by preponderance of military power in strategic areas, while all nations remain sufficiently armed to deter aggression. This is NOT a "new world order." Despite unprecedented technological advances, most persons who have been in charge of international relations during the past 100 years seem very slow to learn the fundamental requirement for world peace.

After the first World War, those who won proceeded to institutionalize the system of armed national sovereignty in the form of the unworkable League of Nations. After the second World War, the victors continued the same obsolete and dangerous system of armed national sovereignty, dominated by the most powerful, in the mis-named United Nations -- under which 100 new nations are still busy arming themselves with modern weapons of mass destruction, along with the U. N. founders.

Now, we have another opportunity to establish the first requirement for peace, survival, and constructive solutions to global problems: A World Federation of disarmed nations, under a Constitution for Federal World Government. Nothing less. The Constitution is already drafted.

If this kind of peace conference and world order makes sense to you, then we welcome your participation in the World Constituent Assembly, and the global ratification campaign to follow. You may serve as a delegate, help send a delegate, publicize the action, give money.

All those desiring to attend as delegates are urged to complete their registration and credentials quickly, including hotel registration. HERE IS YOUR OPPORTUNITY TO HELP ACHIEVE A GOOD FUTURE FOR EVERYBODY ON EARTH,

Philip Isely, Secretary General

"We are as small as our fear and despair, as great as our courage and hope!"

Exhibit F

WCPA Letter to All Heads of State

The letter in Exhibit G, announcing the convening of the 4th World Constituent Assembly, was sent to every Head of State in the world in December 1990. The message is straight forward. "We are forming a World Government, can we count on your support?"

The letter cites Mid-East tensions, the looming threat of war, and various alleged environmental problems as the reasons for why a world government is needed. It then calls for a single global currency and financial system (paragraph 6) as part of the solution.

If the allegations were completely true and if the spiritual motivation behind these arguments was righteous, one might be half inclined to go along with their proposed solution. However, we know that this is not the case. Reading this letter will show you how seductive the rise of the world government will be for those who are not alerted to its dangers in advance.

If the adjacent letter has been sent to every Head of State in the world, why have our leaders not informed us of this plot? It is difficult to imagine that they aren't taking this group seriously considering all the prominent world figures who are involved in it. One need only look at the names of the first three vice presidents listed under the executive cabinet, to realize the seriousness of this threat, (Tony Benn, former Cabinet Minister, United Kingdom; Gordon Bryant, former Cabinet Minister, Australia; and Ramsey Clark, former Attorney General of the United States; see Exhibit A).

There are only a few other possible reasons why we haven't been warned: 1) the letter got intercepted by a top aide and never made it to the Head of State; 2) the letter was taken seriously, but the receiver was fearful of taking a stand—realizing the powerful forces behind this effort; or 3) the letter was taken seriously, but the leader's attempt to expose the conspiracy has failed because of one-world interests who control major press and media communications.

A possible fourth reason is that the Head of State is himself involved in the plot. I wonder how many times a president must publicly mention the phrase "New World Order" before he qualifies for this category?

Whatever the case may be, none of the above scenarios work in our favor. This is why you are urged, once again, to send the letter at the back of this book to your elected officials. We must hold them accountable, or else the world government will soon become a reality!

12th December 1990

To All Presidents, Prime Ministers, Kings, Queens,
   and Other Heads of Governments and National Parliaments

Just when the relaxation of tensions among the super-powers was
giving hope for the dawn of a new era, where the resources of
Earth could be used to serve only peaceful human needs, a new
crisis erupts and rapidly escalates, this time in the Mid-East. By
this, we are forcefully reminded that the world is loaded with
weapons sufficient to kill everybody on the Planet a dozen or
fifty times over again in a few days.

Meanwhile, the mad arming of more nations with more weapons
continues, while new generations of weapons go into production,
and an endless number of crises situations loom on the horizon,
if we survive the current one.

War could end civilization any week. But war is not the only
danger. Climate changes are already creating havoc. If not
turned around, the rise of carbon dioxide in the atmosphere and
surge of climatic changes may soon become irreversible,
culminating in the fatal starvation of most people on Earth --
because of crop failures in most countries resulting from
unfavorable weather.

It is time for all nations to abandon their disastrous pre-occupation
with military power and confrontations, which in the end solve no
problems and can only lead to misery and death for everybody.
It is time to re-direct the resources, the technology, the scientific
talent, the people power, and the money now squandered by
competing military priorities and struggles, into a common global
campaign to save the environment, to reverse climate changes, and
to restore Earth to conditions for healthy living for all inhabitants.

It is time to see that the climate crisis makes the use of fossil
fuels obsolete and dangerous, and war over oil absurd; and
consequently to give, top priority for the immediate transition to
solar and hydrogen technologies and other safe energy sources,
available to all countries without monopolistic conditions.

It is time, also, to escape from the constraints of obsolete
financial accounting, which chain development to the scarcity of
past savings at high interest rates; and to establish the alternative
of a rational global system for abundant low-cost credit based
soundly on the availability of people to work and produce, using
a common global currency.

During the past four-and-one-half decades since the end of
World War II, many unsolved global, regional and supra-national
problems have accumulated. Many unsolved problems have by
now reached extreme crises stages, each complicating the others.
These unsolved problems underlie the emergencies which are now
erupting into armed conflicts.

We are convinced that to solve global problems peacefully, and
to administer human affairs on Earth intelligently, a WORLD
GOVERNMENT is required -- a democratically organized Federal
World Government.

Exhibit G1

Page 2 -- To All Presidents, Prime Ministers, Kings, Queens and other Heads of Governments

Only World Government can provide the security and authority necessary to supervise disarmament, and quickly eliminate all nuclear weapons and other weapons of mass destruction.

Only World Government under a World Constitution can provide the necessary civilian framework for a World Legislature, World Executive Agencies, and mandatory World Courts, all to act directly, decisively and without bias in areas of global and supra-national problems, to achieve peaceful and rational solutions for the mutual benefit of all inhabitants of Earth.

People all over the world are ready for World Government -- a constitutional democratic world government, under which national and local governments retain jurisdiction over strictly internal affairs. Many people have been ready since the end of World War II. People in their capacity as Citizens of Earth have been taking action towards World Government for many years. Some people have, in fact, prepared a complete Constitution for the Federation of Earth.

Upon the initiative of these people, a World Constituent Assembly is now called, to convene at the end of April, 1991. The purposes are: to submit the Constitution for the Federation of Earth for review, and for amendments where improvements may be needed; and then to launch a rapid global ratification campaign. Enclosed is a copy of the Call to the World Constituent Assembly, which invites delegates from the national governments and the people of all countries.

We who sign this appeal to you, are ready for Democratic Federal World Government, under a ratified World Constitution. We have already joined as Honorary Sponsors of the World Constituent Assembly, and as signers of the Call to the World Constituent Assembly. Many of us are also ready to serve as delegates to the World Constituent Assembly.

WE NOW JOIN IN APPEALING TO YOU. AS CUSTODIAN OF THE WELFARE OF THE CITIZENS OF YOUR COUNTRY, WHO, LIKE YOURSELF, ARE RESIDENTS AND CITIZENS ALSO OF ONE EARTH, WILL YOU SUPPORT THIS MOVE FOR A FEDERAL WORLD GOVERNMENT?

SPECIFICALLY, WILL YOU APPOINT OFFICIAL DELEGATES TO THE WORLD CONSTITUENT ASSEMBLY, TO BEGIN ON 29TH APRIL, 1991? Or ask your National Parliament to elect delegates? The Assembly will convene at Alexandria, Egypt, in the Montazah Sheraton Hotel, beginning on 29th April, 1991.

Your Excellency, time is short to avert extreme catastrophe for everybody. Now is the time to assure the dawn and full blooming of a new era for humanity on Planet Earth.

We shall anticipate your affirmative reply, and appointment of delegates!

Dr. Kalman Abraham, Hungary   Tony Benn, M. P., England

Exhibit G2

Call to a World Constituent Assembly

This Call to hold a 4th World Constituent Assembly (Exhibit H) in Alexandria, Egypt (later Lisbon, Portugal), at the end of April 1991, was mailed out by the Preparatory Committee to everyone associated with the WCPA. It was accompanied with a letter, sample advertisements—which we were encouraged to use to promote the convention—and the necessary registration forms (Exhibits I-L).

In this Call, the organizers were even more blatant about their objectives than in preceding documents. Note the paragraph at the bottom of the first column on the first page.

If you had any lingering doubt over whether this organization is a threat to our national sovereignty, consider it gone! Although the document promises to respect "the jurisdiction of national governments over their internal affairs" (col. 2, para. 2), we know that the real power would rest with the world government and those who control it. Furthermore, once a world government is in power, who is to prevent it from forcing its influence upon the internal affairs of nations as well?

The WCPA does not consider the United Nations to be part of the solution. Yet it reproduces the U.N. logo on its proposed world constitution; and more than one-fifth of its members are affiliated with the U.N. How does one account for this?

Apparently the WCPA has been destined to replace the U.N., much like the U.N. replaced the League of Nations. The same group of people were involved in both cases; only the names had changed. This created an illusion of progress.

Behind-the-scenes, the WCPA is connected with the U.N. in a similar fashion (otherwise it would not be using its logo). However, it does not want this fact publicly known. Instead, the WCPA wants to create the false impression that it is something brand new, an independent organization representing only "the people of the world." Such an image is essential if the insiders are to have any hope of pulling their plan off.

In the second column of page one, the document goes on to call for the immediate forming of a world government and implementation of a world constitution . . . which just happens to be waiting in the wings, having had no input from humanity at large. It then announces the convening of the World Constituent Assembly, listing the qualifications for delegates to attend.

Please study this document closely. Notice how every effort has been made to create the appearance that those in charge are acting on behalf of democracy. In the future, remember not to accept something just because it carries a topdressing of democracy. We must always look beyond the surface.

Also enclosed in the registration packet was a cover letter offering further details of the convention and encouraging delegates to publicly advertise the event, indicating that the Preparatory Committee was indeed preparing to launch the final ratification campaign.

The packet included several sample advertisements, which had been designed for our use. Look for these advertisements in occult magazines and newsletters throughout the world, placing like-minded New Agers on alert for the final push. Eventually, as this campaign

CALL TO A WORLD CONSTITUENT ASSEMBLY

To convene on the 29th day of APRIL, 1991

THE PREDICAMENT OF HUMANITY:

At the time of issuing this Call in 1989, Humanity is confronted with many extreme global problems, some affecting the survival of most people on the planet. These problems include:

• Climatic changes already underway, because of excess carbon dioxide and other pollutants in the atmosphere, threaten universal disaster soon, including the possible starvation to death of hundreds of millions or even billions of people.

• No one is safe while nuclear weapons remain aimed and ready to fire at a moments notice, and while other weapons of mass destruction continue to be developed and deployed. As more nations gain nuclear capability, human survival is threatened by wars starting anywhere, either accidental or deliberate, made even more deadly by nuclear fallout and nuclear winter.

• The economies of most countries are crippled by debts, lack of funding, unemployment and inflation. Adequate development and environmental repair cannot go forward until a new global financial system is instituted, designed to serve peaceful human needs.

• Safe and sustainable energy supplies must be developed very rapidly to replace the use of polluting fossil fuels, deforestation for fuel, and nuclear fission reactors which each year produce hundreds or thousands of years of radioactive dangers to all life on the planet.

• Food production per capita of world population is declining for many reasons, while population is increasing

• Earth's oxygen supply is endangered by pollution of the oceans, the death of plankton, and destruction of the rain forests, which together recycle most of the oxygen people depend on for life.

• With increasing production by chemical processes, in both industry and agriculture, toxic wastes are rapidly accumulating, with few (if any) safe places for disposal.

• The capabilities for production with highly advanced technology in a few countries, are increasing the gap between the "haves" and the "have nots", and reducing the employment and livelihood opportunities for most people in many countries to primitive levels.

• The spread of ozone holes in the atmosphere, rapid loss of topsoil and fertility, floods and hurricanes arising from conditions which transcend national boundaries, acid rainfall and snowfall, and expanding deserts, are some of the dozens of environmental problems which have become global problems of common concern to people everywhere.

• Many millions of people are likely to seek refuge from unliveable environments soon, including large percentages of the people of some countries.

• Human welfare, environmental health, and basic human rights are sacrificed everywhere so long as nations allocate large amounts of money, resources and scientific talents for armaments, and give priorities for military purposes. This now costs the people of Earth a trillion dollars (US) per year, with no safety for anyone. The same amount needs to be spent instead on rescuing Earth from climatic and environmental catastrophes, and the production of goods and services for useful peaceful purposes

The global crises and problems mentioned herein, as well as many others, have been accumulating for many years. Solutions are now required quickly, and simultaneously in many cases, in order to avert or minimize global catastrophes. Experience during the past 40 years, and longer, demonstrates that adequate solutions are not possible to negotiate among sovereign nations- neither outside nor inside of the United Nations Organization.

WORLD GOVERNMENT IS REQUIRED:

To devise and implement adequate solutions to these problems and others which transcend national boundaries, as well as for global problems which will continue to arise in the future, requires a World Government immediately, particularly within the time frame allowed by the extreme nature of some of the problems. By World Government we mean a federal world government that is democratic in its own structure and designed for civilian administration. World Government is, in fact, the first practical requirement for survival and progress, not a dream for the future after human civilization has been destroyed by unsolved problems.

The federal World Government must include an elected and fairly representative World Parliament, given authority to enact world legislation directly to solve world problems and provide for the management of global and trans-national affairs; a World Executive and Administration given authority to implement the world legislation directly, while respecting the jurisdiction of national governments over their internal affairs; World Courts which are given mandatory jurisdiction; a World Ombudsmus to protect human rights and to keep governments from becoming tyrannical; adequate means for direct enforcement and financing; and all other agencies of a Government for Earth necessary and appropriate for peaceful, creative and sustainable living during the present and next centuries.

WORLD GOVERNMENT REQUIRES A WORLD CONSTITUTION:

Before federal World Government is established, a World Constitution is required, to define the functions, the powers, the limits, and the structure of the World Government; and to define how all of the organs, parts and agencies of the World Government will be organized and will operate together to serve human needs and the common welfare of all people on Earth. The Constitution for a federal World Government must also protect both universal human rights, cultural diversities, and the peaceful jurisdiction of national governments over their internal affairs. At the same time, the World Constitution needs to define how world government and national governments can work jointly to solve some problems and administer some affairs which have both internal and supra-national aspects.

Preparing a truly adequate World Constitution for Earth takes much time. Fortunately, a very adequate World Constitution has already been prepared over a period of nine years, and during several previous sessions of a world constituent assembly, so that no time need be lost by repeating what has already been accomplished. This World Constitution is known as the CONSTITUTION FOR THE FEDERATION OF EARTH, and is ready for immediate provisional ratification and stage-by-stage implementation, although still subject to amendments. Before final ratification, however, more countries and more people from different parts of Earth need an opportunity to review the Earth Constitution, and see if some improvements by amendment are needed.

WE, THEREFORE, ISSUE THIS CALL FOR A WORLD CONSTITUENT ASSEMBLY TO CONVENE ON THE 29th DAY OF APRIL, 1991.

THE PURPOSES of this World Constituent Assembly shall include the following:

1. To review the Constitution for the Federation of Earth, which shall be taken as the basic document for deliberations at the Assembly;

2. To consider and debate possible amendments, and to adopt those amendments which may be deemed desirable;

Exhibit H1

Call to a World Constituent Assembly - page 2

3. To launch a final and rapid global campaign for ratification of the amended Earth Constitution by the people and governments of Earth;

4. To assist the continued functioning of the Provisional World Parliament and Provisional World Cabinet, already organized under Article 19 of the Constitution for the Federation of Earth, until the Earth constitution has been ratified by a sufficient number of countries or people to go beyond the provisional stage.

5. To assist implementation in first stages of some of the most urgent measures already adopted by the Provisional World Parliament.

THE LOCATION for the World Constituent Assembly shall be decided at a meeting of the Preparatory Committee for the Assembly before the end of 1989.

DELEGATES to the World Constituent Assembly are invited from both the national governments and the people of all countries, on the following basis:

A. From national governments or national parliaments or executive heads of national governments ratifying this Call to the 1991 World Constituent Assembly and accepting the Constitution for the Federation of Earth as the basis for deliberations:

One delegate from countries under 2,000,000 in population;
Two delegates from countries between 2,000,000 and less than 7,000,000 in population;
Three delegates from countries between 7,000,000 and less than 20,000,000 in population;
Four delegates from countries between 20,000,000 and less than 80,000,000 in population;
Five delegates from countries with 80,000,000 or more in population.

B. From people or non-governmental organizations or communities ratifying this Call to the 1991 World Constituent Assembly, and accepting the Constitution for the Federation of Earth as the basis for deliberations:

One delegate from each ratifying non-governmental organization of 5,000 members or more;
One delegate sent jointly by several ratifying non-governmental organizations with combined total membership of 5,000 or more
One delegate elected or appointed by a ratifying community, or by a group of ratifying communities, totaling 25,000 or more in population;
Individual delegates securing 700 or more signatures on election petitions approved by the Preparatory Committee;
Individual delegates who publish advertisements which explain the World Constituent Assembly and announce attendance by the delegates, such advertisements to have the approval of the Preparatory Committee and be placed in periodicals having total combined circulation of 25,000 or more for each delegate so advertising;

Together with five delegates each elected by the World Constitution and Parliament Association, and by the Provisional World Cabinet.

C. Delegates previously accredited to the Provisional World Parliament or previous sessions of the World Constituent Assembly, must obtain renewed credentials by one of the methods defined herein.

D. All delegates must take part in a 2-day pre-session orientation course conducted by the Preparatory Committee, before being seated as accredited delegates in the World Constituent Assembly.

DURATION of the World Constituent Assembly beginning on the 29th day of April 1991, shall be as long as it may take to complete the task, in one session, or in several sub-sessions, as decided by the delegates.

ALL FURTHER DETAILS for the organization, conduct and financing of the 1991 World Constituent Assembly shall be decided and managed by a Preparatory Committee, until the Assembly, itself, assumes full responsibility. The Preparatory Committee shall be composed of delegates appointed or elected by those national governments, parliaments, or heads of national governments, and by those non-governmental organizations and communities which ratify this Call, together with acceptance of the complete plan for the World Constituent Assembly originated by the World Constitution and Parliament Association, and in company with five delegates each from the Provisional World Cabinet and the World Constitution and Parliament Association.

THIS CALL IS FORMALLY ISSUED at a meeting of the Preparatory Committee for the 1991 World Constituent Assembly on 21st July, 1989, in Washington, D.C., with simultaneous press conferences to announce the Call in various countries around the world. Signers are invited both before and after issuance.

THE LOCATION ANNOUNCED for the World Constituent Assembly is Alexandria, Egypt, at the Montazah Sheraton Hotel, beginning on 29th April 1991, and continuing for ten days. Further sessions may be announced.

NOTE: This Call is already signed by thousands of distinguished persons from 80 countries of Earth. Additional signers and ratifiers are invited in the spaces below.

ADDITIONAL SIGNERS:

1. Name _____
Profession _____
Address _____
_____ Date _____

2. Name _____
Profession _____
Address _____
_____ Date _____

3. Name _____
Profession _____
Address _____
_____ Date _____

4. Name _____
Profession _____
Address _____
_____ Date _____

5. Name _____
Profession _____
Address _____
_____ Date _____

6. Name _____
Profession _____
Address _____
_____ Date _____

7. Name _____
Profession _____
Address _____
_____ Date _____

RATIFICATION OF THIS CALL is invited by National Governments, National Parliaments, Executive Heads of National Governments, The United Nations General Assembly, Non-Governmental Organizations, Communities, Political Parties, and other groups.

Ratified by _____
_____
_____

Official Signatures and Seal: _____
_____

Date of Ratification _____

RETURN SIGNED OR RATIFIED CALLS TO THE WORLD CONSTITUTION AND PARLIAMENT ASSOCIATION
1480 Hoyt Street, Suite 31, Lakewood, Colorado 80215 U.S.A.

Exhibit H2

gains momentum and acceptance, these advertisements and related announcements will begin to appear in mainstream publications as well. The most attractive of these articles, entitled "One Earth," will probably be the first to appear in public news magazines.

REGISTRATION FOR THE WORLD CONSTITUENT ASSEMBLY
FOR PEOPLES DELEGATES — 1991 AND ANY SUBSEQUENT SESSIONS

Name_____ Date_____ Telephone_____

Address_____ Telefax_____

City_____ State_____ Postal Zip_____ Country_____

(NOTE: Please check your agreement with each statement, and fill out all blanks which apply to your personal registration.)

1. _____ I hereby declare my acceptance of the draft Constitution for the Federation of Earth as the basic document for review and debate at the World Constituent Assembly, and agree to abide by the Rules of Procedure for the Assembly.

2. _____ I pledge myself to attend the daily sessions of the World Constituent Assembly faithfully, unless prevented by circumstances beyond my control.

3. _____ I expect to obtain my credentials to serve as a delegate by one of the following methods, as checked:

   (a) _____ By advertisements or announcements printed in one or more periodical(s) having total circulation of 25,000 per delegate joining in the same advertisement. (Any advertisement must include the information contained in the model advertisement form provided by the Preparatory Committee or the W.C.P.A. Printed news releases are acceptable, providing they contain the essential information about the World Constituent Assembly, and delegates attending.)

   (b) _____ By resolution of an organization or organizations with membership totaling 5,000, such organization(s) having also ratified the Call to the World Constituent Assembly. (Note: Obtain model resolution form from the Preparatory Committee.)

   (c) _____ By other method defined in the Call to the World Constituent Assembly. Please specify:
   _____

(NOTE: All Peoples Delegates must show proof of credentials obtained by ONE of the above methods, as required by the Call to the World Constituent Assembly. Delegates to previous sessions of the World Constituent Assembly or Provisional World Parliament must obtain renewed and updated credentials by one of these methods. No delegate will be seated without proof of credentials, as well as completion of this Registration Form.)

4. Additional Information:

   Date of Birth_____ Place of Birth_____

   Education_____

   Languages understood_____

   Name of Spouse_____ Children_____

   Profession_____

   Author of _____ _____

   Accor   · Life_____

   —

Exhibit I

PREPARATORY COMMITTEE for the WORLD CONSTITUENT ASSEMBLY

1480 Hoyt Street, Suite 31 / Lakewood, CO 80215, U.S.A.
Phone 303-233-3548; Telefax 303-526-2185 and 303-233-4800

11th January 1991

TO ALL COLLABORATING ORGANIZATIONS AND OTHERS READY FOR A WORLD CONSTITUENT ASSEMBLY

Dear Residents of Earth:

Despite rumblings of war, the time has come for every organization and every person wanting to participate in or assist the World Constituent Assembly, to make definite preparations to come or send delegates to the 1991 WORLD CONSTITUENT ASSEMBLY.

LOCATION -- Montazah Sheraton Hotel, Alexandria, Egypt;
TIME -- 29th April to 9th May, 1991.

Decision on the location was made at the meeting of the Preparatory Committee at Lucerne, Switzerland, in November. A further report on this meeting, together with a ballot for the election of the Directorate for the Preparatory Committee, will be sent soon. My purpose in this letter is to urgently request rapid action to prepare delegates to attend the Assembly. Please take care of the following:

CREDENTIALS: Each delegate must have credentials per the terms of the CALL. Delegates to previous sessions must renew their credentials, since previous credentials are no longer valid. Therefore, be sure to establish your credentials in ONE of the following ways:

1. A Resolution passed by one or more organizations with total membership of 5,000 or more. The resolution must include a statement of support for the World Constituent Assembly and its objectives. A model resolution form for organizations or communities is enclosed. Be sure to complete every part of the resolution, including the number of members of the organization. Please note: delegates to the Preparatory Committee are not automatically delegates to the World Constituent Assembly.

2. An Advertisement or Announcement or News Release published in one or more periodicals, having total circulation of 25,000. The advertisement or announcement must state the purposes of the World Constituent Assembly, the dates and location, and the fact that certain individuals named in the advertisement are attending the World Constituent Assembly as delegates. Three model advertisements or announcements are enclosed for your use:

   a) A long form, headed FIRST PRIORITY FOR SURVIVAL;

   b) A short form, headed "I Am Tired of Wars and Threats of Wars";

   c) Copy of the ad which appears in the February issue of SOUTH magazine, paid for by Philip and Margaret Isely. You may put the same ad in some other magazine, with explanatory note that you will attend the World Constituent Assembly as delegate.

   d) In addition to the model advertisements, we enclose a model news re' ase, which you may be able to get published free of charge. ₁ws relea⌐ ⌐ust include all essenti⌐' ⌐mation ab⌐ ⌐he ⌐em⌐⌐ ⌐rede⌐

Exhibit J

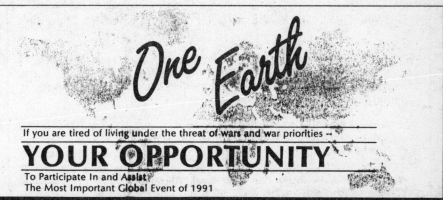

One Earth

If you are tired of living under the threat of wars and war priorities --

YOUR OPPORTUNITY

To Participate In and Assist
The Most Important Global Event of 1991

THE WORLD CONSTITUENT ASSEMBLY

To complete a CONSTITUTION FOR THE FEDERATION OF EARTH and prepare a Federal World Government for Humanity, under which an elected and fairly representative World Parliament will have authority to enact world legislation to solve world problems, a World Executive responsible to the World Parliament will have authority to directly implement the world legislation, and World Courts and a World Ombudsmus will have mandatory jurisdiction, while dis-armed national governments retain legitimate authority within their boundaries.

WHEN: 29th April to 9th May, 1991.

WHERE: Alexandria, Egypt, at the Montazah Sheraton Hotel.

WHO ARE THE DELEGATES?
● NGO or Peoples Delegates: Any qualified person who obtains credentials showing endorsement by organizations (one or several) which endorse the Assembly and have total membership of 5,000 or more; or by public announcements giving full information. Obtain delegates forms from address below.

● Government Delegates: Appointed by the Heads of National Governments which endorse the Assembly, or elected by National Parliaments.

YOUR PART —
1. Attend as a delegate;
2. Nudge your Government to send delegates;
3. Get an organization to send a delegate;
4. Assist another person to attend as delegate;
5. CONTRIBUTE MONEY.
6. Get a copy of CONSTITUTION FOR THE FEDERATION OF EARTH, plus PLANETHOOD, for $10 (U.S.) including airmail postage.

MORE INFORMATION:
WORLD CONSTITUTION & PARLIAMENT ASSN.
1480 Hoyt Street, Suite 31
Lakewood, Colorado 80215, USA
FAX: (303) 526-2185 or (303) 233-4800

(This ad paid for by Philip & Margaret Isely who are delegates to the World Constituent Assembly)

PRACTICAL BENEFITS & REWARDS
● Rapid disarmament under global supervision;

● Use of money and resources saved by disarmament to save the enviroment and serve human needs;

● A new global finance and credit system, giving ample low-cost funding for useful projects and production, whether public or private enterprise, using a single world currency;

● Financial credit based on people available to work, thus guaranteeing full employment; past debts retired without austerity penalties;

● Rapid global transition to safe and sustainable energy; together with a very massive global campaign for reforestation, soil remineralization and all measures necessary to cope with the Climate Crisis and prevent widespread starvation;

● Adminstration of the oceans, seabeds and atmosphere as the common heritage of humanity.

● Peaceful solutions made possible to all supranational problems;

SPONSORSHIP: The growing list of nearly 200 eminent Honorary Sponsors from 80 countries will be sent to every respondent. Sponsors include Nobel Laureates; Supreme Court Presidents; U.N. Ambassadors, M.P.'s, Business Executives, Lawyers, Scientists, Professors, Environmental Leaders, etc.

Name: _____ Date: _____

Address: _____

☐ Rush delegate information to participate in the World Constituent Assembly.
☐ Send draft Constitution for the Federation of Earth, plus Planethood, airmail $10 (U.S.).

☐ Enclosed is $ _____ (U.S. Dollars)
(Checks must show corresponding bank in USA)

Exhibit K

SHORT FORM ——— ADVERTISEMENT OR ANNOUNCEMENT

I AM TIRED OF WARS AND THREATS OF WARS. Therefore,

I _____ of _____
will attend as a Peoples Delegate the World constituent Assembly which
convenes from 29th April to 9th May, 1991, at Alexandria, Egypt, in the
Montazah Sheraton Hotel, with delegates invited from the people and from
national governments of all countries.

Purposes of the Assembly are to review the Constitution for the
Federation of Earth, for which I affirm general support, and to debate
and adopt possible amendments, then to prepare a global ratification
campaign for the inauguration of democratic federal world government
given authority to supervise disarmament and solve supra-national
problems. For a copy of the Constitution for the Federation of Earth
and other information, send $5 plus $3 for postage and handling to the
World Constitution & Parliament Association, 1480 Hoyt Street, Suite 31,
Lakewood, Colorado 80215, U.S.A. The constitution is available in
English, French, German, Spanish, Arabic, Chinese, Italian, Thai, and
a few other languages.

Exhibit L

Plan for Collaboration in Organizing a World Constituent Assembly for 1990 (1991)

The Plan (Exhibit M) was prepared in late 1987, in conjunction
with the proposed 4th convening of a World Constituent Assembly.
The original target date for this meeting was December 1990. However, it was later changed to April 29-May 9, 1991 and the selected
meeting site was moved from Alexandria, Egypt, to Lisbon, Portugal.

According to article 9 of the proposal (Exhibit M2), "Preference
for location shall be given to a country whose national government
or legislature has already given Provisional Ratification to the Constitution for the Federation of Earth." If the Preparatory Committee
abides by its own rules, then apparently, Egypt and Portugal have
already ratified the world constitution, since they were the considered meeting sites.

The final ratification campaign began at the convention in
Lisbon. However, based on what I already know, the WCPA is not
expecting this campaign to bring us into a world government overnight. They realize that it may take a few more years of concerted
effort and preparation. Hence, there will probably be more such
meetings in the near future.

Note the effort to compare the current endeavor of the WCPA to the endeavors of our founding fathers leading up to the acceptance of the U.S. Constitution (Exhibit M3), using this historical event of 1787 as an example of how a Constitutional Convention, held for the purpose of making only minor revisions, can lead to the production of an entirely new constitution.

The document ends by presenting a ten point plan (Exhibit M2) that was to result in the convening of the 4th World Constituent Assembly. Everything went as planned except that the date and location of the meeting was changed. It is hoped, in the not too distant future, a few hitches will develop!

PLAN FOR COLLABORATION
IN ORGANIZING A WORLD CONSTITUENT ASSEMBLY

Considering that various persons and organizations are now getting interested in convening a World Constitutional Convention or World Constituent Assembly, and in drafting of a constitution for World Government, it seems most desirable to have a common plan for this purpose. We have a plan to propose, but before outlining the plan, we should like to make a brief historical review.

Not all persons now proposing a World Constituent Assembly are familiar with the long history of work in this direction carried on by the World Constitution and Parliament Association, beginning in 1958. Others are not familiar with the substantial stages in the development of this project, to the point of the adoption of the Constitution for the Federation Of Earth at the Second Session of the World Constituent Assembly held at Innsbruck, Austria, in June of 1977. Others may not realize the relevance of the subsequent sessions of the Provisional World Parliament to the accomplishment of the objective.

In this brief review, we want to emphasize that the organization of the sessions of the World Constituent Assembly and the drafting of the Constitution for the Federation of Earth was carried forward from stage to stage in an orderly fashion. To begin with, from 1958 onwards, we have at all times sought and invited the participation of both national governments and the people of all countries. The original "Agreement To Call A World Constitutional Convention," circulated from 1958 to 1961, was drawn in terms of inviting both national governments or national parliaments and the people of each country to send delegates. Several thousand eminent persons from all over the world signed this Agreement, including a number of former Prime Ministers and Cabinet Ministers, many Nobel Laureates, and others of like distinction. When the Call to the first session of the World Constitutional Convention was issued in 1963, five Heads of State and Government were among the distinguished signers from more than 50 countries of all continents. As the years

passed, however, and 300 "Peoples Delegates" committed themselves to attend, it became necessary to make the decision to convene the first drafting session in 1968, even if no governments sent delegates, although the invitation remained open.

Under these circumstances, meeting in the City Hall of Wolfach, West Germany, work was begun at the 1968 session by peoples' delegates only, on the task of debating and drafting the world constitution - which came to be known as the Constitution for the Federation of Earth. In this drafting work, the delegates followed an orderly process, using as their guide "The Comprehensive Outline for the Debate and Drafting of a World Constitution," which had been initiated at the 2nd Preparatory Conference at Milan, Italy, in 1965. Following the 1968 session, a special drafting commission, or Committee of Detail, worked intensively for more than two months to complete a first draft. This first draft was then submitted to more than 1,000 persons all over the world for study and comments. After receiving comments, the Committee of Detail met again and prepared a revised draft. The revised draft was then circulated worldwide with a new Call to the second session, now called the World Constituent Assembly. The revised draft, and the call with invitation to send delegates, was sent to all national governments, as well as people.

When the 2nd Session of the World Constituent Assembly met at Innsbruck, Austria, in June of 1977, those delegates concerned with drafting a world constitution went over the submitted draft paragraph by paragraph, sentence by sentence, and made various amendments before submitting to the plenary session. After much debate, the Constitution for the Federation of Earth was adopted with only one dissenting vote and initially signed by 138 participants from 25 countries of 6 continents. At the same time, a Universal Call for Ratification by the Nations and People of Earth was issued. Subsequently, both the Call for Ratification and the Earth Constitution were sent to the United Nations and to all national govern-

Exhibit M1

Before a final ratification campaign, we of the World Constitution and Parliament Association and of the Provisional World Parliament, have anticipated a fourth session of the World Constituent Assembly in the near future, to review the Constitution for the Federation of Earth and to amend where found desirable. In view of both growing world crises and growing interest in a world constituent assembly, we should like to offer now the following proposal for moving ahead rapidly and effectively:

1. All those desiring a World Constitutional Convention or World Constituent Assembly are invited to work together for the next three years, in concert with the World Constitution and Parliament Association and the Provisional World Parliament and Provisional World Government, with the aim to convene the next World Constituent Assembly during the latter part of 1990.

2. Since the Constitution for the Federation of Earth is ready now, is comprehensive, is adequate for the problems of today and also of the 21st century, was developed and agreed at earlier sessions of a World Constituent Assembly with participation by several thousand persons from all continents, has already achieved world-wide circulation and widespread acceptance, therefore the Constitution for the Federation of Earth is taken as the basic document of the Assembly, but open to thorough review and amendments.

3. Any government, group or individual wishing to propose an amendment or amendments to the Earth Constitution shall be invited to prepare precise proposal(s) for amendment in good and competent style in advance of the 1990 Assembly, such proposed amendment(s) to be submitted first to a special committee to review proposed amendments.

4. The 1990 Assembly shall be called the 4th Session of the World Constituent Assembly.

5. The World Constituent Assembly of 1990 shall be composed of delegates invited from both national governments or national parliaments, and from people of all countries.

6. For doing serious work, the 1990 World Constituent Assembly shall be organized to continue for a period of two months, unless the work is satisfactorily completed before then.

7. A budget for the 1990 Assembly shall be prepared which will enable the sessions to continue for two months, covering the expenses of delegates; and a finance drive shall be organized to raise the necessary funds from both governmental and non-governmental sources well in advance.

8. The exact location and date for the 1990 Assembly shall be fixed by the Preparatory Committee (see point #10, below) at least one year in advance.

9. Preference for location shall be given to a country whose national government or legislature has already given Provisional Ratification to the Constitution for the Federation of Earth.

10. The Preparatory Committee for the 1990 4th Session of the World Constituent Assembly, shall include:

A. Five members elected by the Presidium of the Provisional World Government, which has been established under Article 19 of the Constitution for the Federation of Earth.

B. Two members appointed by each National Government or National Legislature which gives provisional ratification to the Constitution for the Federation of Earth in advance of convening the 4th Session of the World Constituent Assembly.

C. Five members elected by the Executive Cabinet of the World Constitution and Parliament Association, as the organization which has made the most substantial and constructive and specific progress towards the objective of democratic world government under a constitution for world federation, during the past 30 years.

D. Two members elected/appointed by each supra-national organization with active members and groups of members in at least seven countries, and agreeing to this plan.

E. One member elected/appointed by each national organization, or international organizations with active groups in less than seven countries, which agree to this plan for the 1990 World Constituent Assembly, and agree to make promotion of the Assembly as defined herein a major part of its program during the next three years.

Those who agree to this plan shall come themselves or authorize others to meet no later than November, 1988, to define all details, to adopt the budget, to issue the definitive Call to the Assembly, and to establish all necessary working sub-committees. The place of this meeting may be Nepal, or such location as shall be determined by June, 1988.

Exhibit M2

Sponsors and Collaborating Organizations

(NOTE: Exhibit N reveals some of those sponsors and collaborating organizations who have endorsed the agenda of the WCPA and are willing to have their names identified with the organization in order to encourage the participation of other people.)

world constitution, together with a World Parliament and a World Government functioning under that constitution.

One further historical reference may be made, on this 200th anniversary of the drafting of the Constitution for the Federal Government of the U.S.A., and that is to the circumstances under which that long enduring constitution was actually produced in 1787. As some of you may recall, that Convention of 1787 was actually convened to correct the defects in the Articles of Confederation, rather than to draft a new constitution for a strong federal government, although a number of the delegates were of the opinion that a strong federal government was required. As it happened, one delegate had the foresight to come to that 1787 Convention with a clear and detailed draft of a new constitution for a strong federal government for the United States.

As may be seen from history, a comprehensive outline or the complete draft of a constitution, if well designed, can serve as a very propitious beginning for effective work by a Constitutional Convention.

Exhibit M3

ORGANIZATIONS WHICH ARE COLLABORATING IN THE PREPARATORY COMMITTEE
FOR THE WORLD CONSTITUENT ASSEMBLY TO CONVENE ON 2ND APRIL 1991

(Partial List -- More Being Added)

Each Collaborating Organization Names Delegate(s) to the Preparatory Committee

ORGANIZATION	Base Country
Africa Network Prof. Dennis Brutus, President	U.S.A.
Agboye Organization High Chief Prof J.O. Agboye, Pres.	Nigeria
All India Camping Association Zulfy Lalani, President	India
All India Crime Prevention Society B. P. Nigam, President	India
All India Fed. Backward Classes, Scheduled Castes and Tribes, and Religious Minorities Ram Awadhesh Singh, President	India
American Movement World Gov't Arnold H. Bergier, President	U.S.A.
Arkadas - Independent Newspaper Yasar Ozturk, Secretary	Turkey
Asian Environmental Society Dr. Desh Bandhu, Secretary	India
Asian Youth Centre Ms. V. Krishnaveni, Secretary	India
Assn. Cultural Concejo Comunero Daniel G. de Culla, President	Spain
Assn. des Etudes Internationales Rachid Driss, President	Tunisia
Association for Voluntary Action Ashutosh Chakrapani, Exec.Secy	India
Association for World Education Aage Rosendal Nielsen, Pres.	Denmark
Bangladesh American Friendship Assn. Kh. Soleman Ahamed, Chairman	Bangladesh
Bangladesh Branch of W.C.P.A. E.A. Anwarul Majid, President	Bangladesh
Bangladesh Human Rights Comm. Akram H. Chowdhury, Secy-Gen.	Bangladesh
Bethel Apostolic Church Rev. Isaac Mensah	Cote d'Ivoire
Buddhist Education Society of India Dr. Dauji Gupta, President	India
Caribbean Action Group Dr. Roy Johnston, President	Jamaica
Centre for Communication & Dev. Swapan Mukhertee, Secy-Gen.	India
Christ Apostolic Church Pastor A.A. Eringuwade, Pres.	Cote d'Ivoire
Christian Youth Fellowship Kingsley Uwuigbe, President	Nigeria
Church of Christ, Inc. Rev. Bessekon Yapi Jean, Pres.	Cote d'Ivoire
Civil Service International Samson Jayasinghe, Nat. Secy	Sri Lanka
Cote d'Ivoire Branch W.C.P.A. Dr. P. K. Glover-Hemans, Pres.	Cote d'Ivoire
Council for Dev., Environmental Studies and Conservation Rajen Awotar, Chairman	Mauritius
Depdikbud Universitas Hasanuddin Ir. Hasan Basri	Indonesia
Desert Environ. Conservation Org. Dr. S. L. Harsha, Secy	India
Earth Light Network Ms. Beverley L. Brenner, Pres.	U.S.A.
Earth Paradise Movement B. S. Gunawardhana, Pres.	Sri Lanka
Eglise Evangelique de Delivrance Rev. Tsiku Koku Dzidonu	Cote d'Ivoire
English Speaking Union S. D. Pandey	India

ORGANIZATION	Base Country
English Speaking Union Dr. T. P. Amerasinghe, Pres.	Sri Lanka
Environmental Conservation Soc. Dr. Tej Prakash Vyas, Pres.	India
Environment Preservation Society Ashutosh Upadhyaya, Chairperson	India
Federation of Christian Churches Johnson S. Khan, Secy-Gen.	Pakistan
Fellowship of Reconciliation, India Mathew George, Secy	India
Free World Republic Emil O. Peter	W. Germany
Fundacao Cidade da Paz Mauricio A. Ribeiro, Exec. V.P.	Brazil
Future In Our Hands Segar Krishnan, President	Malaysia
German Branch of W.C.P.A. Emil O. Peter, President	W. Germany
Gesellschaft fur Bedrohte Volker Tilman Zulch, President	W. Germany
Global Futures Network Rashmi Mayur, President	India
Globe-Lib John R. Ewbank, President	U.S.A.
Gospel Faith Mission Rev. Ebenezer Jackie-Otoo	Cote d'Ivoire
Gram Mangalam Sultanpur Shankarbhai N. Patel, Pres.	India
Grassroots Mufrad Jamal, President	Bangladesh
Green Assn. Protection of Life Earo Palobeime, President	Finland
Groupe Solaire le Bon Samaritan Rev. Dr. Gouin Cedieu, Pres.	Cote d'Ivoire
Humanist Movement of Iran Dr. Adnan Mazarei, Pres.	Iran
Indian Housewives Federation Miss Lianmangi Fanai, Jt. Secy	India
Indian Youth for Dev. & Coop. Ashis Kumar De, President	India
Inst. des Affaires Internationales Rodny Daniel, Chairman	France
Integrated Rural Comm. Dev. Soc. P. Stephen, Programme Coord.	India
Int. Assn. of Educators World Peace Dr. Charles Mercieca, Exec. V.P.	U.S.A.
Int. Council Christian Churches T. F. Hutton, President	Cote d'Ivoire
Int. Federation of Religions Dr. Suchart Kosolkitiwong, Pres.	Thailand
International Friendship League Mario Franco, Coordinator	Portugal
International Keisei Institute Ms. Sumiko Nishino, V.P.	Japan
International Peace Organization Amjad Mahmood, Secretary	Pakistan
Japanese Branch of WCPA Dr. Takeshi Haruki, Pres.	Japan
Japan Womens Council World Fed. Mrs. Sumi Yukama, Pres.	Japan
Justicia y Pau Joan Gomis, President	Spain
Kumasi Youngsters Club Davis Darko, Secretary	Cote d'Ivoire
Lanka Jathika Sarvodaya Shramadana Sangamaya Dr. A.T. Ariyaratne, Pres.	Sri Lanka

Note to Collaborating Organizations: Please examine this list carefully. If any correction is needed, please inform the Secretary of the Preparatory Committee. Please include both the name and position or title of the contact person for an organization, if a change is needed, as well as any change in address. Thank you, The Secretary.

Exhibit N1

COLLABORATING ORGANIZATIONS - Page 2

ORGANIZATION	Base Country	ORGANIZATION	Base Country
League of World Peace Org. A. O. Osaguona, Jr., Pres.	Nigeria	Service Civil International Sanowar Hossain, Nat. Secy	Bangladesh
Madras Group W. J. Arputharaj, Chairperson	India	Servicio Paz y Justicia Nelson Curbelo, Coordinator	Ecuador
Mauritian Branch of WCPA	Mauritius	Smoking & Intoxicant Preventive	Bangladesh
Mauritius Action Disarm. & Peace Soodhakur Ramlallah, President	Mauritius	Human Service Association Md. Maniruzzman, Secy	
Mayan Indigenous Community Hunbatz Men, President	Mexico	Soc. for Northern Samar Dev. Lt. Col. Pedro B. Merida	Philippines
Millennium Project, The Dr. J.A. Kovelman, President	U.S.A.	Soc. Protect. Cruelty to Animals D. H. Balachandra, President	Sri Lanka
Min. Spiritual Soldats de Dieu Rev. Aboua Thomas, Pres.	Cote d'Ivoire	Sotaen Nigeria Limited Solomon O. Aghotaen	Nigeria
Movm't for World Political Union Jorgen Laursen Vig, President	Denmark	Sri Lanka Branch of WCPA T. P. Amerasinghe, Pres.	Sri Lanka
Nat. Council of Christian Churches Apostle J.W. Mensah, Pres.	Cote d'Ivoire	Swedish-Asia Cooperation Ms. Anna G. Eriksson, Pres.	Sweden
National Youth Organization M. Fazlul Haque, Pres.	Bangladesh	Tanzania Environmental Society Hussein J. Chomba	Tanzania
Nepal Branch of WCPA Hon. M. B. Pradan, Pres.	Nepal	Third World Network of Sci. Org. M. H. A. Hassan, Secy-Gen.	Italy
Oduwa Club Odigie T. Felix, President	Nigeria	Twelve Apostles Church Rev. Isaac Mensah, Pres.	Cote d'Ivoire
One World Movement Errol E. Harris, President	England	Union of Arab Jurists Shabib Al-Maliki, Secy-Gen.	Iraq
Oecumenical Social Echo Found. Johnson D. McJonah, Pres.	Nigeria	United Club MD Mozammel Haque, Dir.	Bangladesh
Oscar A. Romero Cathedra Lic. J. Artavia Alpizar, Dir.	Costa Rica	United Globe Association Prof. N. R. Kaley, Pres.	India
Pan-African Peace Congress Chief Akanbi Sanni, Secy	Nigeria	United Nations Assn. of Nigeria Mrs. Tina Uwechue, V. P.	Nigeria
Pan African Reconciliation Council Eben Ade. Adenekan, Secy-Gen.	Nigeria	United Peoples Robert Rosamond	U.S.A.
Papua New Guinea Inst. Med. Res. Dr. Michael Alpers, Pres.	Papua-New Guinea	Universal Correspondence Org. Prof. R. K. Jiwanmitra, Pres.	Nepal
Partido Verde Dr. Jose L. Barcelo, Pres.	Spain	Univ. Great Brotherhood Solar Line Domingo Diaz Porta, Pres.	Venezuela
Paz y Cooperacion Joaquin Antuna	Spain	War and Peace Foundation Ms. Selma Brackman, Pres.	U.S.A.
Int. Foundation for Survival and Development of Humanity	U.S.S.R.	Weltfoderalisten e.V. Gerhard Havel, President	W. Germany
Pentecostal Church of God Bishop K. A. Charles, Pres.	Cote d'Ivoire	World Citizens Assembly Dr. L. W. Green, Chairperson	U.S.A.
People's Inst. Participatory Action and Research R. N. Hota, Adm. Officer	India	World Citizens Registry, Canada Mrs. Helen Tucker	Canada
Progressive Group of Bombay Dr. D. M. Spencer	India	World Constitution & Parliament (Global) Philip Isely, Secy-Gen.	U.S.A.
Provisional World Cabinet Dr. T. Amerasinghe (Sri Lanka) Margaret Isely (USA) Philip Isely (USA) Ratansinh Rajda (India) Reinhart Ruge (Mexico)	GLOBAL	World Democracy News Rick Wicks, President	U.S.A.
		World Federalist Youth Tilak Amerasinghe, Secy	Sri Lanka
		World Gen. Elections Movement B. S. Gunawardhana, Pres.	Sri Lanka
Rainbow Coalition, California Scott J. Starquester	U.S.A.	World Health Found. for Peace Dr. Carlos Warter, Pres.	Chile
Royal Reigns Ministry Rev. Cedric Somian	Cote d'Ivoire	World Muslim Congress Dr. I. Khan, Secy-General	Pakistan
Sakai Citizens' Conference of Peace and Democracy Rev. Dr. B. Tsuchiyama, Pres.	Japan	World Survival Foundation Patrick Fox, Secy	U.S.A.
		World Union International Samar Basu, Secy-General	India
Save Our Shores Ms. Beth S. Leeds, Pres.	U.S.A.	Youth and Students Union Akbar Ali Saleh, President	Comoros
Save the Children Dr. Olaf H. Pongratz, Pres.	Austria	Youth for Dev. & Cooperation Jan Pakulski, Secretary	Netherlands
Humanist Movement of Iran	Iran	South Asia Association of NGOs	Pakistan

OTHER ORGANIZATIONS ARE INVITED to join as Collaborating Organizations.

Please complete the supporting resolution, which may be adopted by any organization in any part of the world desiring to assist this endeavor for the survival and welfare of humanity on Earth. For further information, write to: PREPARATORY COMMITTEE for the World Constituent Assembly, 1480 Hoyt Street, Suite 31, Lakewood, Colorado 80215, USA. FAX 303-526-2185 or 303-233-4800. Phone (303) 233-3548 or 526-0463. (No collect calls.) Contributions invited!

Exhibit N2

RECENT ADDITIONS TO THE LIST OF HONORARY SPONSORS
for the World Constituent Assembly
and the Provisional World Parliament

DR. KALMAN ABRAHAM, Hungary
M.P.; Engineer; Govt. Minister;
Pres. Nat. Authority for Protection
of Environment

DR. MALCOLM S. ADISESHIAH, India
Development Economist; M.P.;
was Dep. Director General UNESCO

FAKHRUDDIN AHMED, Bangladesh
Recent Foreign Secretary; Ambassador
to Italy, FAO, Yugoslavia, Greece,
Portugal; High Commissioner to U.K.

DR. FRANCIS ALEXIS, Grenada
Barrister, Solicitor; M.P., Minister of
Labor; Attorney General; Dean Faculty
of Law, Univ. West Indies

DR. JOSE AYALA-LASSO, Ecuador
Ambassador to the U.N.; was Foreign
Minister of Ecuador; Ambassador to
Belgium, E.E.C., Italy, Peru

DR. KAMAL H. BATANOUNY, Egypt
Prof. of Ecology Cairo Univ.; Pres.
Int. Organization for Human Ecology

DR. PETTER JAKOB BJERVE, Norway
Economist; was Minister of Finance;
Author "Planning in Norway"

DR. GOUIN CEDIEU, Cote d'Ivoire
Docteur au Pedagogie et Theologie;
Author, Le Bon Samaritain

DR. WILBERT K. CHAGULA, Tanzania
Recent Ambassador to United Nations;
former Minister for Water, Economic Affairs
& Development Planning; Chrmn., U.N.
Advisory Cttee Application of Science and
Technology to Development, 1975-79

DR. SRIPATI CHANDRASEKHAR, India and USA
Demographer and Economist; was M.P. and
Minister of State for Health & Family Planning;
Prof. at Universities in India and U.S.A.

ARCHBISHOP FRENCH CHANG-HIM, Seychelles
Bishop of Seychelles and Archbishop of the
Province of the Indian Ocean

DR. PRATAP CHANDRA CHUNDER, India
Lawyer; M.P.; Playwright; Editor; was
Minister Education, Social Welfare and
Culture

DR. KENNETH B. CLARK, U.S.A.
Psychologist; Professor Psychology;
Author; Sidney Hillman Prize Book Award

DR. DAVID DAUBE, Germany and USA
Professor of Jurisprudence and Law,
at Cambridge, Oxford, Univ. Calif., etc.

HON. JUSTICE ENOCH DUMBUTSHENA,
Zimbabwe
Chief Justice, 1984-90; was Lawyer, M.P.,
Member Constitutional Conferences;
Teacher and Journalist

DR. ADEMAYO ADEDEJI, Nigeria
U.N. Under Sec. Gen., and Exec. Sec. U.N.
Economic Comm. for Africa since 1975; Pres.,
African Assn. Public Admin. & Mngt. 74-83;
Author books on New Int. Economic Order.

DR. DAVID EASTON, Canada and U.S.A.
Prof. Political Science, Univ. Chicago,
Univ. California, Queens Univ.; was
Pres. Am. Political Science Assn.;
Author several books on Political Science

W. WILSON GOODE, U.S.A.
Mayor of Philadelphia since 1983

PROF. KAZIMIERZ KAKOL, Poland
Professor, Lawyer, Journalist;
Editor of Law and Life weekly;
Gov't Minister 1974-80

DR. JEROME KARLE, U.S.A.
Nobel Prize Chemistry, 1985; Pres. Int.
Union of Crystallography 81-84; Author
200 scientific articles

DR. DMITRI KAVTARADZE, U.S.S.R.
Principal Ecologist for State Committee
for Peoples Education; Head of Ecology
Lab, Moscow State Univ.

KHURSHED ALAM KHAN, India
Governor of State of Goa; was Foreign
Minister of India

HON. JUSTICE MICHAEL KIRBY, Australia
President, Court of Appeals, Supreme Court
of New South Wales; Chrmn., UNESCO Cttee
Experts on Rights of Peoples; on Exec. Cttee
International Commission of Jurists

DR. DAVID KRIEGER, U.S.A.
Attorney; Pres., Nuclear Age Peace
Foundation

DR. NIKOLAI A. LOGATCHEV, U.S.S.R.
Dir. Inst. of Earth's Crust; Member
Supreme Soviet USSR 1978-89; Chrmn.
Presidium E. Siberian Div. Academy of
Sciences

DR. JUR. ADAM LOPATKA, Poland
Deputy; First Pres. Supreme Court;
Pres. Polish Lawyers Assn. 1972-81; on
Exec. Cttee. Int. Inst. Rights of Man

DR. ABDEL SALAM MAJALI, Jordan
Dir. Gen., National Medical Inst.; was
Minister of Health, and of Education;
Chrmn. U.N. University Council; was
President, University of Jordan

MHLANGANO STEPHEN MATSEBULA,
Swaziland
Mem. National Council; was Minister
State for Foreign Affairs; Min. Labor
and Public Service

DR. ALI A. MAZRUI, Kenya and USA
Prof. Political Sc. and Humanities at
Makerere Univ., Harvard, Northwestern,
Univ. Michigan, State U. New York, etc.
Dir. African Sec. World Order Models
project

DR. RAM CHARAN MEHROTRA, India
Prof. Chemistry; was V. Chancellor Univ.
Rajasthan and Delhi; Pres. Indian Chemical
Soc.; participant in dozens of international
conferences

Exhibit N3

RECENT ADDITIONS TO THE LIST OF HONORARY SPONSORS - Page 2

DR. JUR. LAZAR MOJSOV, Yugoslavia
Mem. Collective Presidency 1984-88;
President, 1987-88; Pres. of 32nd
Session of U.N.; Perm. Rep. to U.N.,
1969-74; Chrmn. Security Council 1973;
Secretary Foreign Affairs, 1974-84.

HON. JUSTICE M.J.A. MOONS, Netherlands
Recent President Supreme Court of Nether-
lands, and of Benelux Court; Advocate
General 1958-66; Judge since 1966

A. T. MOORTHY, Sri Lanka and U.K.
Ambassador or Mem. Embassy to Indonesia,
China, Germany, Thailand, Iraq and
Pakistan; High Commissioner to U.K. 1961-63
and 1981-84; Mem. U.N. Comm. for Asia

DR. I. G. MURGULESCU, Romania
Prof. Physical Chemistry, Univ. Bucharest
(ret.); former Minister Education, and
Pres. Romanian Academy of Sciences; was
V. Pres. Council of State; active in Front
of National Salvation.

JOSEPH A. MURUMBI, Kenya
M. P. since 1963; was Minister of State,
and Minister External Affairs; V.Pres.
of Kenya, 1966; Asst. Sec. Movement
for Colonial Freedom 1952-58

PROF. DR. ENGELBERT MVENG, Cameroun
Sec. Gen. Pan-African Movement of
Christian Intellectuals; Prof. History; Co-
Pres. World Conf. Religion & Peace;
Co-Founder, Union of Black Writers

PROF. GABRIEL OLAKUNLE OLUSANYA, Nigeria
Director General., Nigerian Institute of
International Affairs

AMOS OZ, Israel
Novelist; Winner of France's Best
Foreign Novel of 1988

PROF. LENARD PAL, Hungary
Physicist; Pres. State Office for Technology
Development 1978-85; Gen. Sec. Hungarian
Academy Sciences 1980-84; Pres. Intercosmos
Council 1980-84; Author 275 Scientific Articles

PROF. M. S. RAJAN, India
Dir., Indian School Int. Studies 1965-71, Prof.
Int. Org. at J. Nehru Univ. 1971-onwards;
Sec. Ext. Affairs of Nauru, 1984-86, Author,
India in World Affairs, Studies on Non-Alignment

DR. CHINTAMANI N. R. RAO, India
Chemistry Prof. at many universities India,
U.S.A., and U.K.; Dir., Indian Institute of
Sciences; Founding mem. Third World Academy
Sciences; V. Pres. Indian Acad. Sciences;
Author, 500 research papers

DR. S. K. SAXENA, India and Canada
Director, International Cooperative
Alliance, 1968-81; now Consultant on
International Social & Economic Dev.;
Faculty Environmental Sc., York Univ.

DR. GLENN T. SEABORG, U.S.A.
Nobel Prize Chemistry, 1951; Chrmn. U.S.
Atomic Energy Comm. 1961-71; Professor
and former Chancellor Univ. Calif. at
Berkeley; Assoc. Dir., Lawrence Berkeley
Labs.; Pres. Int. Platform Assn; was Pres.,
Int. Org. Chemical Sciences in Development

PROF. DENNIS BRUTUS, South Africa & USA
Educator and Poet; Prof. at several Univs.
U.S.A. and England since 1939; Chrmn.,
Africa Network; V.Pres. Union of Writers
of African People; Many awards.

DR. KEWAL SINGH, India
Foreign Secretary, 1972-76; Ambassador to
Cambodia, Sweden, Denmark, Finland, U.S.S.R.,
the U.S.A.; High Commissioner to U.K.;
Pakistan; Gov't delegate to numerous Int.
conferences; Prof., Visiting Professor at
Universities in USA

DR. M. S. SWAMINATHAN, India
Dir., Centre for Research on Sustainable
Agric. & Rural Dev.; was Dir. Gen., Int.
Rice Research Inst. in Philippines; Pres.,
Int. Fed. Agric. Research Systems for Dev.;
Author 200 research papers

HOMI J. H. TALEYARKHAN, India
Recent Governor of Sikkim; was Amb. to Italy,
FAO, and Libya; Union Minister of State;
Indian delegate many Int. conferences; Pres.
or Chrmn., various cttees and councils on
ecology, minorities, trade and development,
family planning, etc.; Author, numerous books

ANDIMBA TOIVO YA TOIVO, Namibia
Co-Founder, then Sec.-Gen., Southwest
Africa People's Organization; was leader
SWAPO delegation to U.N.; Now: Minister of
                                   Mines & Industry

TOMOS, China (Mongolia)
Well-known Chinese oil painter; Dean of
Fine Arts, Inner Mongolia Normal College

DR. SANTIAGO TORRES-BERNARDEZ, Spain
Lawyer; Member many U.N. Committees
on legal matters incl. Law of Sea,
Humanitarian Law, etc.; Registrar at
World Court

ARCHBISHOP DESMOND M. B. TUTU,
South Africa
Nobel Peace Prize 1984; Archbishop of
Cape Town, Bishop of Johannesburg;
was Sec. Gen., S. African Council Churches

DR. GEORGE WALD, U.S.A.
Nobel Laureate in Medicine; Prof. Biology at
Harvard since 1935; V.Pres.Permanent Peoples'
Tribunal at Rome since 1980; leading participant,
speaker many peace conventions and movements

DR. DAVID ALAN WALKER, England
Prof. and Dir. Research Institute of
Photosynthesis; Author 150 publications

DR. LYALL WATSON, Ireland
Biologist; Conservationist; Television Producer
and Presenter, BBC; organizer of numerous
expeditions; Author of Earthworks, Super-
nature, and other studies

RICHARD WILBUR, U.S.A.
Prof. English; Poet; Pulitizer Prize 1957;
Pres. and Chancellor Am. Academy Arts
and Letters.

DR. JUR. SYLWESTER ZAWADZKI, Poland
Lawyer; Prof. Constitutional Law, Warsaw
Univ. since 1968; Minister of Justice 1981-83;
Member of Syem since 1972; Chairman
Council Ministers 1981-86; V. Pres. Int.
Assn. of Constitutional Law 1987

DR. LINUS PAULING, U.S.A.
Professor of Chemistry; Nobel Prize in
Chemistry, 1954; Nobel Prize for Peace,.
1962; Lenin Prize, 1970; Pres. Linus
Pauling Inst. of Science and Medicine

HONORARY SPONSORS -- SECOND ADDENDUM, 15 May, 1990

EGIL AARVIK, M.P., Norway
Member Parliament; President of Lagting
several years from 1974; Chairman,
Norwegian Nobel Committee.

EDWARD ASNER, U.S.A.
Actor; Pres. Screen Actors Guild, 1981-85;
recipient 5 Golden Globe and 7 Emmy Awards.

RT. HON. TONY BENN, M.P., United Kingdom
Member Parliament since 1950; was Chrmn.
Labor Party; was Minister of Technology and
Power; was Sec. of State for Industry, and
for Energy.

SHANTI BHUSHAN, LL.B., India
Senior Advocate at Supreme Court; Minister
of Law and Justice, 1977-79; Leader India
Del. to U.N. Confs. Law of Sea; Treas.
Bharatiya Party, 1979-86.

CHEN MINGYUAN, China
Computer Scientist and Poet; Author,
Information Processing of Chinese Language,
Linguistics and Modern Science, etc.; V.Pres.
Beijing Poetry Assn; Prof. Buddhist Culture.

HON. JUSTICE MARK DE WEERDT, Canada
Senior Judge, Supreme Court, Northwest
Territories; Dir., Canadian Inst. Admin. of
Justice, and Canadian Judicial Council;
Adv., Human Rights Institute.

BALKRISHNA V. DOSHI, India
Architect and Planner; Dir., then Chrmn.,
then Dean, Centre for Environmental Planning
and Tech., Ahmedabad, since 1972; Dir. Vastu-
Shilpa Found. for Environmental Design.

ALEXANDER DUBCEK, Czechoslovakia
Pres. of Federal Assembly; Beginning in 1962,
was Mem. Presidium, then Sec. Central Cttee
of CP of Slovakia, then Czechoslovakia; then
Mem. Exec. Cttee Presidium, then Chairman
of Fed. Assembly, 1969, again currently.

PROF. DR. HANS-PETER DUERR, Germany
Physicist; Mem. Directorate Max-Planck
Inst. fur Physik, 1971-on, then Chrmn., from
1977; Chrmn. Bd. Global Challenges Network;
on Exec. Committee Greenpeace.

DR. ROLF EDBERG, Sweden
Journalist; Editor several Newspapers; M.P.,
1941-56; Del. to U.N. 1952-61; Governor,
Varmland Prof. 1967-77; Del. to Disarmament Conf.; Pres. Stockholm Int. Peace Inst.
1973-78; Author, A House in the Cosmos,
and on political, ecological subjects.

NZO EKANGAKI, Cameroon
Sec. Gen., Org. African Unity, 1972-74;
Adviser to Presidency since 1985; M.P. many
years; was Min. Foreign Affairs, Public
Health & Pop., Labour and Social Welfare;
Del. to sev. Int. Labor Confs.; Party Secy.

DR. ANATOLY ANDREYEVICH GROMYKO, USSR
Dir., Africa Inst. of USSR Academy Sciences
since 1976; was Minister Plenipotentiary,
Washington Embassy; Prof. Social Sciences;
Author many books; son of Andrey Gromyko.

DR. H. ROBERTO HERRERA CACERES, Honduras
Prof. Int. Law, Honduras Univ.; Amb. to U.N.
1983-86; V.Chrmn. U.N. Legal Cttee; Mem. Perm.
Court Arbitration, The Hague, since 1977, Spec.
on Law of Sea; Ambassador sev. countries.

BAL RAM JAKHAR, India
M.P.; Speaker of Lok Sabha, 1980-89; was
Pres. Commonwealth Parliamentary Assn.;
Hon. Speaker, 1983 Session of Provisional
World Parliament.

JAN KAROL KOSTRZEWSKI, M.D., Poland
Prof. Epidemiology; Pres. Polish Academy
Sciences, 1984-88; Minister, Health & Social
Welfare, 1968-72; M.P. since 1985; Chrmn.
Presidium, Ecological Social Movement.

BEN M. LEITO, Netherlands Antilles
M.P., 1959-62; Lt. Gov. 1968-70, then
Governor, 1969-83; was Pres., Bank of
Netherlands Ant. 1965-70; now Mem.
Council of State of Netherlands.

DR. MRS. ALLA GENRIKHOVNA MASSEVITCH,
U.S.S.R. - Astronomer; Prof. Astrophysics,
Moscow Univ. since 1946; V.Pres., Astronom-
ical Council, Soviet Acad. Sciences since
1972; Chrmn. Cttee for Space Research;
V.Pres., Soviet Peace Cttee, and USSR-USA
Friendship Society.

HON. KEBA M'BAYE, Senegal
Judge at Int. Court Justice, The Hague, since
1982, V.Pres. since 1987; fmr Pres. Supreme
Court, Senegal; fmr. Chrmn. Comm. on Human
Rights, and Int. Cttee on Comparative Law.

MIHAJLO MIHAJLOV, Yugoslavia, living USA
Former Prof. Zagreb Univ.; later Lecturer and
Prof. Univs. in USA; V.Pres., Democracy Int.;
Commentator, Radio Free Europe; on Ed. Brd.
Kontinent, Tribunia, and Forum Mags.; author
Planetary Consciousness.

MOHAMED EZZEDINE MILI, Tunisia
Dpty Sec. Gen., then Sec. Gen., Int. Telecommunications Union, 1965-82; Chief Del.
of Tunisia to I.T.U. Conferences.

RAM NIWAS MIRDHA, India
M.P., Rajya Sabha, since 1967; fmr. Minister
Home Affairs, of Supply and Rehabilitation,
of External Affairs, of Communications, of
Textiles, of Health & Family Welfare; Hon.
Pres. World Fed. of U.N. Associations.

GERARD PIEL, U.S.A.
Founder, Publisher and Editor of Scientific
American since 1947; then Chrmn. Board;
Trustee many human welfare organizations.

DR. BLAGOVEST CHRISTOV SENDOV, Bulgaria
Prof. Computer Sciences, 1963-67, then
Dean Math., then Rector Univ. Sofia, 1973-
79; M.P. Since 1976; now Pres. Bulgarian
Acad. Sciences; Hon. Pres. Int. Assn. Univ.;
Ex. Cttee Int. Foundation for Survival and
Development of Humanity.

PROF. JOSEF SIMUTH, Czechoslovakia
Prof. Molecular Biology, specialist Gene-
ingenering of Food, Int. Legis. for Control
of Recombinant DNA.

HON. ROBERT D. G. STANBURY, P.C., Q.C.,
Canada - Lawyer; fmr, Member Parliament;
fmr. Minister Commun., and of Revenue;
Del. to U.N. 1974-76; Gen. Counsel and CEO,
Firestone Canada; Chmn/CEO Globescope, Inc.
Globescope, Inc.

OLIVER STONE, U.S.A.
Film Dir. and Screen Writer; Academy Award,
Best Dir., "Born on 4th of July," 1990, also
Best Picture, Best Dir., "Platoon," 1986; other
pictures: Salvador, Wall Street, Talk Radio.

Exhibit N5

HONORARY SPONSORS — ADDENDUM, 20 April, 1990

ATIKU ABUBAKAR, Nigeria
Business Executive, Politician.

DR. SAMIR AMIN, Egypt and Senegal
Dir., U.N. African Inst. Economic Dev.
and Planning; African Bureau in Senegal
of Third World Form; Prof. Economics.

DR. NASSIR EL-DIN EL-ASSAD, Jordan
Pres., Royal Academy Islamic Civilization
Research; former Minister of Higher
Education; Pres., Univ. of Jordan, 1962-80.

DR. HENRY R. CASSIRER, France
Dir., Mass Media in Education for UNESCO;
producer TV documentaries, and Univ.
Teacher of TV and public affairs program-
ming; consultant to many developing
countries on use of Mass Media.

PIETER VAN DIJK, S.J.D., Netherlands
Prof., International Law at Utrecht Univ.
and Univ. Michigan; Chrmn. Netherlands
Institute Human Rights since 1982; Delegate
to U.N. 1981, 1983, and 1986; author.

MAJHEMOUT DIOP, Senegal
Sec-Gen, then President of Parti Africain
de l'Independence; active in many
organizations; pharmacist; politician.

EMMANUEL U. EMOYON, Nigeria
Prof. Chemistry; recent Minister of Science
& Technology; was V.Chan., Univ. of Jos;
recent Pres. Nigerian Academy of Sciences.

DR. MRS. PHULRENU GUHA, India
Social Worker, welfare of women and
children; Mem. Parliament, 1964-70;
Minister for Social Welfare, 1967-70; was Sec.
Gen. and V. Pres. All India Women's Conf.

JOHN HERSEY, U.S.A.
Writer; former editor, Time; author many
books; V.Pres., Author's League of America,
1948-54, then Pres., 1975-80; Professor at
Yale, since 1976; Chancellor, American
Academy Arts and Letters, 1981-84.

RYSZARD KAPUSCINSKI, Poland
Journalist; with Sztandar Mlodych, then
Polityka until 1961, then corres. Polish
Press Agency, and Kultura; Deputy Chrmn
Poland 2000 Cttee, Polish Acad. Sciences.

DR. JUL LAG, Norway
Prof. of Soil Science; Rector Agric. Univ.
Norway, 1968-71; then Chmn. Agric. Council
Norway; Pres., Norwegian Acad. Science
and Letters, 1976-84; author 8 books.

DR. BAL KRISHNA MADAN, India
Economist and Banker; Exec. Dir. Int.
Monetary Fund, 1946-50; was Exec. Dir.
then Deputy Gov. Reserve Bank of India;
on many U.N. and India Committees on
Economic Dev.; Chrmn Man. Dev. Inst.

JEAN-CLAUDE PECKER, France
Astronomer at Paris Observatory, then
Dir. of Nice Observatory; Gen. Sec., Int.
Astronomical Union 1961-67; then Dir.
Inst. Astrophysique, Paris; and Chrmn.
Nat. Cttee. Scientific and Tech. Culture

DR. RAMENDRA KUMAR PODDAR, India
Prof. Nuclear Physics at Saha Inst., then
Prof. Biophysics at Calcutta Univ., and
Vice Chancellor 1977-83; Member Parlia-
ment since 1985; V. Chrmn. Rajya Sabha.

DR. NICHOLAS POULIN, CBE, Switzerland
Pres., Foundation for Environmental Conservation, and World Council for Biosphere;
Editor, Environmental Conservation, since
1974; Sec.-Gen. several Int. Confs. on
Environmental Future; Prof. at many universities; author many books; Leisure interest:
developing new ideas into plans for action.

DR. JULIO PRADO-VALLEJO, Ecuador
Lawyer; Prof. at Univ. Cen. del Ecuador
since 1958; Minister Foreign Affairs, 1967-
68; was Pres. Inter-American Comm. Econ.
Cooperation; Mem. UN Human Rights Comm.

DR. ALEX QUAISON-SACKEY, Ghana
Barrister before Supreme Court; Ambassador
to U.N. 1959-65; Pres. U.N. General
Assembly 1964-65; Minister Foreign Affairs,
1965-66; was Ambassador to USA, Mexico,
and Cuba; Pres. Chana U.N. Assn.

DR. SAYE QASSEM RESHITIA, Afghanistan
Historian, Writer, Diplomat; was Editor,
Kabul Mag.; Minister of Information, 1956-
64; Pres., Gov't Economic Planning Brd.;
then Minister Finance; V.Chrmn., Constitution Drafting Comm.; Ambassador to U.N.
and to 8 countries; Del. to Non-Aligned
Conf.

JIRI SEQUENS, Czechoslovakia
Film and TV Director; Head film dept.,
Union of Czech. Dramatic and Film Artists;
Head Dept. Film & TV Directing of Acad.
Performing Arts; Director many films, TV
serials, documentaries.

DAVID SHAHAR, Israel
Writer; was Pres., Assn. Hebrew Writers;
Award from City of Jerusalem, Bialik
Prize of Tel-Aviv, Newman Prize of N.Y.
University.

IDOWA SOFOLA, Nigeria
Lawyer, Senior Advocate of Nigeria; recent
General Secretary, Nigerian Bar Assn., and
of International Bar Assn.

DR. MONKOMBU S. SWAMINATHAN, India
Geneticist; Dir. Gen., Indian Council Agric.
Research and Educ.; Dir. Gen. Int. Rice
Research Inst.; Chrmn. UN Advis. Cttee on
Science and Tech. for Dev.; Pres., Int. Fed.
of Agric. Research Systems for Dev.

DR. SOL TAX, U.S.A.
Prof. Emeritus Anthropology Univ. Chicago;
Editor, Current Anthropology and World
Anthropology; Pres., Int. Union Anthropo-
logical and Ethnological Sc., 1968-76; Dir.,
Council for Study of Mankind, 1963-79.

DR. WALTER E. THIRRING, Austria
Prof. of Physics, Universities of Berne,
of Vienna, of Mass. Inst. Tech., of
Washington; Author 120 scientific papers.

DR. DIMITRIOS J. DELIVANIS, Greece
Prof. Economics; fmr. Pres. Greek Econ.
Assn., Pres. Mediterranean Social Sc. Re-
search Cen., Rector, Univ. Salonika.

Exhibit N6

Design and Action for a New World

Design and Action For a New World, is the principal document being circulated by the WCPA to promote its global agenda (Exhibit O). The publication reproduces bills that have already been passed and enacted into World Law by the Provisional World Parliament. By showing how much progress has already been made toward the forming of a world government, it is hoped that credulous personalities from around the world will begin to support the Plan, creating a bandwagon effect.

The eleven bills that have been enacted at the first three sessions of the Provisional World Parliament are listed on the front cover. Bills 1 through 5 were enacted as World Law in Brighton, England, in September 1982 at the first session of the Provisional World Parliament. Bills 6 through 8 were enacted at the second session held in New Delhi, India, in March 1985. The final three bills became World Law in June 1987 at the third session of the Provisional World Parliament in Miami Beach, Florida. Bills 2, 7, and 11 deal with global finances and Bill 5 concerns the establishment of a World Court System. These four bills would most adversely affect Christians.

These acts and others yet to be proposed will become enforceable once national governments ratify the world constitution. They cannot become legally effective within a given nation unless that nation suspends its existing constitution (or significantly alters the same) and accepts the new world constitution. This would most likely occur in the United States through the holding of a constitutional convention.

The WCPA itself realizes that the ratification process "may take five or ten years or longer." Thus, according to its own projections, the formation of the world government would occur sometime between 1993 and 1998, since this document was printed in 1988.

On page one of *Design and Action* you will notice a "Partial List of World Problems" (Exhibit O2), which the WCPA cites as reasons for needing a world government. Of the forty-nine problems listed, a total of fifteen deal with the environment; seven relate to military concerns (disarmament, prevention of war and terrorism), six have to do with world hunger or poverty; and four deal with international monetary matters.

Notice that the WCPA cannot make up its mind as to whether we are heading into a global warming or a global ice age (Exhibit O2; Problem #15). . . . But whichever the case may be, it is a reason for a world government.

The WCPA effort to form a New World Order is not based on need but on the hidden agenda of the occult secret societies to bring the world under their control in order to usher in the reign of their "World Teacher": the Antichrist.

Exhibit O1

Design and Action For A New World

CHARTING THE ROUTE BY WHICH PEOPLE WHO WANT PEACE AND EQUITY CAN TAKE CHARGE OF WORLD AFFAIRS

Eleven Major Bills Enacted Into World Law At The First Three Sessions Of The

Provisional World Parliament

Organized under Article XIX of the Constitution for the Federation of Earth, meeting on 4th to 17th September, 1982, at Brighton, England; on 15th to 25th March, 1985, at New Delhi, India; and 18th to 28th June, 1987, at Miami Beach, Florida, U.S.A.

Bill #1, to Outlaw Nuclear Weapons and Other Weapons of Mass Destruction, and to Create a World Disarmament Agency	pages 3 - 6
Bill #2, for a World Economic Development Organization, to inaugurate a New World Economic Order	pages 7 - 8
Bill #3, for the Ownership, Administration and Development of the Oceans and Seabeds of Earth as the Common Heritage of the People of Earth	page 9
Bill #4, for a Graduate School of World Problems, as part of a World University System	pages 10 - 11
Bill #5, for Provisional District World Courts	pages 12 - 13
Bill #6, for an Emergency Earth Rescue Administration, particularly to save the Environment, together with a list of 35 benefits resulting from the implementation of Bill #6	pages 14 - 19
Bill #7, for a World Government Funding Corporation, to finance the entire program indicated by all measures defined in this booklet	pages 20 - 25
Bill #8, for a World Commission on Terrorism	page 26
Bill #9, to Protect Life and Nature on Planet Earth, and to Create a Global Ministry of Environment	pages 27 - 29
Bill #10, for a World Hydrogen Energy System Authority	pages 30 - 31
Bill #11, for an Earth Financial Credit Corporation	pages 32 - 35
Call for Ratification of the Constitution for the Federation of Earth, together with a diagram for World Government	pages 39 - 40
Call to the Provisional World Parliament	inside front and back covers

"Let us Raise A Standard To Which The Wise And The Honest Can Repair!"

PARTIAL LIST OF WORLD PROBLEMS

(which require a world legislature and a world government to devise and implement adequate solutions)

DEFINITION: World problems are problems which transcend national boundaries, and require that solutions be worked out and implemented on a global or trans-national basis, either in part or entirely. Most world problems overlap and are related to other world problems, and require inter-related solutions.

1. Nuclear weapons, spread of nuclear capability, threat of nuclear war and nuclear winter.

2. Other weapons of mass death and destruction.

3. International trade in armaments; many local wars which could escalate; constant military R&D creating pressure for new generations of weapons.

4. The entire process of disarmament: by what stages? unilateral or multilateral? how supervised? the strategy of nuclear freeze? what world political requirements for disarmament?

5. Conversion from armaments to a peaceful world economy. The decentralization and sub-contracting of weapons production and military R&D, pervading all aspects of society, which creates great pressure against disarmament.

6. Nearly a trillion dollars spent annually on war preparations, dominating government and civilian priorities, wasting money and resources, and sub-verting the world's scientific talents.

7. Nuclear energy production, which spreads the capability to produce nuclear weapons, has unsolved waste disposal problems, and opens doors for terrorists to get nuclear weapons.

8. Third world debt and development: Impossibility to continue re-cycling loans and debts under austerity conditions. Imminent collapse of global financial infra-structure without basic changes.

9. Transition to New World Economic Order: How can this be accomplished? What kind of new world finance, credit and money system, which can assure adequate development, full employment at useful work for all, and global economic equity?

10. Rapid increase of carbon dioxide in atmosphere, which may result in cataclysmic climatic changes. CO_2 increase coming from burning fossil fuels, massive de-forestation, and de-mineralization of soils.

11. Acid rain, and trans-national air pollution.

12. Soil erosion, loss of topsoil, increase of floods, decrease of agricultural productivity, but more people: global crises brewing.

13. Use of wood and animal dung for fuel, causing spreading deserts and loss of soil fertility.

14. Rapid cutting of rain forests for wood and agriculture, leading to loss of species and global climatic disaster because forests are needed to absorb CO_2.

15. Threat of a new ice age or melting polar caps: Which? How soon? Consequences? Can this be prevented? The global campaign required.

16. Global transition from fossil fuels and nuclear energy to safe and sustainable energy supplies.

17. Development of means of transportation not dependent on oil, coal or nuclear power.

18. Use of land to produce tobacco, alcoholic beverages, harmful drugs, sugar, and to satisfy meats diets, making shortage of land for essential food production.

19. Drought conditions which are increasing and spreading, resulting in starvation and migration of millions of people: Causes and cure?

20. Pressure of population on resources, and difficulties of birth control: How many can Earth carry?

21. Mal-distribution of world food supply, resulting in widespread mal-nutrition, resulting in widespread mental malfunctioning: threat to civilization.

22. Transnational pollution of fresh water supplies. Transnational demands on limited fresh water supplies.

23. Ocean pollution which threatens Earth's fish and oxygen supplies. Pollution of oceans from transport, drilling and pumping of oil: How long can this go on before death of the oceans?

24. Claims by nations of 200 miles offshore (the exclusive economic zone under proposed law of seas) which contain most of easily accessible ocean resources.

25. Worldwide use of pesticides harmful to people, which enter into world trade in food, while pests get more virulent.

26. Growing dependence of world food supply on mining water acquifers, plus increase of population in hot dry areas plus air conditioning: crises situations soon.

27. Rapidity of technological changes, resulting in technological unemployment, social and community instabilities, unforseen adverse ecological impacts.

28. Displacement of natural raw materials by synthetics, resulting in disruption of livlihoods of people in raw materials producing areas.

29. Vast disparities between hi-technology economies and manual labor or low-technology economies. The process of technology transfer so as to benefit everybody.

30. Worldwide rural poverty, excessive urbanization, unemployment, partial employment, social unrest.

31. Brain drains, and opportunities for educated people in less developed countries.

32. How to prevent technological mistakes (e.g., nuclear power, off-shore oil well drilling) and ensure the selective use of technology for life-betterment and ecologically safe purposes.

33. Tariffs, trade barriers, vast disparities in wage levels, inequitable access to resources and markets, movement of industries to low wage countries.

34. Regulation of multi-national corporations.

35. Global planning for wise use of natural resources as common heritage of humanity. Global priorities for investment and development.

36. Ownership of atmosphere and stratosphere. Space exploration as a global project.

37. Ethnic, religious, racial and political intolerances, regional wars, and problem of refugees.

38. Migrations or movements of people across national boundaries. Is freedom of travel and choice of place to live and work possible?

39. Violations and protection of human rights. Protection of minority rights. Do people also have global responsibilities for each other and posterity?

40. Terrorism: many forms and many causes.

41. Co-existence of differing political and economic systems: under what global conditions?

42. Unsolved local problems due to supra-national factors, leading to instabilities and dictatorships.

43. Attempts to escape from global problems by rationale that big is bad and that all problems can be solved locally or by individual transformation.

44. Teaching about history and world problems so that people will be prepared to live together peacefully and work out problems for the common good.

45. Language barriers, world communications, access to basic research, fair reporting of the news.

46. Difficulties for leaders of national governments and national parliaments to conceive of the kind of global political structure which is required to solve world problems peacefully, and to help take the necessary action to establish the required global political structure.

47. General lack of well informed and well motivated people with humane and global outlook to cope adequately with inter-related problems of living on Earth.

48. Big dams which silt up quickly, cause ecological damage.

49. Lack of funding for solving world problems.

DIAGRAM OF WORLD GOVERNMENT under the CONSTITUTION FOR THE FEDERATION OF EARTH

(The full text of the Constitution for the Federation of Earth is available from the World Constitution and Parliament Asssociation, 1480 Hoyt Street, Suite 31, Lakewood, Colorado 80215 U.S.A. 1 to 4 copies, $5.00 each; 5 or more copies, $3.00 each.)

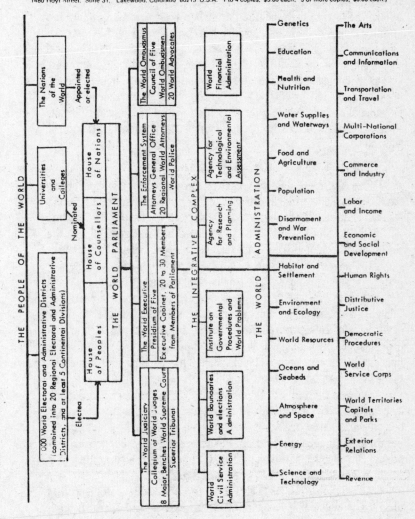

Exhibit O3

The proposed organizational structure of the world government is revealed on page 40 of *Design and Action* (Exhibit O3). According to the diagram, "We, the People" would sit alone at the top of this New World Order.

Do Christians really believe that they would have freedom of speech and worship under such a system? There has been only one other time during the post-flood era when the world became unified under a single system; this occurred at the building of the Tower of Babel in ancient Babylon. God responded by dispersing mankind and causing him to speak different languages. Had God not intervened, mankind would have become enslaved under the first Luciferic priesthood, established by Nimrod, the founder of the Ancient Mysteries and of pantheism. Is it a pure coincidence that Freemasonry, by its own admission, traces its roots through the Ancient Mysteries to Nimrod?

Climate Crisis

The single greatest propaganda effort by New Agers over the past few years has come in the area of the global environment. Countless environmental problems have been cited as reasons for needing world government. *Climate Crisis*, printed in February 1989 by the WCPA, offers "global solutions" to these alleged crises (Exhibit P).

On pages 2 through 8 of this publication is a "World Patriot Letter," which was sent to all Heads of State on 10 February 1989. (According to the WCPA, it is no longer acceptable to be a patriot of one's own country. We must now become patriots of the world in order to save the environment.) This letter (excerpts of which are reproduced in the exhibit) was the fourth appeal of its kind sent to world political leaders since July 1988; yet we have heard nothing about the WCPA from our leaders.

On pages 2 and 3 of the letter, the WCPA lists a chain reaction of events, which, it warns, will occur soon to the earth's climate if our environmental problems aren't solved at once. The letter continues on a lengthy discourse about the severity of the crisis, before proposing the WCPA's solution which is, of course, the formation of a world government (point B, page 6 of letter).

As part of its efforts in this direction, the WCPA points out that the Provisional World Parliament has already passed World Bill #6, creating the Emergency Earth Rescue Administration (Exhibit P3).

The WCPA is basing its main argument for a New World Order on its weakest cases—the threat of an impending climate crisis. To present his case, Isely relies on information from such alarmist New

Age organizations as the Earth Regeneration Society, the Institute for a Future and the Worldwatch Institute (bottom of page 7; see Exhibit P4) of which Isely is himself a member.

Many of the supposed environmental crises listed by the WCPA are scientifically debatable; others are completely unfounded. While there are legitimate concerns regarding the environment, the severity of the situation has been drastically overstated to create a "climate of panic," which is necessary for the acceptance of a world government.

Isely's gloomy scenario is constructed on the Theory of Inter-glacial Periods. This theory holds that ice ages last about ninety thousand years and are separated by brief inter-glacial periods of ten to twelve thousand years. According to Isely, we are nearing the end of one such period and are rapidly approaching the next ice age. In order to reverse this trend before it is too late, we must therefore establish a world government that will save us from destruction.

The problem with Isely's inter-glacial theory is that it is based on theories that are based on other theories. At some point, these theories began to be presented as fact in order to support the hidden agenda of globalists. Isely is quick to argue, "This is fact, not theory." (page 4, paragraph 2)

The most logical and scientific explanation of how the world's geography and climate have gotten to the present point is offered by Dr. Walter Brown, former National Science Foundation Fellow with the Massachusetts Institute of Technology. His book, entitled *In the Beginning*, is available for $9.00 (plus 10% shipping) by writing to:

Center for Scientific Creation
5612 N. 20th Place
Phoenix, Arizona 85016

Dr. Brown's evidence may surprise you. It contradicts Isely's conclusions by revealing that the earth is much younger than previously thought. Brown's conclusions, based on years of scientific research, contradict Isely's theories of inter-glacial periods.

Plan for an Earth Financial Credit Corporation

The following plan is being referred to by the WCPA as "The Key to a New World Economic Order" (page 1 along with other parts are excerpted in Exhibit Q). The plan offers unlimited, interest free credit to "all worthy projects" and proposes a single global monetary system and currency, while guaranteeing jobs for all. Many of these jobs would be in the area of cleaning up the environment. The plan also promises billions of dollars of annual savings resulting from zero

PROVISIONAL WORLD GOVERNMENT Including the PROVISIONAL WORLD PARLIAMENT

(This letter, individually addressed, has been sent to the Presidents, Prime Ministers, Kings, Queens, Sultans, and other Heads of Governments of all countries on Earth.)

Telefax: 303-526-9504, Attn. WCPA

1480 Hoyt St., Suite 31 / Lakewood, CO 80215 USA / 303-233-3548

10th February, 1989

Organized under THE
CONSTITUTION FOR THE
FEDERATION OF EARTH

*Serving until the
next session of the
PROVISIONAL
WORLD PARLIAMENT*

WORLD PRESIDIUM
Dr. Terence P. Amerasinghe
Sri Lanka
Margaret Isely
U.S.A
Hon. Shettima Ali Monguno
Nigeria
Shri Ratansinh Rajda, x-M.P.
India
Ing. Reinhart Ruge
Mexico

CABINET MINISTERS
EDUCATION
Dr. Terence P. Amerasinghe
EMERGENCY EARTH
RESCUE
Philip Isely
ENVIRONMENT
Dr. Rashmi Mayur
FINANCE
Philip Isely
HUMAN RIGHTS
Dr. Roy Johnstone
RATIFICATION
Ram Awadhesh Singh, M.P.
WORLD CITIZENSHIP
Helen Tucker

*Other Cabinet Ministries
in process of formation*

WORLD TREASURY
Served by World Government
Funding Corporation

Your Excellencies
Presidents, Prime Ministers, Kings, Queens, Sultans,
and other Heads of Governments of All Countries on Earth

Your Excellency and Decision Maker:

We wish to report a successful first meeting of the Preparatory Committee for the World Constituent Assembly, which is to convene at the end of 1990. We mentioned this meeting to you in our previous letters appealing for World Patriots, under dates of July 5, August 18, and September 1, 1988. The meeting was held in the Sky Garden room of the St. Moritz Hotel in New York, on 19 and 20th November, 1988.

A feature of the meeting was a special luncheon on November 19, attended by the United Nations Ambassadors or Deputy Ambassadors for twenty countries. At the luncheon, the plan for the World Constituent Assembly to convene near the end of 1990 was fully explained, and the draft of the Constitution for the Federation of Earth was given to each one present. Special emphasis was given to the problem of global climate change. A report on this first meeting of the Preparatory Committee was later sent to the Ambassadors at the United Nations of all countries, including yours.

In this fourth letter to Heads of Governments, appealing for action by World Patriots, we wish to give particular attention to the problem of climate change, which has been widely publicized during the past two years. Contrary to most warming predictions, however, there are very good reasons, as well as extensive scientific documentation and reports in the news, to believe that a different scenario is most likely, and therefore different strategy required to deal with the problem.

First, we will summarize the most likely sequence of events, and then analyze the situation in greater detail:

The much reported slight increase in average global temperature means very little. Any scientist should suspect gross error when basing predictions on the averaging of extremely variable temperatures of different latitudes. Rather than a general global warming, there is already evident and documented both a warming at lower latitudes and a cooling at higher latitudes. The cooling originates from increased cloud cover because of moisture-laden air moving polewards. The sun's rays will not get down long enough to melt the ice caps. The sea levels are not likely to rise. Lowlands are not likely to get flooded. Grain growing and agricultural production cannot shift to higher latitudes because increased snow cover and shorter growing seasons will make crop failures more and more certain.

"Let Us Raise A Standard To Which The Wise And The Honest Can Repair!"

Exhibit P1

sno\
.ure on 1.   .nic .   .g \
.ntinental pla   .nge on .   e faults

- Volcanoes will begin to erupt mo.   .ntly because   this pressure. The/ are
  already doing so. Earthquakes wi.   .ome more frequ.nt and violent. Read all
  about it in the daily news.

- Erupting volcanoes will emit great amounts of carbon dioxide into the atmosphere,
  and will also spread smoke and dust over wide areas, thus reducing the amount of
  sunlight reaching earth.

- By this time, rapid descent into the next ice age will be irreversible, if not long
  before. The ice age will probably last about 90,000 years, the same as previous ice
  ages.

- Although civilization will be mostly destroyed, a few million people may survive to
  begin again, provided nuclear weapons are not exploded also during the turbulence of
  the next two decades.

- It may be noted that with the increasing snow and ice, vast amounts of water
  absorbed from the oceans will be stored in snow and glaciers. The sea levels will
  then recede, not get higher.

Exhibit P2

..

..   .ajor .   .along with . .eral other actr. .iot describe .erein,
.imans n. oe able to . .g carbon dioxide levels back down to around 270 parts per
million, and maintain this inter-glacial balance for many thousands of years, with the
elimination of climate-changing chlorofluorocarbons.

These are the major elements of the emergency Earth rescue campaign which must go
forward quickly if we are to survive. The same sort of combined remedy would be
required even if the "greenhouse" effect was going to result in melting the ice caps
during the next few years. However, the reality of what is already happening with
both warming and cooling at the same time, requires much speedier action. Rather
than melting ice caps and flooding lowlands, the main hazards to overcome in 50 or
100 years are universal crop failures, food shortages and starvation, hurricanes and
forest fires, all in the context of a terminating inter-glacial period, unless corrective
measures are implemented very rapidly.

A more detailed outline of the necessary action (except for CFC control) is given in
the enclosed World Legislative Bill #6, recently adopted by the Provisional World
Parliament, to put into effect an EMERGENCY EARTH RESCUE ADMINISTRATION.
Please study World Legislative Bill #6. At least 30 other environmental problems are
also solved at the same time by implementing Bill #6.

To carry out this emergency campaign on the massive global scale that is essential,
three conditions are required:

A. The campaign must be conceived, organized, and carried out as a global trillion-
    dollar-a-year public and private works campaign, continuing over a period of at
    least 20 years. The first couple of years may start with less than a trillion.
    The campaign can employ all available persons, including those unemployed and
    those in national armies.

B. The campaign can be fully and successfully carried out only in the context of the
    organization and the practical emergence of a Federal World Government, which
    is given sufficient constitutional authority and finances to do all that is necessary.
    Otherwise, civilization is finished.

C. The resources, money, and human talents now used for national military purposes
    must be diverted to a global campaign for our mutual survival on Earth.

Our appeal and request, therefore, is that you as a Head of Government will take the
following immediate steps:

Exhibit P3

4th World Patriot Letter - page 7

1. Please study what we have written very carefully.

2. Invite the Heads of Governments of other countries to an emergency meeting where the problem and the remedy can be discussed very honestly, and action planned accordingly.

3. Join with other Heads of Government to convene such a meeting, if you believe a joint invitation to the meeting is better -- but please do not wait too long.

4. Invite some members of our initiative to the meeting to explain and to serve as consultants.

5. Come to such a meeting yourself, even if it is convened by the Heads of Governments of some other countries.

6. Plan on sending delegates, or come yourself, to participate in the World Constituent Assembly which will begin at the end of 1990. We will send further details. Please study the draft of the Constitution for the Federation of Earth beforehand.

Please reply without delay, directly or through your Ambassador. Let us know what you will do. There is no time to lose.

Most sincerely yours, for adequate action in time for the Survival of Humanity on Earth,

Philip Isely, U.S.A.
Integrative Engineer

Reinhart Ruge, Mexico
Civil Engineer

Ratansinh Rajda, India
Member Parliament 1977-84

Dr. Terence P. Amerasinghe, Sri Lanka
Attorney-at-Law

Margaret Isely, U.S.A.
Businesswoman

HELEN TUCKER
World Citizens Leader

SHETTIMA ALI MONGUNO
U.N. Delegate 9 Sessions
Nigeria

DR. RASHMI MAYUR
President, Global Futures Network
India

NOTE: Much of the factual and scientific basis for the analysis in this letter is drawn from the comprehensive and well documented book, SURVIVAL OF CIVILIZATION, by engineer John Hamaker, written together with Don Weaver; research by the Earth Regeneration Society, and by the Institute For A Future; several (but not all) studies published by the WorldWatch Institute; and corroborated by daily news reports during the past five years in the New York Times and elsewhere.

ADDITION: To fully and expeditiously implement the rescue from climate catastrophe, as defined herein, requires also the simultaneous introduction of a new global finance and credit system, which will be fully explained in the next letter.

Exhibit P4

military spending. All of this sounds incredibly inviting to a debt ridden, war-torn society . . . at first glance.

The main portion of the plan has to do with World Legislative Act #11, authorizing the establishment of the Earth Financial Credit Corporation. Here are some highlights of the bill:

Article 1 states that the new global money and banking system will be activated as soon as ten nations have ratified the world constitution along with Bills # 1, 2, 6, 7, and 11.

Article 3 reveals that the amount of credit available to a given nation will be dependent upon its birth rate. Those countries with 2 percent or more annual population increase (which includes the poorest nations of the world) would receive the least help, while those with zero or less population growth would be eligible for the most credit.

(I wonder what this would do to the already alarming abortion rate since developing countries would be forced to choose between life and money. This bill would hurt third world countries and would further widen the gap between rich and poor.)

Article 5 sets forth the conditions for credit eligibility. Note the following provisions of the article.

1. Receiving credit would be dependent upon whether or not the applying nation has ratified the world constitution.

3. Any request for credit would have to be approved by the Earth Financial Credit Corporation.

7. The new monetary system would be based on Earth Dollars.

8. Each participating country could have any existing external debt cancelled by handing the responsibility for repayment over to the Earth Financial Credit Corporation (EFCC). The EFCC would then pay the loans back to lenders in Earth Dollars, according to its own terms.

(This action would prompt national governments to join the New World Order, otherwise their banks would end up with worthless Earth Dollars, which could not be used in their local economies.)

Article 7 addresses the question of leadership. According to Part A of the article, the first twenty-five national governments to participate in the new global system would be able to name one representative each to the board of directors of the EFCC. There is a catch, however . . . Part B of the same article reveals that an additional thirty members of the board of directors would be appointed by the various organs of the world government itself. The bottom line is that those who originated the world government would always retain control, holding a majority interest.

(Those countries, whose leaders are part of the plot, would obviously be among the first twenty-five to join the New World Order, and would therefore help to run the system; while those countries that would not join in right away, would suffer enormous economic consequences. This prospect, insiders hope, will provide a strong incentive for nations to rapidly join the new system.)

Article 10 authorizes the establishment of a Procurement Agency whose purpose would be to expedite "the widespread and universal acceptance of the Earth Dollar global financial system." In other words, this agency would be charged with the task of promoting and implementing the system as rapidly as possible, making it a very powerful organization. It would oversee the development of global trade and commerce on a regional basis. Article A-3 (d) of the charter goes on to state: "The solicitation, sales, and contracts to accept and use Earth Dollar Credit Accounts and Lines of Credit may be comparable to the manner in which the acceptance and use of any credit card system is now achieved."

(It is my projection that international credit card companies will be among the first to join the system. This will produce a chain reaction, forcing other institutions to rapidly follow suit.)

Article 14 discusses the subject of monetary valuation in making the transition from the old system to the new. According to this proposal, those existing financial institutions that join the new world system within two years would "be integrated with the new system on the basis of 100% valuation. . . ." Each year thereafter, the valuation rate would drop by 10 percent for new financial institutions joining the system. Those corporations holding out twelve years or longer would therefore have no transfer value left.

This would, in effect, put institutions run by "uncooperative Christians" out of business within a few years, except for the transactions that they might be able to conduct with other uncompromising Christians. Such transactions would probably have to be in the form of bartering arrangements.

You are encouraged to review this plan carefully. Be skeptical. Even though it sounds appealing, remember who is behind the planning of all of this. Ask yourself, "What will it be like when the system forces everyone to take an invisible mark in order to buy or sell?" How will Christians be treated by a predominantly pantheistic (occult) world leadership when they refuse to cooperate by taking such a mark? Please do not allow yourself to be deceived into supporting this effort. (Read Revelation 13 and 14.)

THEREFORE —

Article 1: As soon as ten national governments have given provisional ratification to the Constitution for the Federation of Earth, and have also ratified World Legislative Bills #1, #2, #6, #7, and #11 (this act), then an Earth Financial Credit Corporation shall be organized and activated as a division of the World Economic Development Organization, for the purpose of introducing the new Earth finance, credit, money and banking system.

Article 3: Initial revolving lines of credit in Earth Dollars shall be calculated on the basis of $1 billion dollars for each million of population for countries having natural population increase rates by birth of more than 2% annually, $1.5 billion dollars per million of population for countries having natural population increase rates of between 1% and 2%, $2 billion dollars per million of population for countries having natural population increase rates of between 0% and 1%, and $2.5 billion dollars per million of population for countries having zero or less population growth.

Article 5: The manner of extending the revolving Lines of Credit shall be in the form of an offer to each country defining the total amount of the Line of Credit per Article 3, to be activated under the following terms:

1. Provisional ratification of the Constitution for the Federation of Earth is a prerequisite to activating the Line of Credit.

3. Specific proposals and projects for the use of credit or funds advanced per the Line of Credit must be submitted for approval by the Earth Financial Credit Corporation.

7. The Line of Credit will be accounted in terms of Earth Dollars, which shall at no time have a lower value than U.S.A. Dollars or international SDRs (Special Drawing Rights), whichever is higher in value at the time of exchange.

8. Each country accepting a Line of Credit under the conditions specified herein may turn over current external debts for repayment to creditors by the Earth Financial Credit Corporation, under the following procedure:

a) Announce to creditors that the country is accepting the Line of Credit from **EFCC**, and is assigning its approved external debts for repayment to creditors by the **EFCC**.

b) Approved current external debts are defined as the balance due on original principal amounts of loans for valid projects, excluding loans for military projects or purposes, and excluding re-cycled interest and interest currently due.

c) No further external debts may be contracted except through the **EFCC**, or other agencies of the World Economic Development Organization (WEDO) or of the emerging World Government under the Constitution for the Federation of Earth .

d) The debts assumed by the **EFCC** shall be repaid to creditors in Earth Dollars, which shall never be valued below par with U.S. Dollars, and shall be paid on an installment basis during the next 20 years after assumption of the debts by the **EFCC**.

e) All subsequent interest on debts assumed by the **EFCC** shall be at no more than 2% of the assumed principal.

Article 7: The Board of Directors for the EFCC shall be composed as follows:

Part A — The first 25 national governments to accept Revolving Lines of Credit extended by the Earth Financial Credit Corporation may each name one representative to the Board of Directors of the EFCC each to serve a five year term. After more than 25 countries have accepted Lines of Credit, then for the election of successive terms for Directors, each national government shall nominate one candidate and the total of 25 Directors shall be elected by a combined vote of the national governments.

Part B — Thirty additional members of the Board of Directors of the EFCC shall be elected as follows:

10 elected by the Provisional World Cabinet

5 elected by the Board of Directors of the World Economic Development Organization;

5 elected by the Board of Directors of the World Government Funding Corporation;

5 elected by the Board of Directors of the Emergency Earth Rescue Administration;

5 elected by the Board of Trustees of the World Disarmament Agency.

The Directors to be elected under Part B of Article 7, may be elected in whole or in part prior to the naming of members of the Board of Directors by participating national governments.

Article 10: To expedite the inauguration and successful and rapid development of the EFCC, a Procurement Department may be established under separate legislation by the Provisional World Parliament. When established, the Procurement Department shall work in close co-operation with the EFCC in order to expedite widespread and general acceptance of the Lines of Credit and of all financial procedures being introduced by the Earth Financial Credit Corporation, as well as by other financial agencies established by the Provisional World Parliament.

Article 14: To encourage the cooperation of existing banks and financial institutions in making the transition to the new financial system, which is not based on prior savings and does not require prior savings to extend Lines of Credit or make loans, recognition shall be given to the net cash assets of cooperating banks and financial institutions in the following manner:

The net cash assets of those banks and financial institutions which agree by contract to join in and co-operate with the new financial system within 2 years from the date of operative launching of the EFCC, shall be integrated with the new system on the basis of 100% valuation of their net cash assets in terms of Earth Dollars, together with interest to be paid at 10% for 10 years on such net cash assets integrated and used in the new system. The net cash assets of those banks and financial institutions which agree to join during the 3rd year of operation of EFCC shall be accounted at 90% of valuation, together with 9% interest for 9 years. The net cash assets of those which agree to join during the 4th year shall be accounted at 80% of valuation together with interest at 8% for 8 years. And so on, until the 12th year, when the old system will have no transfer value to the new system.

Exhibit Q2

A Constitution for the Federation of Earth

The Constitution for the Federation of Earth (excerpts of which appear in Exhibit R) was first adopted during a meeting of the World Constituent Assembly in June 1977 at Innsbruck, Austria. The document was signed by approximately 135 participants from twenty-five countries and is intended to replace the U.N. charter to become the centerpiece of the New World Order. This intent of the WCPA is clearly described in the following statements, appearing on pages A and B of the document:

> . . . Whatever illusions remain that adequate progress can be made through negotiations among sovereign national governments for the solutions to the inter-related global crises confronting humanity, must also be discarded.
>
> The inescapable alternative for humanity today is the establishment of a democratic federal world government, given adequate powers and means to provide the framework within which supra-national problems can be solved for the good of all . . .(page A, paragraph 2 and 3)
>
> But before democratic world government can be established, agreement is first required upon a World Constitution which defines the powers, the structure, the composition and the functioning of the world government—as well as the procedure by which it shall be inaugurated—while at the same time protecting the legitimate jurisdiction of national governments over their internal affairs.
>
> One approach is to amend the Charter of the United Nations. But after 30 years of proposing amendments, the progress of humanity under the U.N. remains stalled in the dark ages of only slightly modified international anarchy, entrenched by the military establishments of rich and poor nations alike. While we support every humanitarian effort under the U.N. to alleviate world problems, the fact is that the United Nations is organized throughout to preserve national sovereignty. Even the least change is blocked by veto powers of each permanent member of the Security Council.
>
> Another way to achieve world government is for people and statesmen of vision to act directly to convene a new set of delegates who are given a mandate to prepare and to begin the implementation of a constitution for world government—specifically designed to serve the welfare

of humanity. This line of action was developed by a
series of calls and conventions during recent years, and
must now be completed to give new and practical hope
to mankind. (page B, col. 2)

These words make it clear that the WCPA expects the lead role
for establishing World Government to be passed from the U.N. to The
Federation of Earth. Once the world government, authorized by this
Constitution, is in power, it could expand its role at anytime it chooses.
Nothing would be able to prevent if from doing so.

The Preamble to the Constitution (Exhibit R3) reads like a page
out of a new age/occult manual. It states that we are on the threshold of a new world order, a new age of peace and unity, where the
interdependence of all life and the oneness of humanity will finally
be achieved. In closing, it submits that "the greatest hope for the
survival of life on earth is the establishment of a democratic world
government."

The following excerpts from the articles reveal the comprehensive nature of the constitution's provisions:

Article I, point 4 reveals that the world government would regu-
late virtually every aspect of life.

Article II, point 1. The world government would be all-encompassing. The information provided resembles the description of the
beast's authority given in Revelation 13:7-8.

Points 4-7 reveal the political and administrative structure of
the government. The world would be divided into twenty World Elec-
toral and Administrative Regions and ten Magna-Regions.

Point 8. The new political boundaries will not necessarily con-
form to existing national boundaries—meaning that nations could be
split up.

Article III, point 2 may lead to the seizure of all personal weapons required for self-defense.

Points 14 & 17. The world government would control all aspects of international trade, banking and finance.

Point 21 relates to plans for controlling population growth and
solving problems of population distribution.

Point 37 relates to the designation of a world language.

Article V, sec. A, point 3 permits the World Parliament to "reject the international laws developed prior to the advent of World
Government."

Article VIII, sec. G pertains to the establishment and operation
of a Planetary Accounting Office, Planetary Banking System, and Planetary Monetary and Credit System.

Article IX. The World Judiciary branch of the world government would interpret the rights of world citizens (including Christians) and would issue rulings regarding the sentencing of those who refuse to concede to the demands of the world system (possibly due to religious convictions).

Article X. The Enforcement System branch of the world government would enforce the decisions of the World Judiciary and other governing bodies. One means of enforcement would include the denial of financial credit to those who fail to comply with world law (Sec. D, point 2).

Article XV, sec. A. A total of twenty World Federal Zones will be established for the purpose of the location of various organs of the world government.

Sec. B. Five World Capitals will be established, with the World Presidium proposing the locations for the same. One of these capitals will be designated as the Primary World Capital. The other four will serve as Secondary World Capitals.

Article XVII, sec. A. The World Constitution will be transmitted to the U.N. General Assembly and to each of the national governments for approval, with a final ratification vote held in a popular referendum of the people (points 1 & 3). If a national government fails to submit the Constitution for ratification within six months, then the agency of the Provisional World Government, which is responsible for the worldwide ratification campaign could override the national government by conducting direct referendums with the people.

The contents of this document are blatant enough that no further explanation is required. Discerning Christians will recognize the implications.

If you are not a Christian and remain skeptical as to whether there would be any real danger in embracing such a one-world system, please bear in mind the occult forces behind this movement—a fact which is well established. Whether one cares to admit it or not, the very existence of this international occult endeavor indicates that life consists of more than a physical realm that can be touched or seen. It comes down to a war between good and evil, a battle between God and Satan over our souls. Our struggle, therefore, is not against other humans but against the demonic principalities and powers that are secretly directing this effort through misguided, but willing vessels.

A CONSTITUTION FOR THE FEDERATION OF EARTH

Contents

Exhibit R1

Exhibit R2

PREAMBLE

Realizing that Humanity today has come to a turning point in history and
that we are on the threshold of a new world order which promises to usher in an
era of peace, prosperity, justice and harmony;

Aware of the interdependence of people, nations and all life;

Aware that man's abuse of science and technology has brought Humanity to the
brink of disaster through the production of horrendous weaponry of mass destruction
and to the brink of ecological and social catastrophe;

Aware that the traditional concept of security through military defense is
a total illusion both for the present and for the future;

Aware of the misery and conflicts caused by the ever increasing disparity
between rich and poor;

Conscious of our obligation to posterity to save Humanity from imminent and
total annihilation;

Conscious that Humanity is One despite the existence of diverse nations,
races, creeds, ideologies and cultures and that the principle of unity in
diversity is the basis for a new age when war shall be outlawed and peace prevail;
when the earth's total resources shall be equitably used for human welfare; and
when basic human rights and responsibilities shall be shared by all without
discrimination;

Conscious of the inescapable reality that the greatest hope for the survival
of life on earth is the establishment of a democratic world government;

We, citizens of the world, hereby resolve to establish a world federation
to be governed in accordance with this Constitution for the Federation of
Earth.

Exhibit R3

Letter of Concern

The letter on the following page is intended to serve as a sample
of what you may wish to send to your congressman and senator. If
you would take the time to write a similar letter in your own words,
it would be more effective, particularly if written by hand. Your elected
officials will see that you cared enough to take the time to personally correspond, rather than just sending a form letter. However, if
necessary, you may rewrite or type this letter word for word. Whatever you choose to do, please act now!

Although we will probably be unable to stop the forming of the
New World Order, there are things we can do to help slow it down.
Writing a letter is just one step. If the people of this nation would
wake up and repent and call out to God, perhaps He would intervene

and push back the plans of the adversary. I therefore exhort every individual reading this book to abandon sin, to lead a holy life, to pray to God on behalf of our nation and world, and help elect Godly men and women to public office.

In addition to writing letters and getting your own life in order, you can help by sharing this message with as many people as possible. Inform you friends, relatives, and neighbors. They will not be able to deny the evidence in this book. If you are a pastor or leader of an organization, take the time to inform those entrusted to your care. You can make a difference! Commit yourself to prayer, and God will show you what to do.

If you would like information on obtaining copies of this book for mass distribution, or if you would like to have this writer share on your radio program or at your church, please contact Huntington House Publishers at 1-800-749-4009.

Also, if you do not have the addresses of your elected officials, you can obtain them by calling their offices. You will find their office number listed in the Blue Pages of your phone book, under United States Government–Congressional and Senate offices.

Dear (name of elected official),

In recent months there has been much talk by the president, leaders of the U.N., and various members of Congress about a New World Order. As one who has become enlightened to the real meaning of this term (a one-world government), I wish to express to you my personal grave concern over the implications thereof.

As a citizen of the United States of America whose rights are protected by our unique Constitution, I do not wish to become a "World Citizen" placed under the authority of a world government and a world constitution. It is not the obligation of this country to come under the rule of the United Nations or any subsequent global governing body. To do so would not only be unamerican and unconstitutional but extremely dangerous to the religious and political freedoms of our citizens.

I therefore urge you to do whatever possible in your position of power to protect the sovereignty of this nation. This includes opposing any calls to (hold) a Constitutional Convention or other attempts to significantly alter our Constitution.

We are not part of a "Community of Nations." Rather, we are an independent, sovereign nation. Our forefathers came to the shores of this land to escape the religious persecution and lack of freedom in other countries. Would it make sense for us now, after two hundred years of struggling to remain free, to betray our founding principles and to once again submit ourselves to the authority of others?

This position does not mean that we shouldn't share our material blessings and God-given resources to help the less fortunate in other countries. To the contrary, American Christians and Jews have done more to help others than any group of people in history. This, however, is a far cry from yielding our national sovereignty to a one-world government.

Please be reminded that as an elected official of the U.S. Government, your Constitutional duty is to faithfully represent the interests of the citizens in your district. As a voter to whom you are responsible, I have taken this opportunity to voice my concern and to urge you to take appropriate action.

Rest assured, if you support U.S. involvement in the emerging New World Order in any way, I, along with a growing number of voters in your jurisdiction, will respond accordingly at election time.

If, on the other hand, you remain loyal to the Constitution of the United States and to the people protected by it, you will receive my utmost support at the polls. I will be watching closely.

May God grant you wisdom in your decision!

A Concerned Constituent,

(Your signature)

The Lord foils the plans of the nations; he thwarts the purposes of the peoples. But the plans of the Lord stand firm forever, the purposes of his heart through all generations.
Psalm 33:10-11

A Note from the Author:

I am currently considering the publication of a monthly or quarterly newsletter to keep interested readers up-to-date on new developments concerning the matters discussed in this book. At this point, I am merely trying to determine whether or not a need for this type of publication exists. As it is extremely costly and time consuming to do a quality Christian newsletter, I do not want to make a hasty decision for the sake of good stewardship.

Assuming there would be enough interest and that it is truly God's will for us to proceed, I would most likely begin publishing a newsletter within twelve to eighteen months of the publication of this book. If you would like to be placed on the mailing list for such a news bulletin, please print your name and complete mailing address on a piece of paper and enclose it, along with any suggestions or comments you might have, in an envelope addressed to:

Gary Kah
P.O.Box 509283
Indianapolis, IN 46250-9283

I will personally make an effort to read each letter, as your thoughts and input are greatly appreciated.

Since it could be some time before we would launch such a publication, we ask that you keep us posted of any change in your address.

Also, if you or any friends possess significant information related to the topics discussed in this book, you are encouraged to mail your information along with the appropriate documentation to the preceding address. Please highlight or underline the specific information that you are wanting to call to my attention. Your information could be used in future books or publications to keep the American people and Christians throughout the world informed. Although I have a small network of researchers already in place, it is impossible for a few people to stay current on everything that is going on in the one-world movement. For this reason your help is needed.

In order to save time, I will only write back if I have a major question; otherwise, you may assume that your information has been received and reviewed. Thanks for your input!

Notes

Chapter 1—Global Economics

1. Archibald E. Roberts, *The Most Secret Science* (Fort Collins: Betsy Ross Press, 1984), 56.
2. Ibid.
3. Ralph Epperson, *The Unseen Hand* (Tucson: Publius Press, 1985), 165.
4. Myron Fagan, *The Illuminati—CFR*, Emissary Publications, TP-107, 1968. (Fagan, now deceased, was a well-known Hollywood film producer and playwright. His lectures on the history and activities of the Illuminati resulted from his personal experience with Illuminists who came to dominate key areas of the internatinal motion picture industry.)
5. William Hoffman, *David* (New York: Lyle Stuart, 1971), 45 (according to information provided in the book *America's Sixty Families*, by Ferdinand Lundberg, 1937).
6. Gary Allen, *The Rockefeller File* (Seal Beach, CA: '76 Press, 1976), 29-31. (According to Professor James Knowles who prepared the detailed study "The Rockefeller Financial Group.")
7. Ibid., 24.
8. "Exxon Corporation," *Moody's Industrial Manual* (New York: Moody's Investors Service—A Dun & Bradstreet Corp.), 1986 ed., Vol. 1, 2823.
9. Hoffman, *David*, 35.
10. Allen, *The Rockefeller File*, 26.
11. Ibid., 26-33; and Hoffman, *David*, 121.
12. Gary Allen, *Rockefeller—Campaigning for the New World Order* (Belmont, MA: American Opinion, 1974), 15.
13. Allen, *The Rockefeller File*, 32-33.
14. Allen, *Rockefeller—Campaigning for the New World Order*, 15.
15. Catherine B. Dalton, *Constitutional Money and the Banking Procedure* (Oreana, IL: Illinois Committee to Restore the Constitution, 1985), 4.
16. Dr. John Coleman, *The Federal Reserve Bank, Greatest Swindle in History*, 26-27.
17. Allen, *The Rockefeller File*, Introduction.
18. Rene A. Wormser, *Foundations—Their Power and Influence* (New York: The Devin-Adair Company, 1958), 32, 100-105.
19. Ibid., 214-218.
20. Ibid., 201.
21. Ibid.
22. Ibid.

Chapter 2—Global Politics

1. John Robison, *Proofs of a Conspiracy* (Boston: Western Islands, 1967), 74, 84. This book was originally published in 1798.

2. Nesta H. Webster, *World Revolution* (London: Constable and Company, 1921), 18.

3. Ibid.

4. Ibid., 20.

5. Count Egon Caesar Corti, *The Rise of the House of Rothschild* (Boston: Western Islands, 1972), ix. Originally published by Cosmopolitan Book Corporation in 1928.

6. Nesta H. Webster, *World Revolution*, 25.

7. Ibid.; and Albert G. Mackey, *An Encyclopedia of Freemasonry Vol. 2* (New York: The Masonic History Co., 1921), 843. Originally published in 1873, and more commonly known as *Mackey's Encyclopedia of Freemasonry*.

8. U.S. George Washington Bicentennial Commission, *The Writings of George Washington Vol. 20* (Washington, DC: U.S. Government Printing Office, 1941), 518; and Ralph Epperson, *The Conspiratorial View of History* (Tucson: Epperson, 1986), 2.

9. Louis T. McFadden, *Collective Speeches of Congressman Louis T. McFadden* (Hawthorne, CA: Omni Publications, 1970), 2.

10. Archibald E. Roberts, *Emerging Struggle for State Sovereignty* (Fort Collins: Betsy Ross Press, 1979), 148.

11. Catherine B. Dalton, *Constitutional Money and the Banking Procedure* (Oreana, IL: Illinois Committee to Restore the Constitution, 1985), 3.

12. McFadden, *Collective Speeches*, vi.

13. John Steinbacher, *Senator Robert Francis Kennedy—The Man, the Mysticism, the Murder* (Los Angeles: Impact Publishers, 1968), 51; and Ralph Epperson, *The Unseen Hand* (Tucson: Publius Press, 1985), 166-168.

14. Catherine B. Dalton, *Constitutional Money and the Banking Procedure*, 4.

15. Gary Allen, *Rockefeller—Campaigning for the New World Order* (Belmont, MA: American Opinion, 1974), 15.

16. Eustace Mullins, *The World Order* (Staunton, VA: Ezra Pound Institute of Civilization, 1985), 33-34.

17. Ibid.

18. Ralph Epperson, *The Unseen Hand*, 196.

19. Ibid., 196-197.

20. *Council on Foreign Relations, 1990 Annual Report*, New York, 185.

21. Ibid., 185-186.

22. Ibid., 184, 187.

23. Ibid., 202.

24. Rene A. Wormser, *Foundations—Their Power and Influence* (New York: The Devin-Adair Company, 1958), 209.

25. *Council on Foreign Relations 1987 Annual Report*, New York, 103; and *Council on Foreign Relations Report 1990 Annual Report*, 142.

26. *CFR 1987 Annual Report*, 104; and *CFR 1990 Annual Report*, 141.

27. *CFR 1990 Annual Report*, 6.

28. Ibid., 4.

29. James J. Drummey, "The Internationalist," *The New American* (12 March 1991): 27.

30. William E. Dunham, "Correction, Please!" *The Review of the News* (9 April 1980): 37-38.

31. Phoebe Courtney, *The CFR, Part II* (Littleton, CO: The Independent American, 1975), 4.

32. Roberts, *State Sovereignty*, 203.

33. Gary Allen, *The Rockefeller File* (Seal Beach, CA: '76 Press, 1976), 77.

34. Christian Warner, "World Dictatorship and the New Age Movement," *Newswatch Magazine* (September 1986): 26.

35. Gary Allen, "Who They Are, The Conspiracy to Destroy America," *American Opinion* (October 1972): 65.

36. Steinbacher, *Senator Robert Francis Kennedy*, 17-18.

37. Ibid., 23.

38. CFR 1990 Annual Report, 176..

39. Wormser, *Foundations—Their Power and Influence*, 209.

40. Archibald E. Roberts, "Bulletin—Should the United States Participate and Encourage Development of the United Nations Organization," Committee to Restore the Constitution (July 1986): 4-5.

41. Ibid., 5.

42. Ibid.

43. Epperson, *The Unseen Hand*, 198.

44. Lester B. Pearson, "The United Nations," *The World Book Encyclopedia*, 1969 Edition, Vol. 19: 25, 37. (John D. Rockefeller, Jr., gave $8.5 million to the U.N. in 1946 to buy the site along the East River where the headquarters would be built.)

45. James J. Drummey, "The Internationalist," *The New American*, 29.

46. Edmund Jan Osmanczyk, "United Nations Charter, 1945," *The Encyclopedia of The United Nations and International Relations*, 2d Edition, 948.

47. Epperson, *The Unseen Hand*, 206.

48. Roberts, *State Sovereignty*, 185.

49. Ibid.; and Epperson, *The Unseen Hand*, 207.

50. David J. Smith, "Ten Kingdoms Along with the Beast," *Newswatch Magazine* (March-April 1984): 7.

51. Ibid.

52. Jim Lucier, "Bilderbergers," *American Opinion* (November 1964): 62.

53. Epperson, *The Unseen Hand*, 207; and Roberts, *State Sovereignty*, 186-190.

54. Roberts, *State Sovereignty*, 189.

55. Ibid., 189-190; and Epperson, *The Unseen Hand*, 207.
56. Dennis L. Meadows, Donnella H. Meadows, Jorgen Randers and William W. Behrens III, *The Limits to Growth—A Report for the Club of Rome's Project on the Predicament of Mankind*, 2d. Edition (1972; rpt. Washington DC: Potomac Associates; New York: Universe Books, 1974), 9.
57. Christian Warner, "World Dictatorship and the New Age Movement," *Newswatch Magazine* (September 1986): 19.
58. Shirley West, "History of the Club of Rome," *The Eagle Forum* (Summer, 1989): 7.
59. Mihajlo Mesarovic and Eduard Pestel, *Mankind at the Turning Point—The Second Report to the Club of Rome* (New York: E.P. Dutton & Co., Inc./Reader's Digest Press, 1974), 9-10.
60. Christian Warner, "World Dictatorship and the New Age Movement," *Newswatch Magazine* (September 1986): 19.
61. David J. Smith, "Ten Kingdoms Along With the Beast," *Newswatch Magazine* (March-April 1984): 12-15.
62. Mesarovic, *Mankind at the Turning Point*, 203, 205.
63. Ibid., 201.
64. West, "Club of Rome," 7.
65. Meadows, *The Limits to Growth*, 196-197.
66. Mesarovic, *Mankind at the Turning Point*, 143, 147.
67. Ibid., 206.
68. The Trilateral Commission, *The Trilateral Commission—Questions and Answers* (New York: North American Office, 1986), 2.
69. Dalton, *Constitutional Money*, 5.
70. Zbigniew Brzezinski, *Between Two Ages—America's Role in the Technetronic Era* (New York: Penguin Books, 1970), 300, 304.
71. Epperson, *The Unseen Hand*, 239.
72. Robert W. Lee, "Confirming the Liberal Establishment," *American Opinion* (March 1981): 35.
73. *The Review of the News* (21 July 1976): 32.
74. Congressional Record—Senate, 15 December 1987, p. S18146.

Chapter 3—America's Shadow Government

1. "The Rockefellers," narr. Walter Cronkite, CBS Reports, 28 December 1973.
2. William Hoffman, *David* (New York: Lyle Stuart, 1971), 164-165.
3. United Press International, "Big Bank Dominance of Firms Described," *Arizona Republic* (7 January 1974).
4. Gary Allen, *The Rockefeller File* (Seal Beach, CA: '76 Press, 1976), 69.
5. Alvin P. Sanoff, "Behind the Demise of Family Newspapers," *U.S. News and World Report* (11 February 1985): 59.
6. Allen, *The Rockefeller File*, 75.
7. Hoffman, *David*, 50.
8. Ralph Epperson, *The Unseen Hand* (Tucson: Publius Press, 1985), 386;

and Allen, *The Rockefeller File*, 44.

9. "Occasional Letter, No. 1," General Education Board (1904).

10. Hoffman, *David*, 51.

11. Allen, *The Rockefeller File*, 45.

12. Ibid.

13. Epperson, *The Unseen Hand*, 298.

14. Ibid., 386; and Hoffman, *David*, 51.

15. Epperson, *The Unseen Hand*, 386.

16. Allen, *The Rockefeller File*, 46.

17. Rene A. Wormser, *Foundations—Their Power and Influence* (New York: The Devin-Adair Company, 1958), 142-143.

18. Allen, *The Rockefeller File*, 45-46.

19. Catherine B. Dalton, *Constitutional Money and the Banking Procedure* (Oreana, IL: Illinois Committee to Restore the Constitution, 1985), 7.

20. Adam Ulam, *A History of Soviet Russia* (New York: Draeger Publishers, 1976), 102.

21. Gary Allen, *Rockefeller—Campaigning for the New World Order* (Belmont, MA: American Opinion, 1974), 9; and Dalton, *Constitutional Money*, 7.

22. Allen, *Rockefeller—New World Order*, 9.

23. Wormser, *Foundations*, 163-164.

24. Eustace Mullins, *The World Order* (Staunton, VA: Ezra Pound Institute of Civilization, 1985), 35.

25. "The CFR/Trilateral Commission Connection" (Kerrville, TX: F.R.E.E., 1990).

26. Mullins, *The World Order*, 35.

27. "State of the Union—Bush Seeks to Inspire Support for his Persian Gulf Mission," *Congressional Quarterly* (2 February 1991): 308-310.

Chapter 4—The New Age Movement

1. *Webster's New Collegiate Dictionary*, 1977 ed., s.v. "mystic."

2. Nevill Drury, *Dictionary of Mysticism and the Occult* (San Francisco: Harper and Row, 1985), 76, 212.

3. John Steinbacker, *Senator Robert Francis Kennedy—The Man, the Mysticism, the Murder* (Los Angeles: Impact Publishers, 1968), 29.

4. Ibid., 29-31.

5. *Encyclopedia of Occultism and Parapsychology*, 2d ed., s.v. "Thule Society," and Joseph J. Carr, *The Twisted Cross* (Lafayette, LA: Huntington House, 1985), 107, 109.

6. Steinbacker, *Senator Robert Francis Kennedy*, 30.

7. Christian Warner, "World Dictatorship and the New Age Movement," *Newswatch Magazine* (September 1986): 26.

8. Ibid., 13.

9. Steinbacker, *Senator Robert Francis Kennedy*, 12.

10. *Council on Foreign Relations, 1990 Annual Report*, New York, 196.

11. *Who's Who in the World*, 8th Edition (Chicago: Marquis Who's Who, 1987-88), 499.

12. Warner, "World Dictatorship," 26.

13. *CFR 1990 Annual Report*, 191, 201, 203.

14. *Who's Who in the World*, 8th Edition, 499.

15. Dennis L. Meadows, Donnella H. Meadows, Jorgen Randers and William W. Behrens III, *The Limits to Growth—A Report for the Club of Rome's Project on the Predicament of Mankind*, 2d ed. (1972); (rpt. Washington, DC: Potomac Associates; New York: Universe Books, 1974), 196-197.

16. Warner, "World Dictatorship," 20.

17. Peter LaLonde, "Special Report—The World Future Society's Worldview '84," The Prophecy Newsletter (1984): 12; and Warner, "World Dictatorship," 21. (The Prophecy Newsletter is today known as the Omega Letter.)

18. LaLonde, "Special Report," 12.

19. Ibid.

Chapter 5—Freemasonry

1. *Thirty Year's Work—The Books of Alice Bailey and the Tibetan Master Djwhal Khul* (New York: Lucis Publishing Company, date unknown), 29.

2. Alice A. Bailey, *The Externalisation of the Hierarchy* (New York: Lucis Publishing Company, 1957), 511.

3. *Thirty Year's Work—The Books of Alice A. Bailey and the Tibetan Master Djwhal Khul*, 29.

4. Cardinal Caro y Rodriguez, *The Mystery of Freemasonry Unveiled* (Hawthorne, CA: Christian Book Club of America, 1971), 226.

5. Ibid., 238.

6. Ibid., 227.

7. Ibid., 226.

8. *Facts of Scottish Rite* (Lexington, MA: Northern Masonic Jurisdiction, 1984), 3; and *Freemasonry—A Way of Life* (Indianapolis: Grand Lodge Free and Accepted Masons of the State of Indiana), 2-3.

9. *Facts of Scottish Rite*, 3.

10. Ibid., 5, 12.

11. *Ancient Arabic Order Nobles of the Mystic Shrine* (Tampa: International Shrine Headquarters, 1982), 2.

12. *The New Encyclopedia Britannica*, 15th ed., s.v. "Freemasonry."

13. *The Encyclopedia Americana*, 1986 ed., s.v. "Masons."

14. *The New Encyclopedia Britannica*, 15th ed., s.v. "Freemasonry."

15. *The World Book Encyclopedia*, 1986 ed., s.v. "Masonry."

16. J.S.M. Ward, *Freemasonry and the Ancient Gods* (London: Simpkin, Marshall, Hamilton, Kent & Co., 1921), 342-344.

17. Albert Pike, *Morals and Dogma of the Ancient and Accepted Scottish Rite of Freemasonry* (Washington, DC: House of the Temple, 1966), 207-208. Originally published in 1871, in Charleston, SC.

18. Ibid., 329.

19. Thomas Smith Webb (Past Grand Master), *The Freemason's Monitor* (Cincinnati: The Pettibone Bros., 1797), 39.

20. Henry. C. Clausen (Sovereign Grand Commander), *Masons Who Helped*

Shape Our Nation (San Diego: Neyenesch Printers, 1976), 111. Printed under the authority of The Supreme Council (Mother Council of the World), House of the Temple, Washington, DC.

21. H.L. Haywood, *Famous Masons and Masonic Presidents* (Richmond, VA: Macoy Publishing and Masonic Supply Co., 1944), 97.

22. Albert Pike, *Morals and Dogma*, 248.

23. Nesta H. Webster, *Secret Societies and Subversive Movements* (Hawthorne, CA: Christian Book Club of America, originally published in 1924), 32-34, 63.

24. Ibid., 63.

25. Ibid., 49.

26. *Collier's Encyclopedia*, 1985 ed., s.v. "knights templars."

27. *World Book Encyclopedia*, 1969 ed., s.v. "knights templars."

28. Ibid.

29. Ibid.

30. *Collier's Encyclopedia*, s.v. "knights templars."

31. *World Book Encyclopedia*, 1969 ed., s.v. "knights templars."

32. Ibid.

33. *Collier's Encyclopedia*, s.v. "knights templars."

34. Ibid.

35. Ibid.

36. Pike, *Morals and Dogma*, 819-820.

37. *Webster's New World Dictionary*, 2d College Edition, s.v. "seignior" and "seigniory."

38. Edith Starr Miller, *Occult Theocrasy* (Hawthorne, CA: The Christian Book Club of America, first published in 1933), 143.

39. Ibid., 144.

40. *Collier's Encyclopedia*, s.v. "knights templars."

41. *World Book Encyclopedia*, 1969 ed., s.v. "knights templars."

42. Webster, *Secret Societies*, 51-52.

43. Ibid., 52. This information was taken from Michelet, *Proces des Templiers*, *II*, 1841, 284-364. This work consists largely of the publication in Latin of the Papal bulls and trials of the Templars before the Papal Commission in Paris contained in the original document once preserved at Notre Dame.

44. Ibid., 53. This information was taken from G. Mollat, *Les Papes d'Avignon*, 1912, 241.

45. Ibid., 51. Taken from Michelet's *Proces des Templiers*.

46. Ibid., 53.

47. Ibid.

48. Ibid.

49. Ibid., 53-54.

50. Pike, *Morals and Dogma*, 817-818.

51. Webster, *Secret Societies*, 54.

52. Ibid.

53. *World Book Encyclopedia*, 1969 ed., s.v. "knights templars."

54. Miller, *Occult Theocrasy*, 144.

55. *World Book Encyclopedia*, 1969 ed., s.v. "knights templars."

56. Miller, *Occult Theocrasy*, 144.

57. Ibid., 145.

58. Pike, *Morals and Dogma*, 820.

59. Ibid., 821.

60. Ibid.

61. Albert G. Mackey, *An Encyclopedia of Freemasonry* (New York: The Masonic History Co., 1921), 639. Originally published in 1873, and more commonly known as *Mackey's Encyclopedia of Freemasonry*.

62. Ibid., 640.

63. Pike, *Morals and Dogma*, 816.

64. Ibid., 821.

65. *Mackey's Encyclopedia of Freemasonry*, 346.

66. Ibid., 842.

67. Ibid., 843.

68. H.L. Haywood, *Famous Masons and Masonic Presidents* (Richmond, VA: Macoy Publishing and Masonic Supply Co., 1944), 152.

69. John Robison, *Proofs of a Conspiracy* (Boston: Western Islands, 1967), 60. Originally published in 1798.

70. Ibid., 106.

71. Nesta Webster, *World Revolution* (London: Constable and Company, 1921), 20.

72. *Mackey's Encyclopedia of Freemasonry*, 346-347.

73. Webster, *World Revolution*, 20; and Count Egon Caesar Corti, *The Rise of the House of Rothschild* (Boston: Western Islands, 1972), ix. Originally published by Cosmopolitan Book Corporation in 1928.

74. Haywood, *Masonic Presidents*, 151-152.

75. Robison, *Proofs of a Conspiracy*, 86.

76. Ibid., 87.

77. Webster, *World Revolution*, 13.

78. Robison, *Proofs of a Conspiracy*, 86.

79. *Facts of Scottish Rite*, 4.

80. Ibid.

81. Chuck Sackett, *What's Going On in There?* (Thousand Oaks, CA: Sword of the Shephard Ministries, 1982), 13. As taken from *History of the Church* [D.H.C.], Vol. 4, 550, 552.

82. Ibid.

83. Ibid.

84. W.J. McCormick, *Christ, the Christian, and Freemasonry* (Belfast: Great Joy Publications, 1984), 96. As quoted from Official First Day of Issue: Mormon Temple, Salt Lake City, UT. (Brigham Young: inset), 5 April 1980. (USPS)

85. Ibid., 18.

86. Miller, *Occult Theocrasy*, 207-208.
87. Pike, *Morals and Dogma*, 1-2.
88. *Mackey's Encyclopedia of Freemasonry*, 563.
89. Miller, *Occult Theocrasy*, 210.
90. Haywood, *Masonic Presidents*, 132; and Salem Kirban, *Satan's Angels Exposed* (Rossville: Grapevine Book Distributors, 1980), 159.
91. *Mackey's Encyclopedia of Freemasonry*, 564.
92. Haywood, *Masonic Presidents*, 133.
93. Ibid.
94. Kirban, *Satan's Angels Exposed*, 159.
95. *Mackey's Encyclopedia of Freemasonry*, 564.
96. Miller, *Occult Theocrasy*, 208.
97. Ibid., 220.
98. Haywood, *Masonic Presidents*, 133.
99. Ibid.
100. *Mackey's Encyclopedia of Freemasonry*, 564.
101. Kirban, *Satan's Angels Exposed*, 157-158; and Ralph Epperson, *The Unseen Hand* (Tucson: Publius Press, 1985), 223.
102. Miller, *Occult Theocrasy*, 215.
103. Ibid.
104. Ibid.
105. Ibid., 216-217.
106. Ibid., 217-218.
107. Ibid., 208-209.
108. Kirban, *Satan's Angels Exposed*, 159.
109. Miller, *Occult Theocrasy*, 222.
110. Ibid.
111. Ibid., 216.
112. Ibid.
113. Ibid., 220.
114. Ibid., 221.
115. Pike, *Morals and Dogma*, 817.
116. Kirban, *Satan's Angels Exposed*, 157.
117. Miller, *Occult Theocrasy*, 219.
118. Ibid., 218.
119. Gerald Winrod, *Adam Weishaupt* (Clackamas, OR: Emissary Publications, 1937), 48.
120. Webster, *World Revolution*, 178.
121. Ibid., 179.
122. Ibid.
123. Ibid.
124. Ibid.
125. James Guillaume, *Karl Marx, pan-Germaniste* (Librairie Armand Collin, 1915), 9 as quoted in Nesta Webster, *World Revolution*, 180.
126. Nesta Webster, *World Revolution*, 180.

127. E.E. Fribourg, *L'Association Internationale des Travailleurs*, 1871, 31 as quoted in Nesta Webster, *World Revolution*, 181.

128. Webster, *World Revolution*, 181.

129. Ibid., 182-183.

130. John Steinbacher, *Senator Robert Francis Kennedy—The Man, the Mysticism, the Murder* (Los Angeles: Impact Publishers, Inc., 1968), iv. Originally printed in the *Sunday Illustrated Herald*, 8 February 1920.

131. McCormick, *Christ, the Christian, and Freemasonry*, 116.

132. "Now at War: 1 in Every 4 Nations," *U.S. News and World Report* (28 March 1983): 11.

133. James J. Drummey, "The Internationalist," *The New American* (12 March 1991): 29.

134. Ibid.

135. Ibid., 30.

Chapter 6—The Secret Teachings of the N.W.O.

1. "Freemasonry on Its Own Terms," The John Ankerberg Show—News and Views, No. 0586, 1986, 1.

2. News and Views, 1.

3. Albert Pike, *Morals and Dogma of the Ancient and Accepted Scottish Rite of Freemasonry* (Washington, DC: House of the Temple, 1966), 213. Originally published in 1871 in Charleston, SC.

4. Albert G. Mackey, *An Encyclopedia of Freemasonry* (New York: The Masonic History Co., 1921), 618. Originally published in 1873, and more commonly known as *Mackey's Encyclopedia of Freemasonry*.

5. Thomas Smith Webb (Past Grand Master), *The Freemason's Monitor* (Cincinnati: The Pettibone Bros., 1797), 92.

6. Manly P. Hall, *The Lost Keys of Freemasonry* (New York: Macoy Publishing and Masonic Supply Co., 1931), 48.

7. Edith Starr Miller, *Occult Theocrasy* (Hawthorne, CA: The Christian Book Club of America, 1933), 220-221.

8. Joseph Fort Newton, *The Builders—A Story and Study of Freemasonry* (New York: Macoy Publishing and Masonic Supply Co., first published in 1914; latest printing 1951), 242.

9. Ed Decker, *The Question of Freemasonry* (Issaquah, WA: Saints Alive), 9.

10. Captain William Morgan, *Illustrations of Masonry—By One of the Fraternity Who Has Devoted Thirty Years to the Subject* (Batavia, NY: Col. David C. Miller, 1827), 21-22.

11. Ibid., 3 of Introduction, written by the publisher, Col. David C. Miller.

12. Rev. Charles G. Finney, *The Character, Claims, and Practical Workings of Freemasonry* (Chicago: E. Cook Publications, 1986), 17. Originally published in 1869, by the Western Tract and Book Society.

13. Henry Wilson Coil, *Coil's Masonic Encyclopedia* (New York: Macoy Publishing and Masonic Supply Co., 1961), 58.

14. W.J. McCormick, *Christ, the Christian, and Freemasonry* (Belfast: Great

Joy Publications, 1984), 27.

15. Finney, *Practical Workings of Freemasonry*, 1.

16. Dr. Alva J. McClain, "Freemasonry and Christianity," *The Sword of the Lord* (5 December 1975): 9. Dr. McClain was the long-time president of Grace Brethren Seminary in Winona Lake, Indiana. This article was a reprint of an earlier lecture delivered by McClain.

17. McCormick, *Christ, the Christian, and Freemasonry*, 141.

18. Ibid., 111-112.

19. H.L. Haywood, *Famous Masons and Masonic Presidents* (Richmond, VA: Macoy Publishing and Masonic Supply Co., 1944), 128.

20. McCormick, *Christ, the Christian, and Freemasonry*, 112.

21. Ibid.

22. Ibid.

23. McClain, *The Sword of the Lord*: 9.

24. Louis L. Williams, "Universality and Christianity," *The Northern Light*, Vol. 18, No. 1 (February 1987): 6-7.

25. Ibid., 7, 18.

26. Associated Press, "Church Calls Freemason Rituals Blasphemous," *The Indianapolis Star* (14 July 1987): 10.

27. Ibid.

28. Ibid.

29. Decker, *The Question of Freemasonry*, 8.

30. Ibid.

31. Anton Szandor LaVey, *The Satanic Rituals—Companion to the Satanic Bible* (New York: Avon Books, 1972), 21.

32. Ibid., 54.

33. Ibid., 59.

34. Ibid., 56.

35. Ibid., 56, 58.

Chapter 7—The Coming World Crisis

1. U.S. Department of Defense, *Soviet Military Power 1986* (Washington, DC: U.S. Government Printing Office, 1986), 133.

2. Post Diplomatic Correspondent, "Jerusalem Incomprehension at Syrian Nervousness," *The Jerusalem Post* (12 April 1984): 1, col. 1-2.

3. Ibid.

4. "Israel's Nuclear Prowess—A Leak by Design?" *U.S. News and World Report* (10 November 1986): 8.

5. Salem Kirban, *Satan's Angels Exposed* (Rossville, GA: Grapevine Books, 1980), 158-161.

6. Myron Fagan, *The Illuminati—CFR*, Emissary Publications, TP-107, 1968. This letter between Pike and Mazzini is now catalogued in the British Museum in London (according to Salem Kirban, *Satan's Angels Exposed*, 164). Parts of this letter are also quoted in *Descent Into Slavery* by Des Griffin.